11+ Non-Verbal Reasoning
For the CEM test

This CGP book is brilliant for children aged 9-10 who are working towards the CEM 11+. It's set at a slightly easier level than the real test — perfect for building confidence.

The first few sections are packed with accessible questions that'll help them get to grips with each crucial skill. Once they've mastered those, they can move on to the mixed-topic Assessment Tests for more realistic 11+ practice.

There's also a detailed pull-out Answer Book to make marking as simple as possible!

How to access your free Online Edition

This book includes a free Online Edition to read on your PC, Mac or tablet.
You'll just need to go to **cgpbooks.co.uk/extras** and enter this code:

0621 5086 6360 8571

By the way, this code only works for one person. If somebody else has used this book before you, they might have already claimed the Online Edition.

Practice Book — Ages 9-10
with Assessment Tests

How to use this Practice Book

This book is divided into three parts — Spotting Patterns, 3D Shapes and Folding, and Assessment Tests. There are answers and detailed explanations in the pull-out section at the back of the book.

Spotting Patterns

- Each section contains practice questions focusing on one of the main concepts your child will need to understand for the Non-Verbal Reasoning part of the test.
- These pages can help your child build up the different skills they'll need for the real test.
- Your child can use the smiley face tick boxes in this section and in the 3D Shapes section to evaluate how confident they feel with each topic.

3D Shapes and Folding

- This part concentrates on the skills your child will need for the 3D and folding questions in the test.

Assessment Tests

- The third part of the book contains eight assessment tests, each with a mix of question types.
- You can print off multiple choice answer sheets from cgpbooks.co.uk/11plus/answer-sheets, so your child can practise taking the tests as if they're sitting the real thing.
- Use the printable answer sheets if you want your child to do each test more than once.
- If you want to give your child timed practice, give them a time limit of 20 minutes for each test, and ask them to work as quickly and carefully as they can.
- The tests get harder from 1 to 8, so don't be surprised if your child finds the later ones more tricky.
- Talk your child through the answers to the questions they got wrong. This will help them understand questions that work in a similar way when they come up against them in later tests.
- Your child should aim for a mark of around 85% (37 questions correct) in each test. If they score less than this, use their results to work out the areas they need more practice on.
- If they haven't managed to finish the test in time, they need to work on increasing their speed, whereas if they have made a lot of mistakes, they need to work more carefully.
- Keep track of your child's scores using the progress chart on the inside back cover of the book.

Published by CGP

Editors:
David Broadbent, Ceara Hayden, Sharon Keeley-Holden, Rachel Kordan and Rebecca Tate.

With thanks to Glenn Rogers and Amanda MacNaughton for the proofreading.

Please note that CGP is not associated with CEM in any way.
This book does not include any official questions and it is not endorsed by CEM.

ISBN: 978 1 78908 150 3
Printed by Elanders Ltd, Newcastle upon Tyne
Clipart from Corel®

Based on the classic CGP style created by Richard Parsons.

Text, design, layout and original illustrations © Coordination Group Publications Ltd. (CGP) 2018
All rights reserved.

Photocopying this book is not permitted, even if you have a CLA licence.
Extra copies are available from CGP with next day delivery • 0800 1712 712 • www.cgpbooks.co.uk

Contents

Tick off the check box for each topic as you go along.

Spotting Patterns

Shapes .... 2 ✓
Counting 4
Pointing 6
Shading and Line Types 8
Order and Position 10
Rotation 12
Reflection 13
Layering 14

3D Shapes and Folding

Rotating 3D Shapes 16
2D and 3D Shapes 18
Folding 20

Assessment Tests

Test 1 22
Test 2 32
Test 3 42
Test 4 52
Test 5 62
Test 6 72
Test 7 82
Test 8 92

Glossary 102

Spotting Patterns

Shapes

When you see a question about shapes, counting their sides is often a good place to start.

Warm Up

1. How many **sides** does each of these shapes have?

   a. □ — 4   b. △ — 3   c. ✦ — 8   d. ⬆ — 8   e. ⬠ — 6   f. ⏢ — 4   g. ⋈ — 10

2. How many **lines of symmetry** does each shape have?

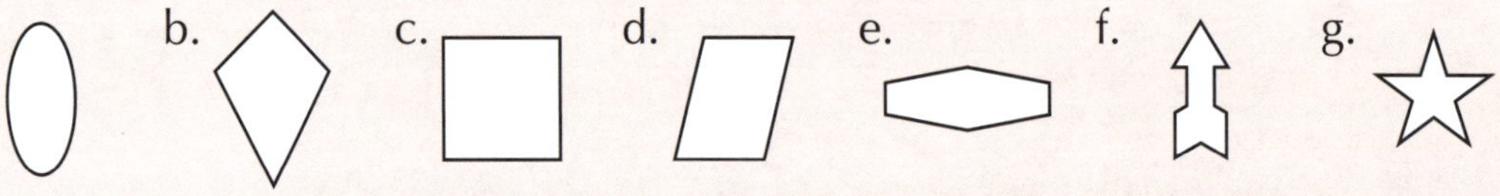

   a. ⬭ — 1   b. ◇ — 1   c. □ — 3   d. ▱ — 2   e. ⬡ — 2   f. ⬆ — 1   g. ★ — 5

3. Find one thing that the shapes in each set have **in common**.

   a. They each have 6 sides

   b. They all have a curved side

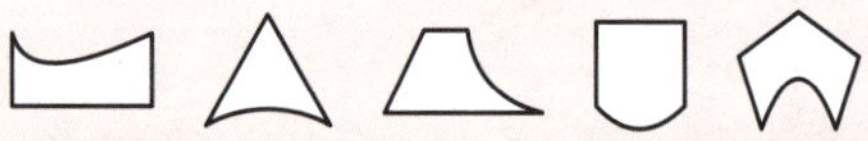

Odd One Out

Find the figure in each row that is most <u>unlike</u> the other figures.

Example:

   a   b   c   d   e   (_d_)

   All the other big diamonds have four-sided shapes inside them.

4.   a   b   c   d   e   (_A_)

5.   a   b   c   d   e   (~C~ _B_)

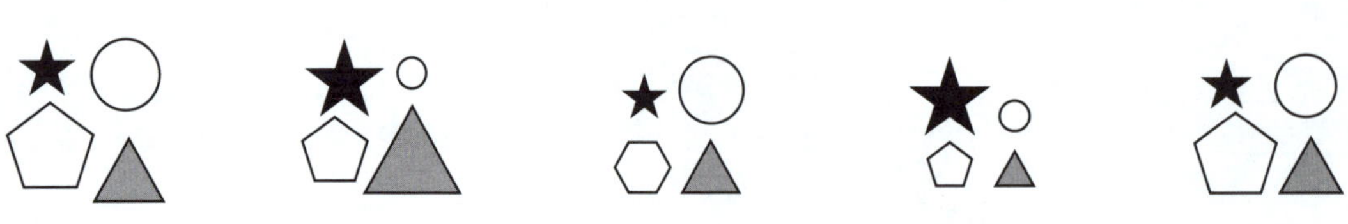

Spotting Patterns

6. a b c d e (b)

7. a b c d e (b)

Complete the Series

Work out which of the options best fits in place of the missing square in the series.

Example:

a b c d (c)

Each new star gets an extra point.

8. a b c d (B)

9. a b c d (D)

10. a b c d (D)

Spotting Patterns

4

Counting

Sometimes questions that look really tricky can be answered by counting things.

Warm Up

1. How many **circles** are there in each of these figures?

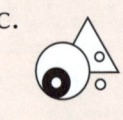

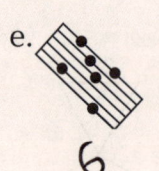

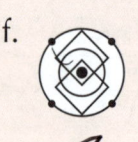

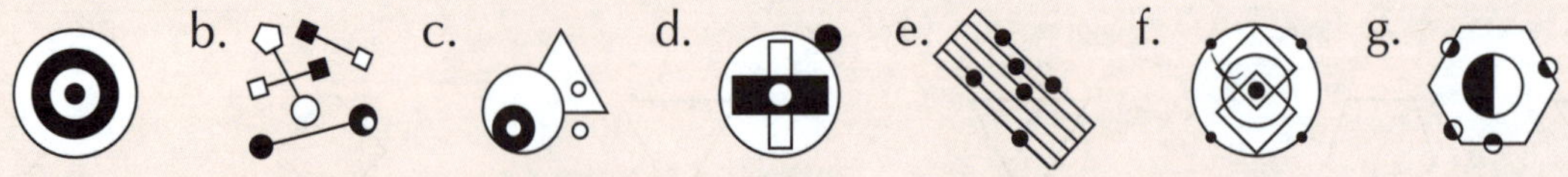

   a. _4_ b. _4_ c. _5_ d. _3_ e. _6_ f. _7_ g. _5_

2. In these figures, how many **more stars** are there than **squares**?

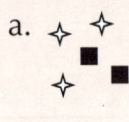

   a. _1_ b. _4_ c. _2_ d. _5_ e. _2_ f. _3_ g. _7_

3. What is the **total number** of shapes in each figure?

   a. _6_ b. _4_ c. _4_ d. _6_ e. _6_ f. _4_ g. _2_

   What do all of these numbers of shapes have in common? _There all even_

Find the Figure Like the First Two

Work out which option is most like the two figures on the left.

Example:

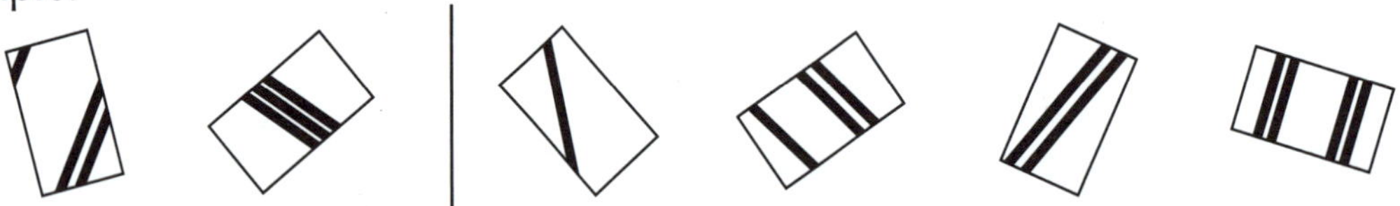

a b c d   (_b_)

All of the rectangles must have three lines through them.

4. a b c d   (_A_)

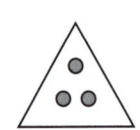

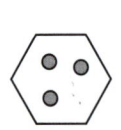

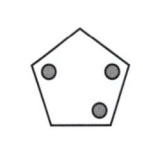

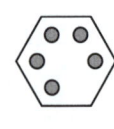

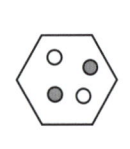

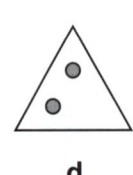

5. a b c d   (_D_)

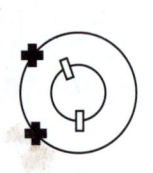

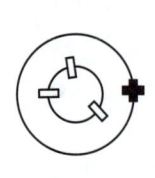

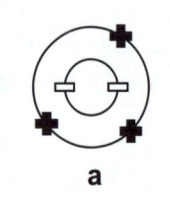

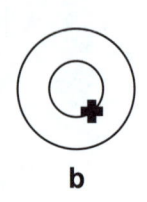

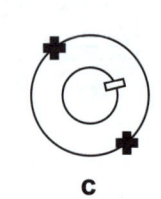

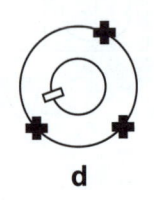

Spotting Patterns

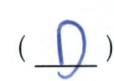

6. (D)

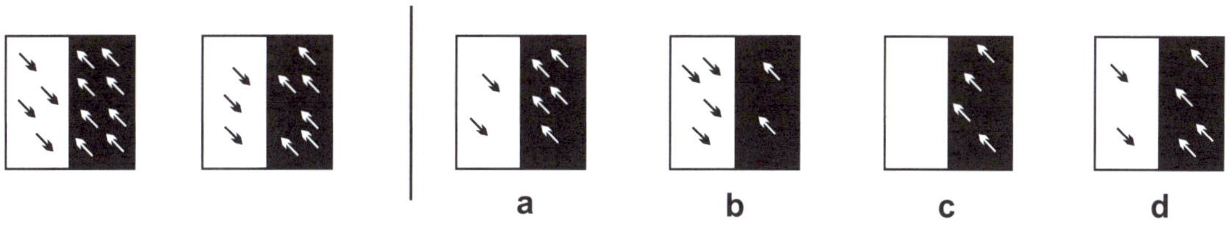

7. (D)

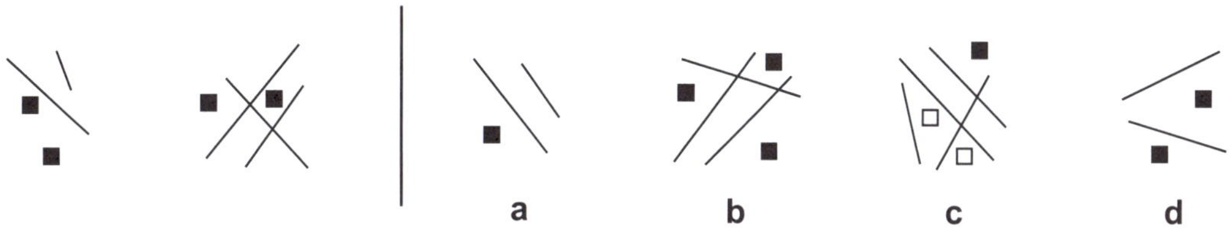

Complete the Square Grid

Work out which of the options best fits in place of the missing square in the grid.
Example:

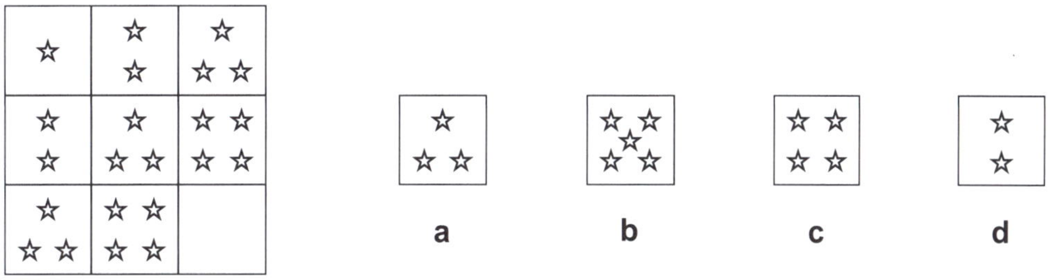

(b)

Working from left to right, the number of stars increases by one in each grid square.

8. (b)

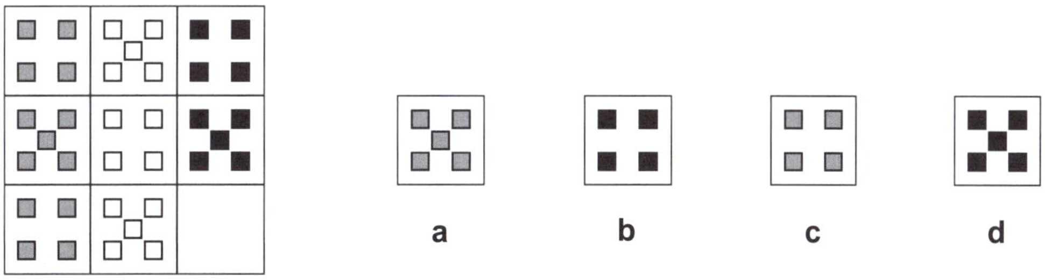

9. (C)

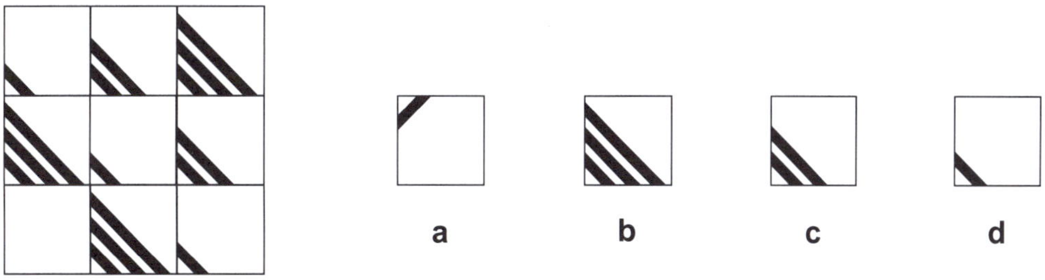

10. (b)

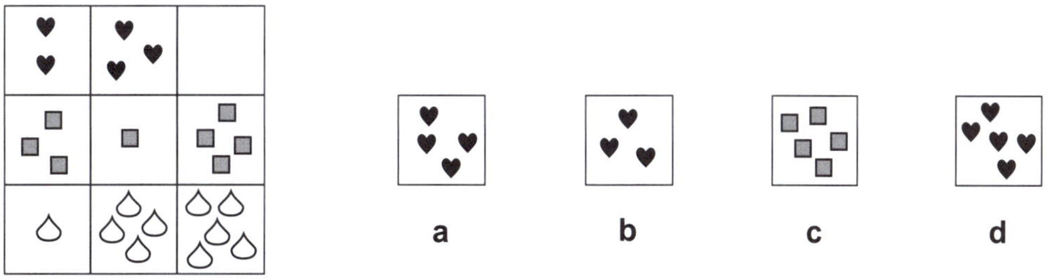

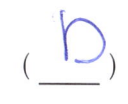

Spotting Patterns

Pointing

Look out for arrows or other shapes which point in different directions — they could be useful.

Warm Up

1. What **shape** is the arrow pointing at in each figure?

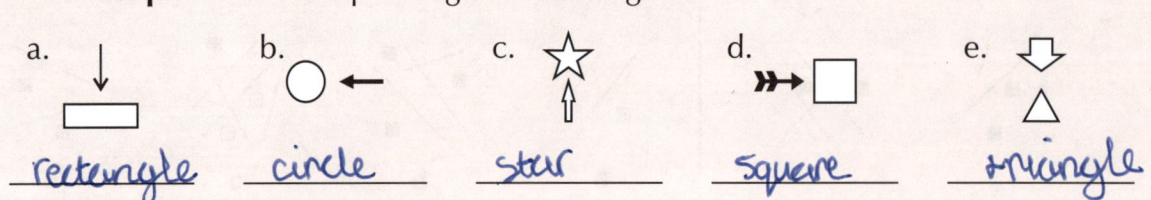

   a. _rectangle_   b. _circle_   c. _star_   d. _square_   e. _triangle_

2. Which **direction** (up, down, left or right) is each arrow pointing in?

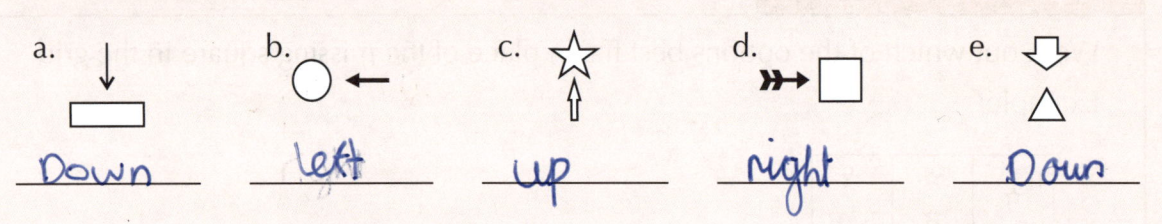

   a. _Down_   b. _left_   c. _up_   d. _right_   e. _Down_

3. How many arrows in this figure point **clockwise**? How many point **anticlockwise**?

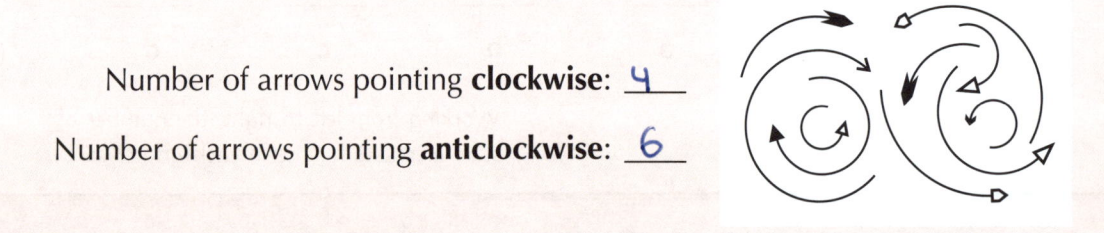

   Number of arrows pointing **clockwise**: _4_

   Number of arrows pointing **anticlockwise**: _6_

Find the Figure Like the First Three

Work out which option is most like the three figures on the left.
Example:

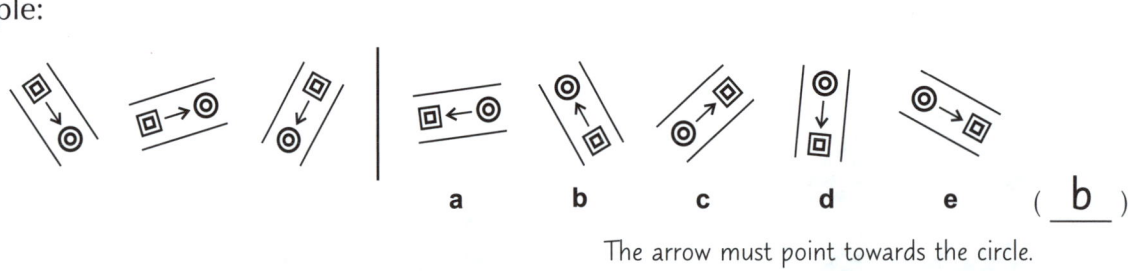

a   b   c   d   e   (_b_)

The arrow must point towards the circle.

4.   a   b   c   d   e   (_E_)

5.   a   b   c   d   e   (_C_)

Spotting Patterns

6. (e)

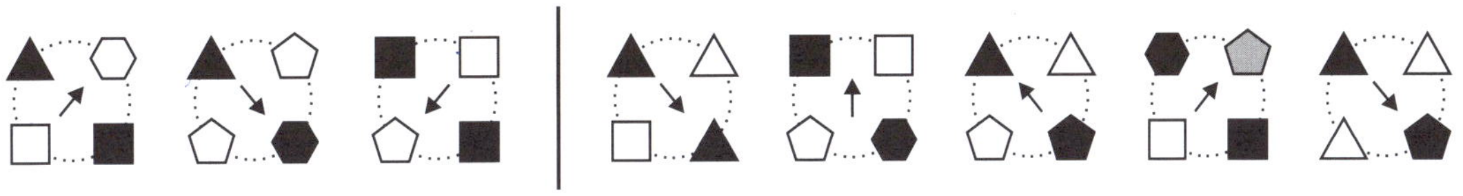

7. (c)

Odd One Out

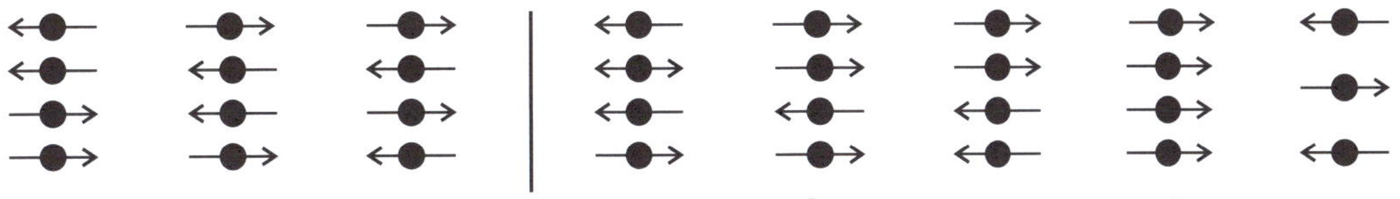

Find the figure in each row that is most unlike the other figures.

Example:

(b)

In all other figures, the arrows all go in the same direction (either clockwise or anticlockwise).

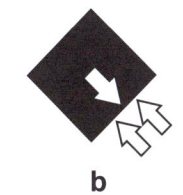

8. (D)

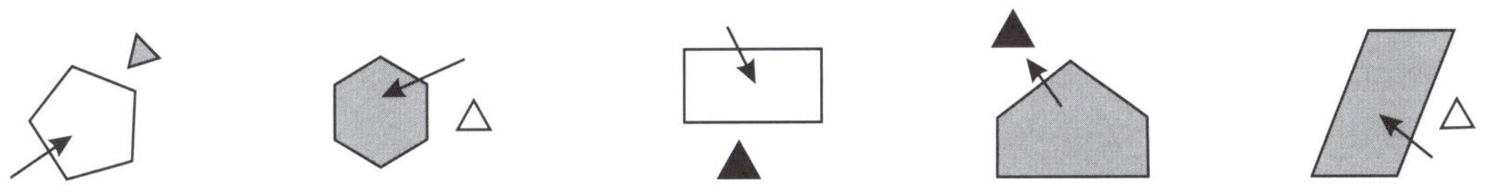

9. (c)

10. (E)

Spotting Patterns

# Shading and Line Types

Look out for shapes that have different shadings, or lines that are dashed, dotted or wavy.

Warm Up

1. How many **different types of line** are there in each figure?
   a. 1   b. 3   c. 2   d. 3   e. 3   f. 3   g. 3

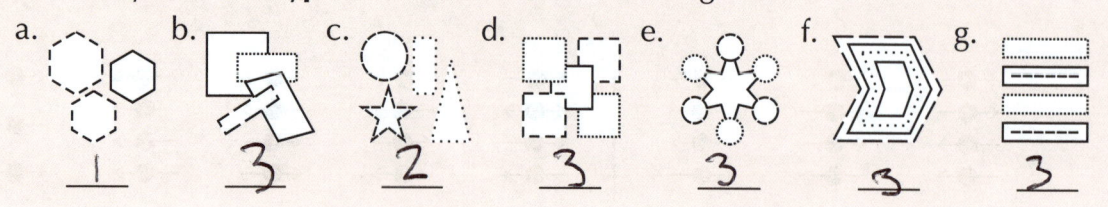

2. Write down the number of the **circle** with the **same shading** as each shape (a-g).
   a. 1   b. 3   c. 4   d. 2   e. 1   f. 4   g. 1

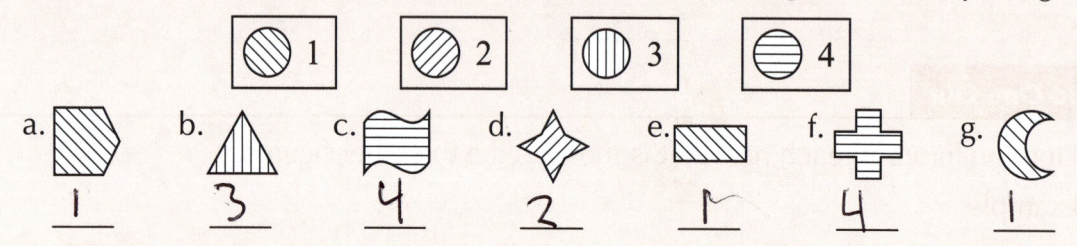

3. How many shapes in this figure have **grey** shading? How many are **spotted**?
   Number of **grey** shapes: 5
   Number of **spotted** shapes: 6

Complete the Pair

Look at how the first two figures are changed, and then work out which option would look like the third figure if you changed it in the same way.

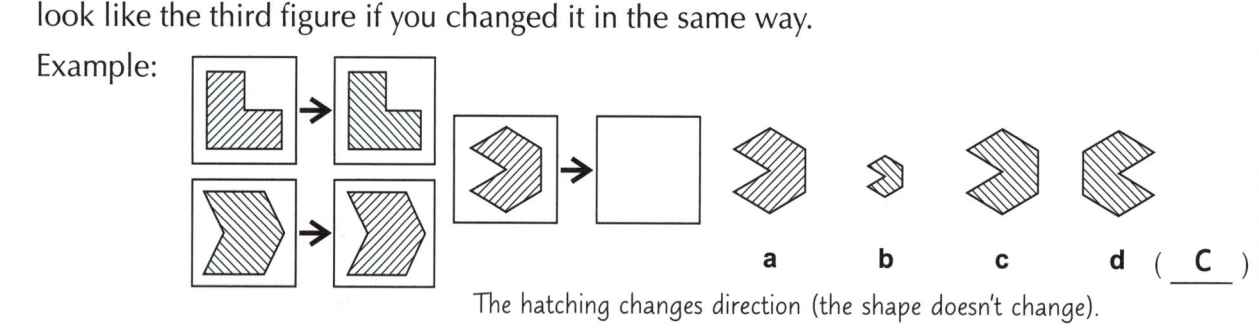

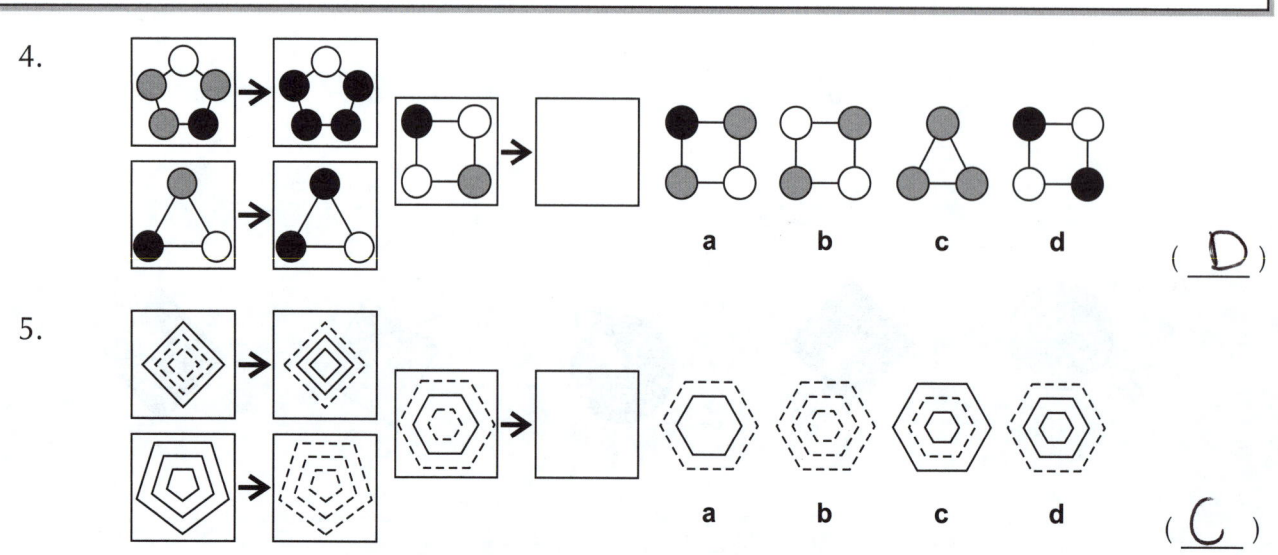

Example: (C)
The hatching changes direction (the shape doesn't change).

4. (D)

5. (C)

Spotting Patterns

6. (b)

7. (C)

Complete the Square Grid

Work out which of the options best fits in place of the missing square in the grid.
Example:

(a)

Going down each column, the shapes stay the same.
Each type of shading appears once in each row and column.

8. (B)

9. (B)

10. (d)

Spotting Patterns

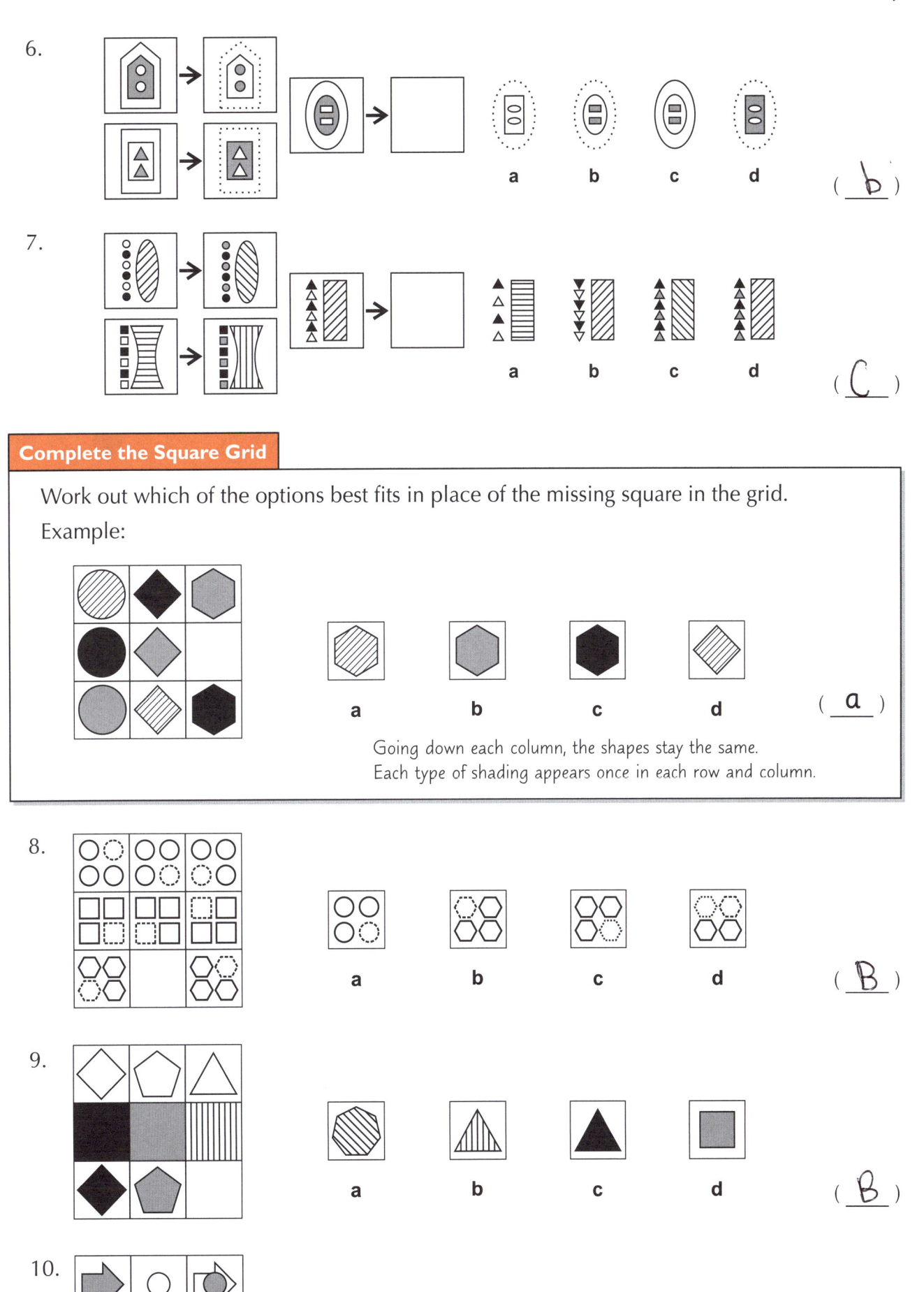

Order and Position

If a figure has more than one shape, look at the order of the shapes are in, as well as their positions.

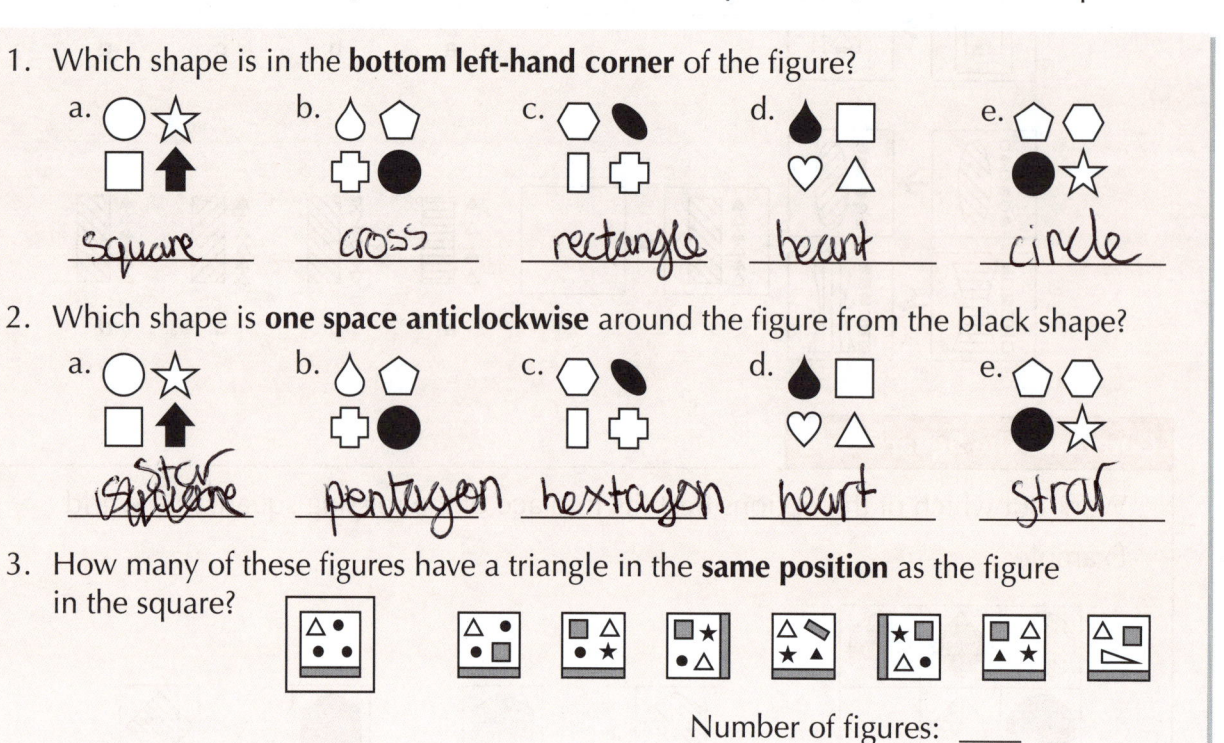

Warm Up

1. Which shape is in the **bottom left-hand corner** of the figure?

   a. square   b. cross   c. rectangle   d. heart   e. circle

2. Which shape is **one space anticlockwise** around the figure from the black shape?

   a. square   b. pentagon   c. hexagon   d. heart   e. star

3. How many of these figures have a triangle in the **same position** as the figure in the square?

   Number of figures: ____

Complete the Hexagonal Grid

Work out which of the options best fits in place of the missing hexagon in the grid.

Example:

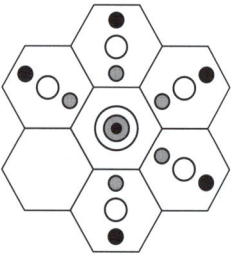

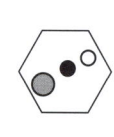

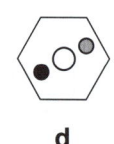

(d)

The circles are always in the order: grey, white, black, with the grey circle closest to the central hexagon.

4.   a   b   c   d   (___)

5.   a   b   c   d   (___)

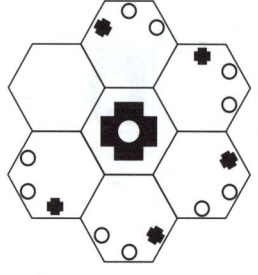

Spotting Patterns

6.

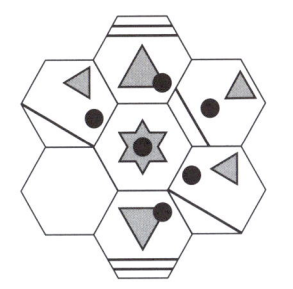

7.

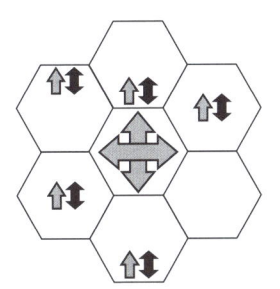

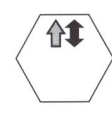

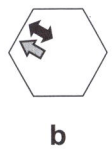

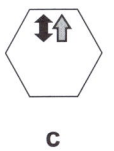

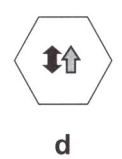

Find the Figure Like the First Three

Work out which option is most like the three figures on the left.

Example:

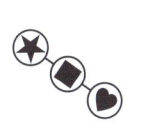

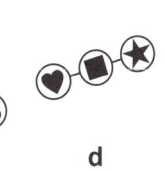

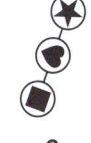

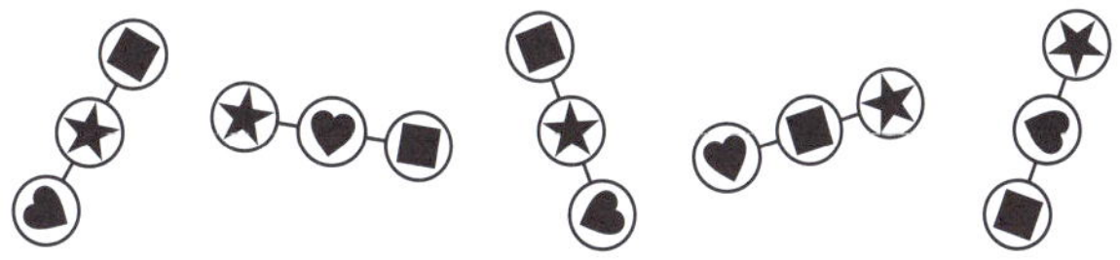

The square must be in the middle circle. (_d_)

8.

9.

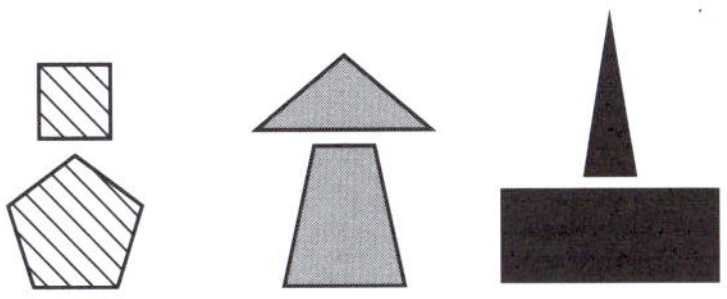

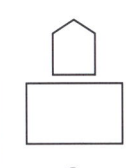

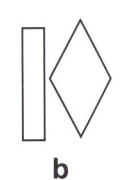

10.

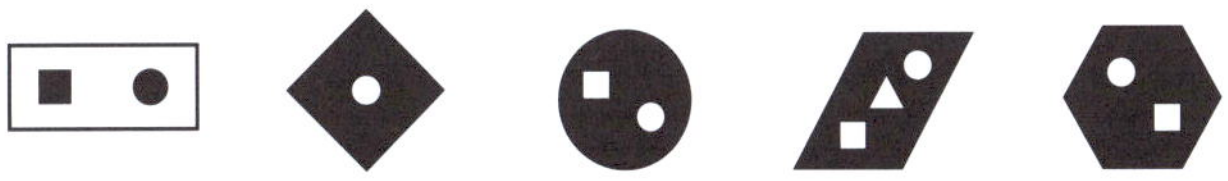

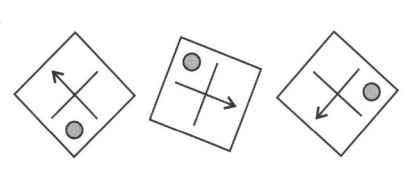

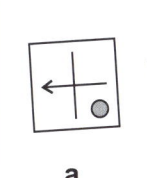

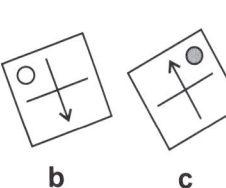

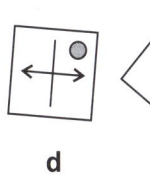

Spotting Patterns

Rotation

Shapes will get rotated in a lot of questions, so practise working out what they'll look like.

Warm Up

1. The **black** arrow has **rotated 90 degrees** away from the **white** arrow. Has it rotated **clockwise** or **anticlockwise**? Write **C** for clockwise or **A** for anticlockwise.

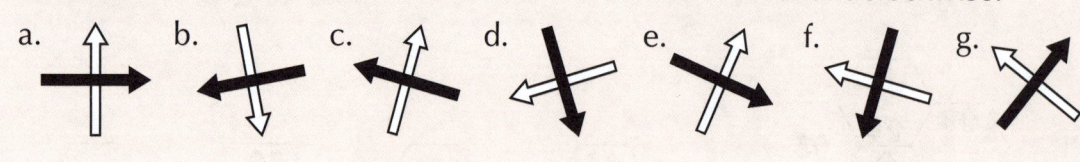

   a.   b.   c.   d.   e.   f.   g.

   ___   ___   ___   ___   ___   ___   ___

2. Has the first shape been rotated **45**, **90** or **180 degrees** to make the second shape?

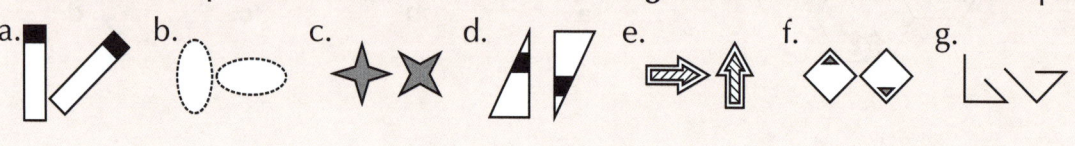

   a.   b.   c.   d.   e.   f.   g.

   ___   ___   ___   ___   ___   ___   ___

Complete the Series

Work out which of the options best fits in place of the missing square in the series.
Example:

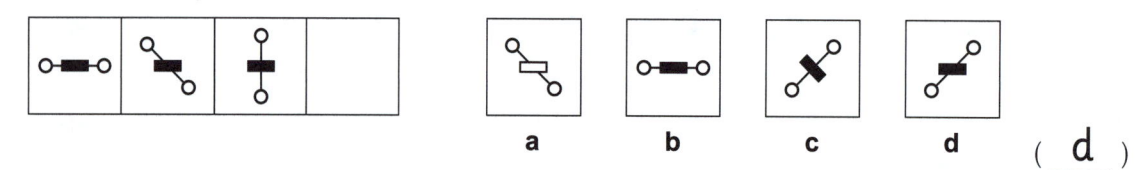

   a   b   c   d   (_d_)

In each series square, the line rotates 45 degrees clockwise. (The black rectangle does not change.)

3.

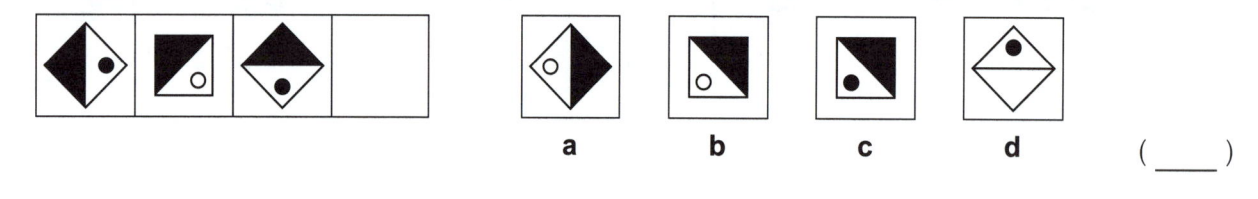

   a   b   c   d   (___)

4.

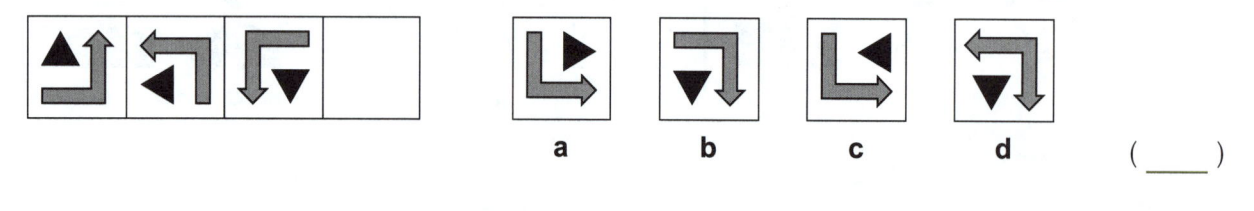

   a   b   c   d   (___)

5.

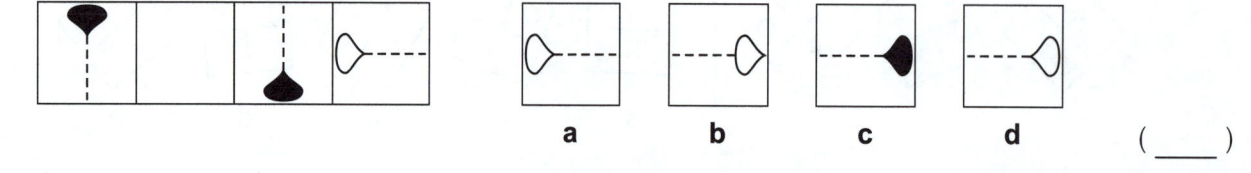

   a   b   c   d   (___)

Spotting Patterns

Reflection

If you find reflection tricky, it might help you to imagine how the shape would look in a mirror.

Warm Up

1. If each figure is **reflected** across the line, will it still look identical to the original?

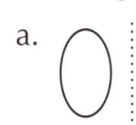

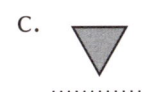

   a. ⬭   b. ★   c. ▽   d. ▭   e. ◆   f. ◐

2. Has the first shape been **reflected** or **rotated** to make the second shape?

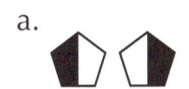

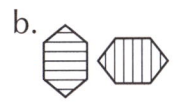

   a.   b.   c.   d.   e.

Reflect the Figure

Work out which option would look like the figure on the left if it was reflected over the line.

Example:

Reflect

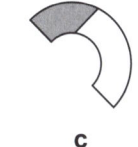

a   b   c   d   (b)

Options A, C and D are rotations instead of reflections.

3. **Reflect**

   a   b   c   d   (__)

4. **Reflect**

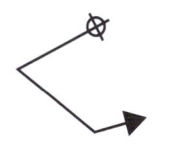

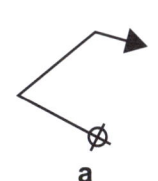

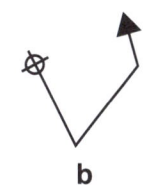

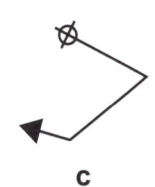

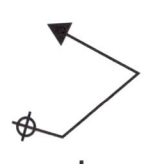

   a   b   c   d   (__)

5. **Reflect**

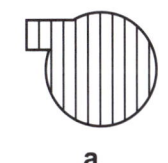

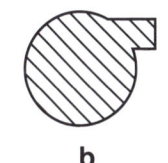

   a   b   c   d   (__)

Spotting Patterns

Layering

Watch out for questions where the shapes overlap each other in different ways.

Warm Up

1. Which **shape** is in **front** of the other shapes?

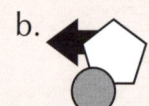

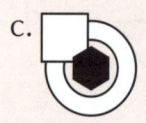

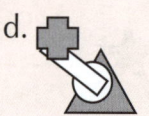

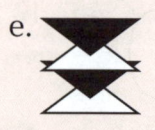

   a.   b.   c.   d.   e.   f.

   _____   _____   _____   _____   _____   _____

2. What **colour** is the shape at the **back**?

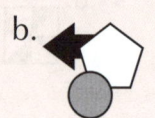

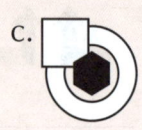

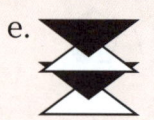

   a.   b.   c.   d.   e.   f.

   _____   _____   _____   _____   _____   _____

3. In the figures below, **extra shapes** have been made where the two shapes **overlap**. How many **sides** does each extra shape have?

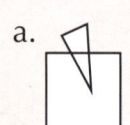

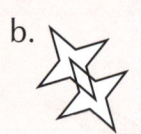

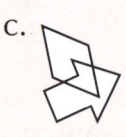

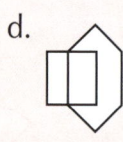

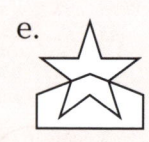

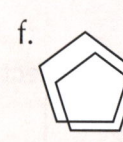

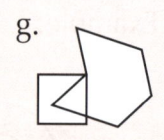

   a.   b.   c.   d.   e.   f.   g.

   _____   _____   _____   _____   _____   _____   _____

Odd One Out

Find the figure in each row that is most unlike the other figures.

Example:

a   b   c   d   e   (**C**)

In all the other figures, the black shape is at the front.

4.

a   b   c   d   e   (___)

5.

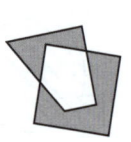

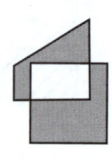

a   b   c   d   e   (___)

Spotting Patterns

6.

   a   b   c   d   e   (___)

7.

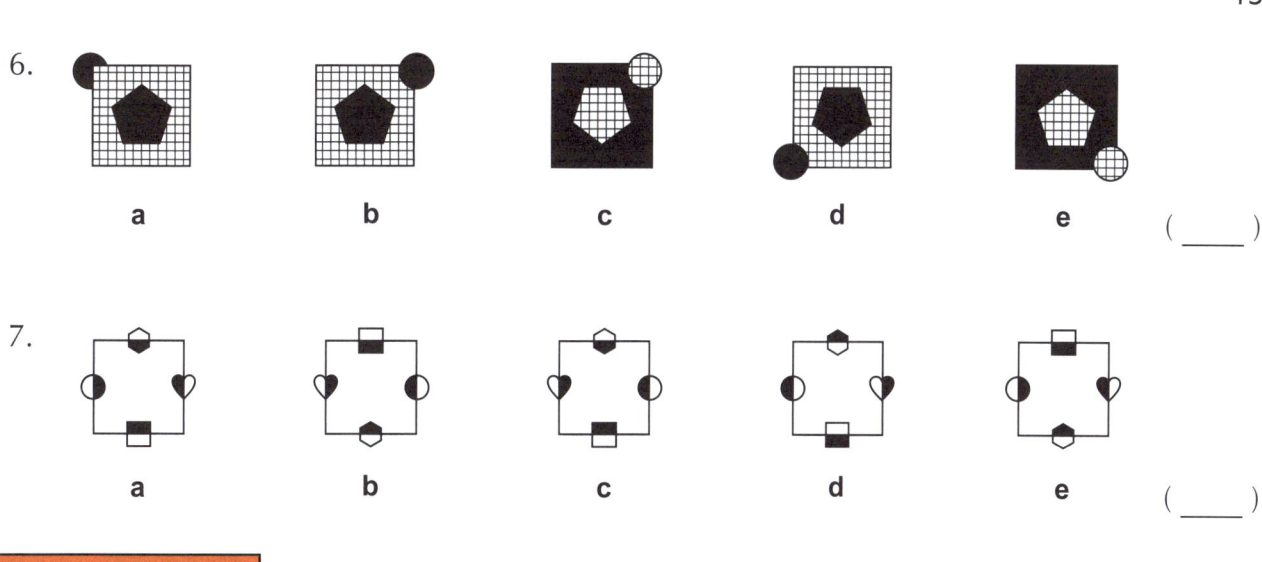

   a   b   c   d   e   (___)

Complete the Pair

Look at how the first two figures are changed, and then work out which option would look like the third figure if you changed it in the same way.

Example:

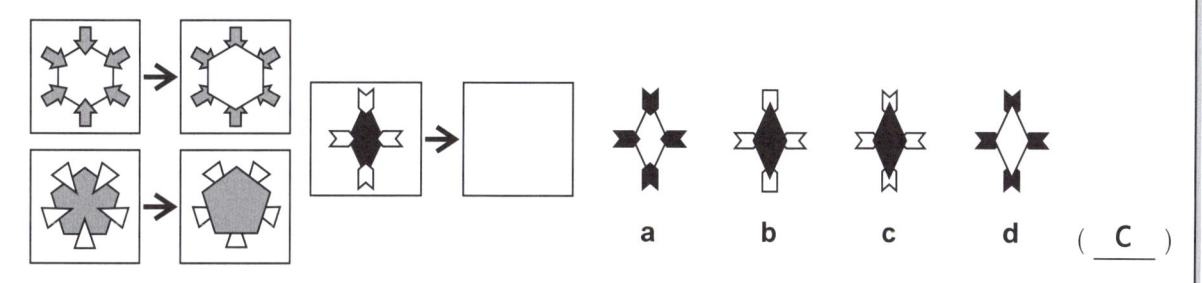

   a   b   c   d   (C)

The arrows move to the back of the figure and the central shape moves to the front.

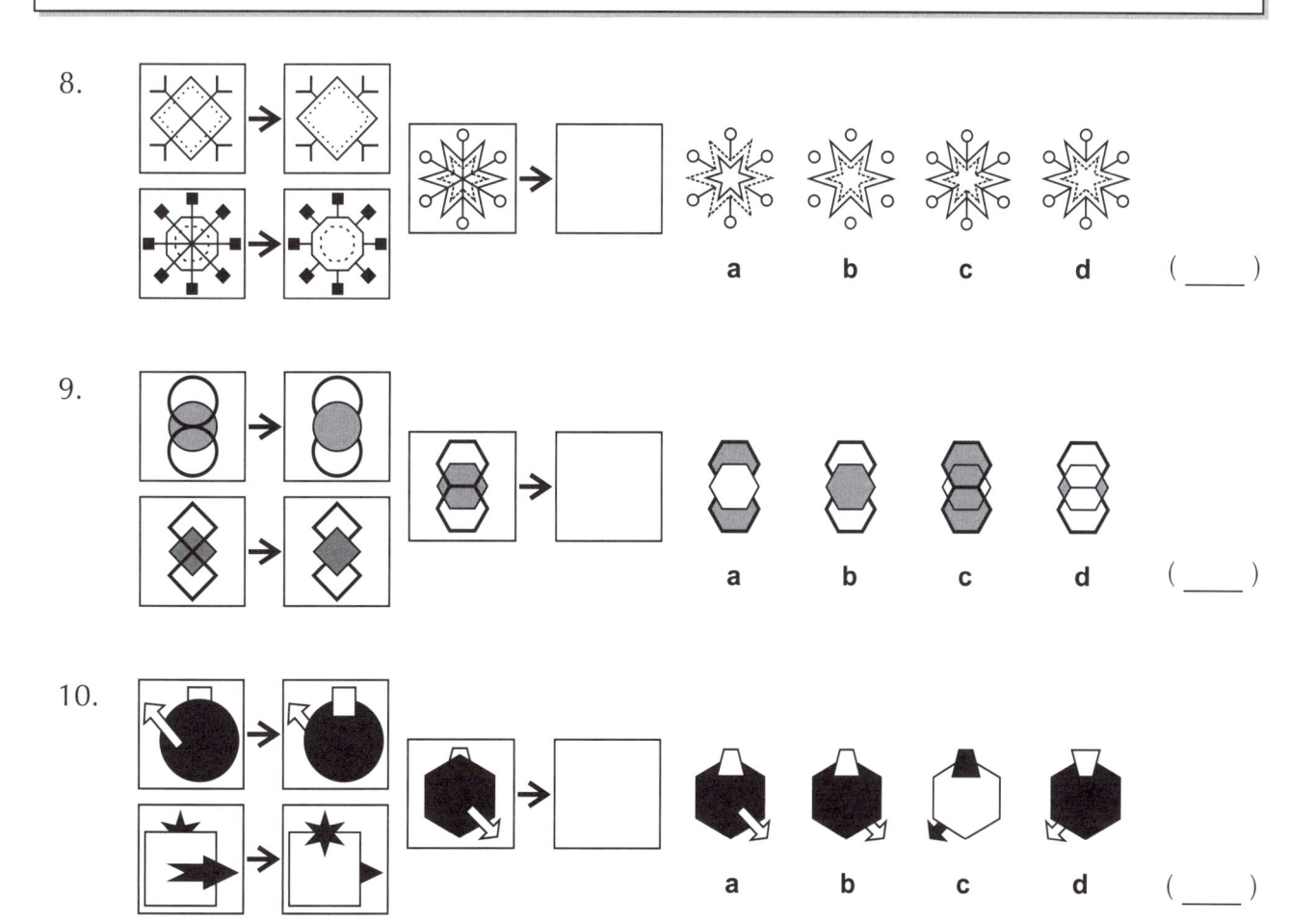

8.

   a   b   c   d   (___)

9.

   a   b   c   d   (___)

10.

   a   b   c   d   (___)

Spotting Patterns

3D Shapes and Folding

Rotating 3D Shapes

3D shapes sometimes look very different when you turn them around.

Warm Up

1. How **many** of the figures below contain the block inside the square?

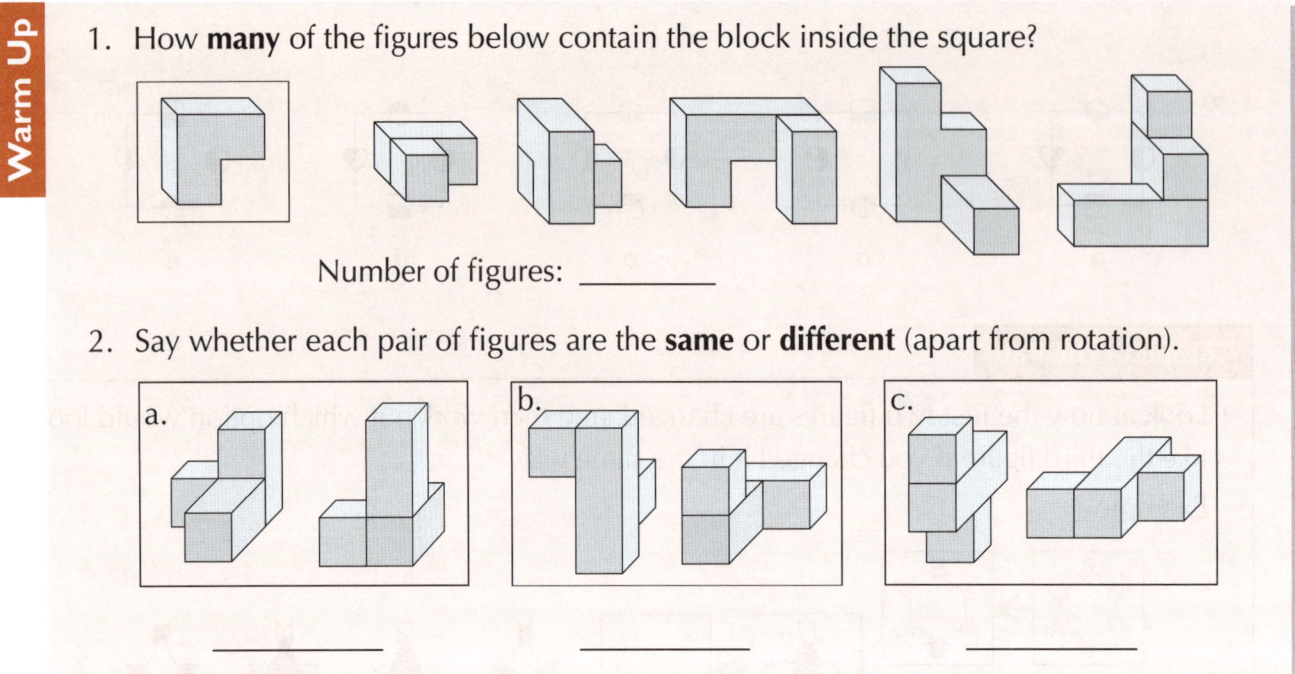

    Number of figures: _____

2. Say whether each pair of figures are the **same** or **different** (apart from rotation).

    a. _____   b. _____   c. _____

3D Building Blocks

Work out which set of blocks can be put together to make the 3D figure on the left.

Example:

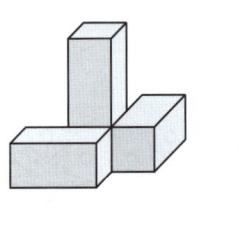

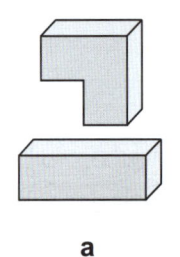

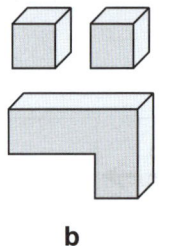

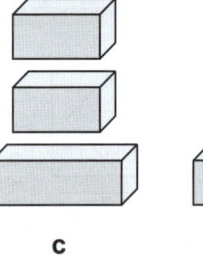

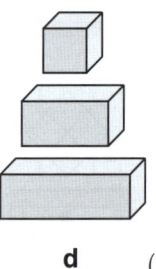

a   b   c   d   (**C**)

The longer block rotates to stand upright and the shorter blocks are positioned around its base.

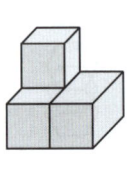

3. a   b   c   d   (___)

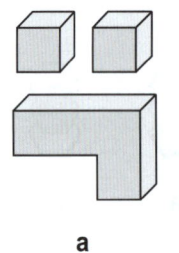

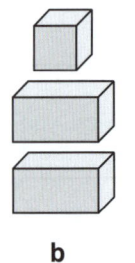

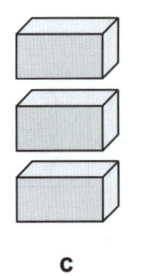

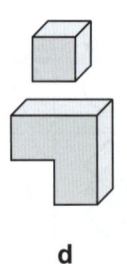

4. a   b   c   d   (___)

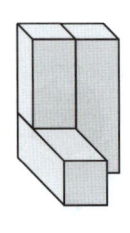

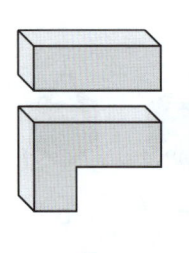

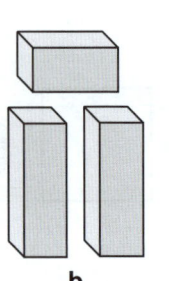

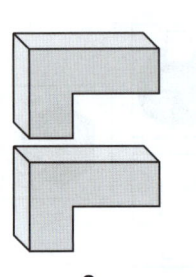

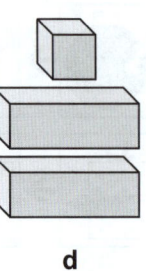

5.

        a   b   c   d   (____)

3D Rotation

Work out which 3D figure in the grey box has been rotated to make the new 3D figure.

Example:

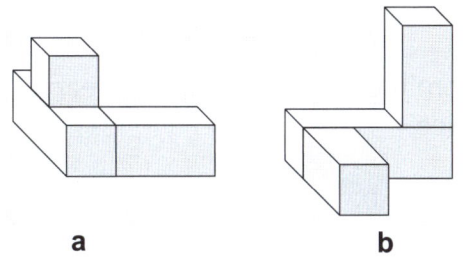

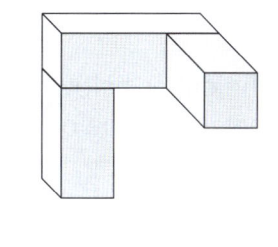

    a   b   (b)

Shape B has been rotated 90 degrees towards you, top-to-bottom.

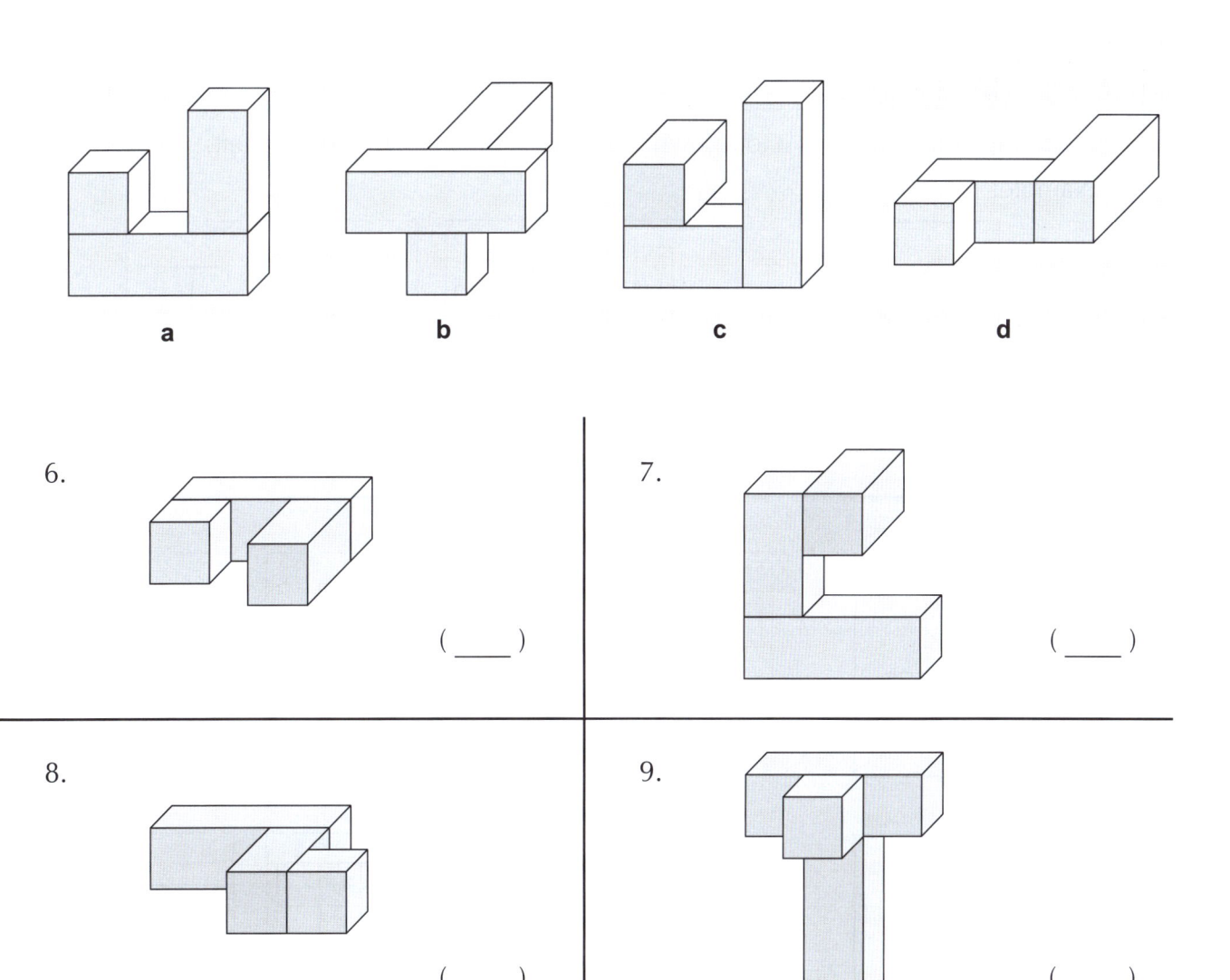

    a   b   c   d

6. (____)

7. (____)

8. (____)

9. (____)

3D Shapes and Folding

2D and 3D Shapes

These pages are about imagining 2D shapes in three dimensions and 3D shapes in two dimensions.

Warm Up

1. If you looked at each figure from **directly above**, how many **cubes** could you see?

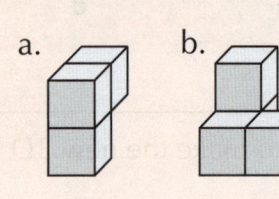

   a.   b.   c. 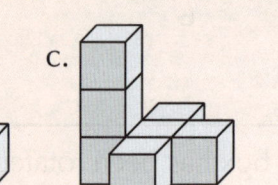   d. 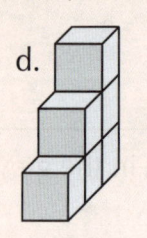   e. 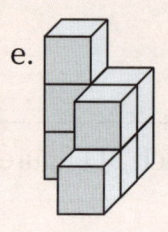   f.

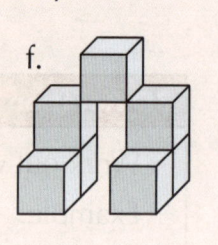

2. The cubes below are made from the net on the left. For each cube, give the **letter** that should be on the **blank face**.

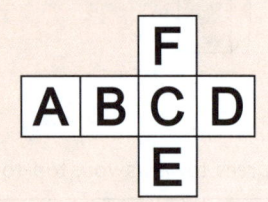

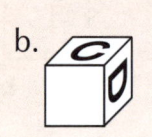

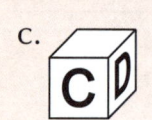

2D Views of 3D Shapes

Work out which option is a top-down 2D view of the 3D figure on the left.

Example:

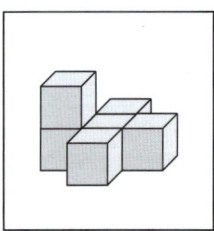

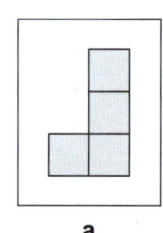

a 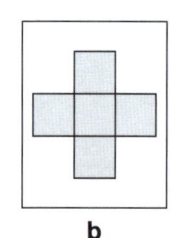   b 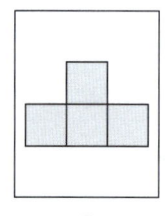   c 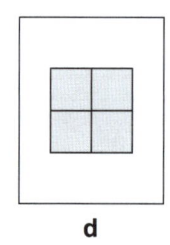   d   (**b**)

There are five blocks visible from above, which rules out options A, C and D.

3. 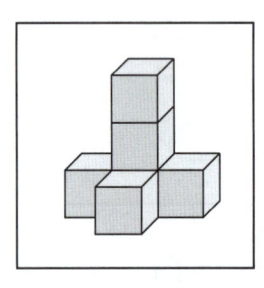 a 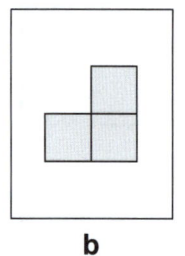   b 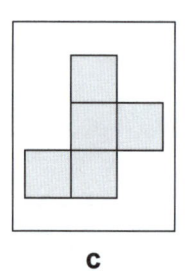   c 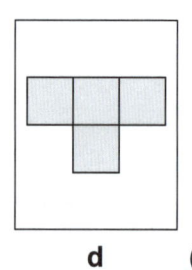   d   (___)

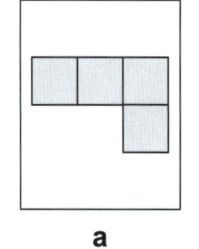

4. 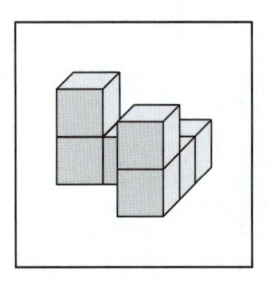 a 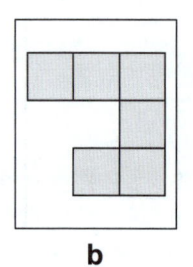   b 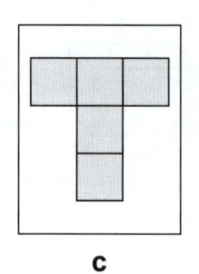   c 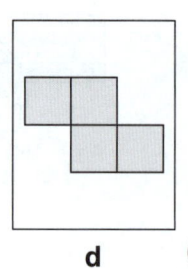   d   (___)

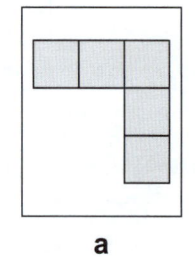

3D Shapes and Folding

5.

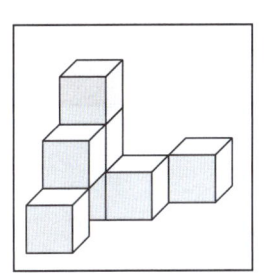

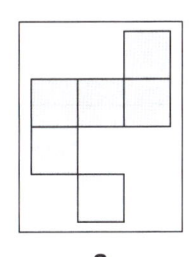

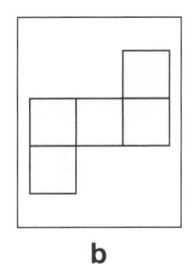

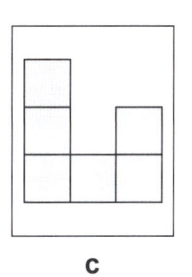

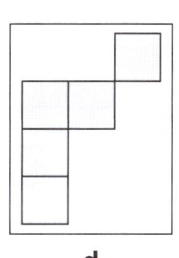

  a   b   c   d   ( )

Cubes and Nets

Work out which of the four cubes can be made from the net.

Example:

  a   b   c   d

(b)

There is only one star, which rules out option A. The number 3 and the thick black circle must be on opposite sides, which rules out option C. There are no black diagonal lines, which rules out option D.

6.

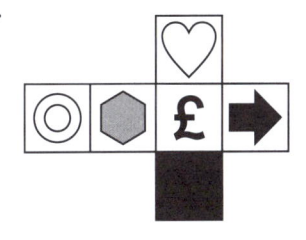

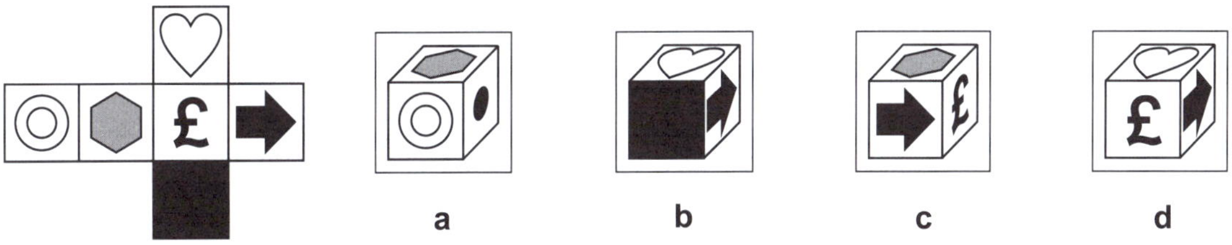

  a   b   c   d   ( )

7.

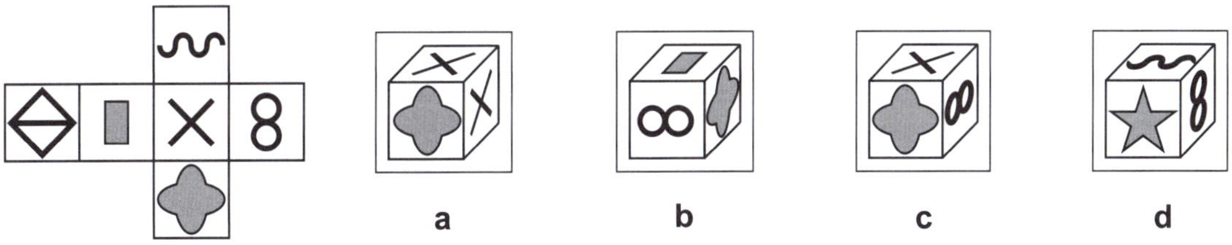

  a   b   c   d   ( )

8.

  a   b   c   d   ( )

3D Shapes and Folding

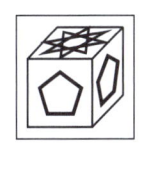

# Folding

You might get questions asking you to imagine folding 2D shapes.

Warm Up

1. Which shape (a to d) **can't** be made by folding the shape on the left once?

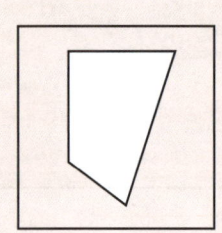

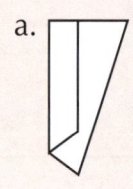

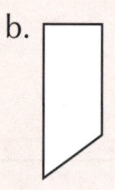

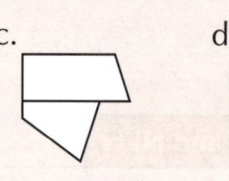

   a.   b.   c.   d.

   Figure: _____

2. The first figure is folded to make the second figure.
   Give the smallest amount of folds that this can be done in.

   a. →   Number of folds: _____

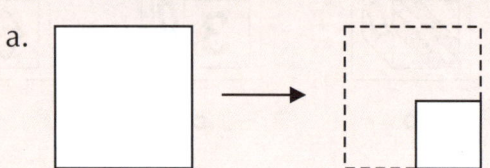

   b. →   Number of folds: _____

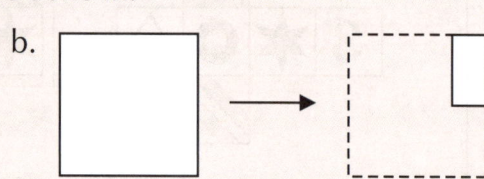

Fold Along the Line

Work out which option shows the figure on the left when folded along the dotted line.

Example:

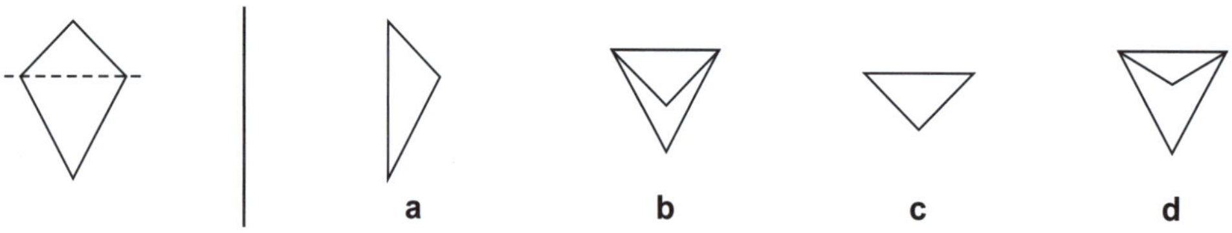

   a   b   c   d   (b)

In option A, the fold line has moved. In option C, the part of the figure originally below the fold line should still be visible. In option D, the part of the figure that has been folded is the wrong shape.

3.   a   b   c   d   (___)

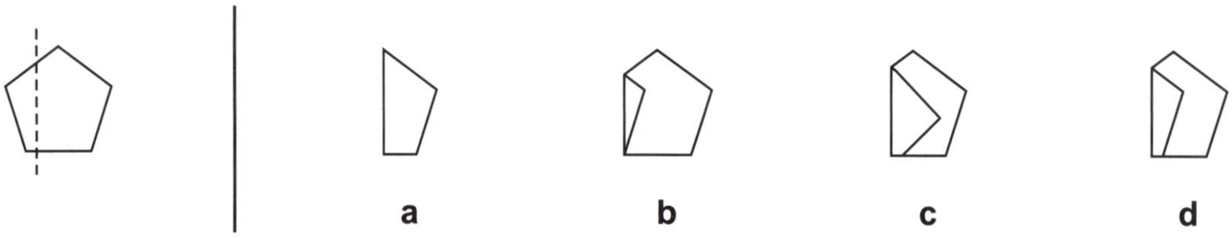

4.   a   b   c   d   (___)

3D Shapes and Folding

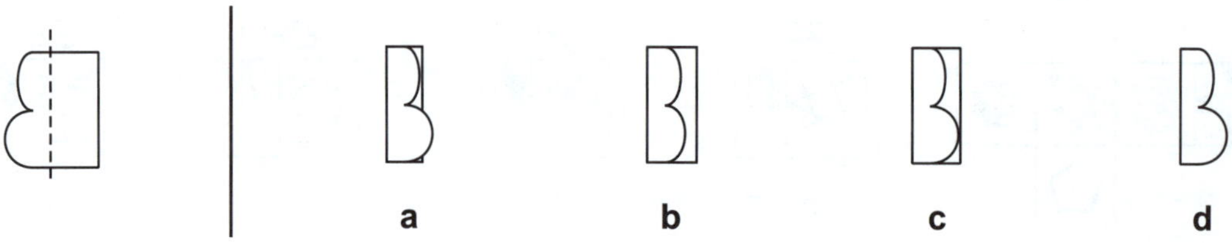

5.

        a   b   c   d

(___)

Fold and Punch

A square is folded and then a hole is punched, as shown on the left.
Work out which option shows the square when unfolded.

Example:

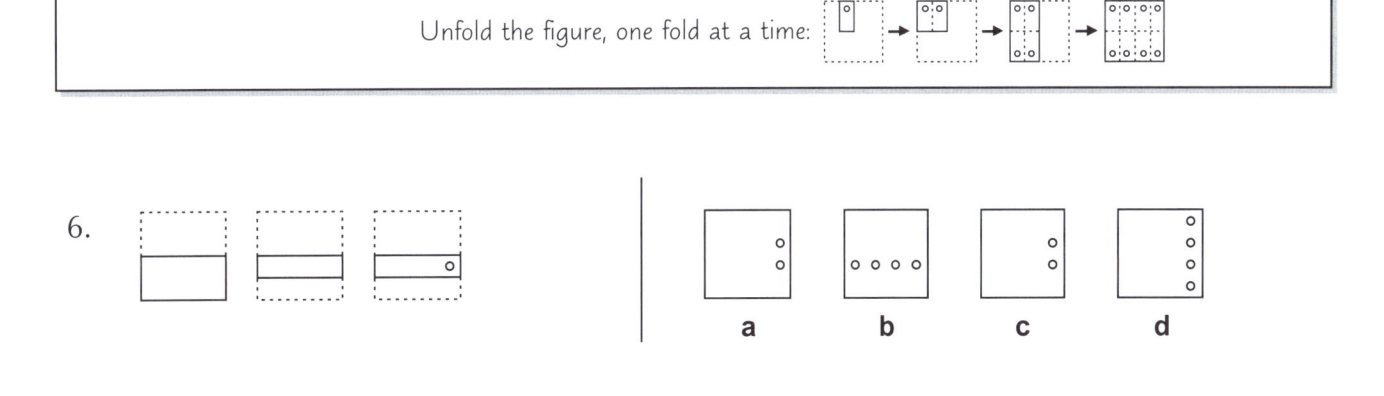

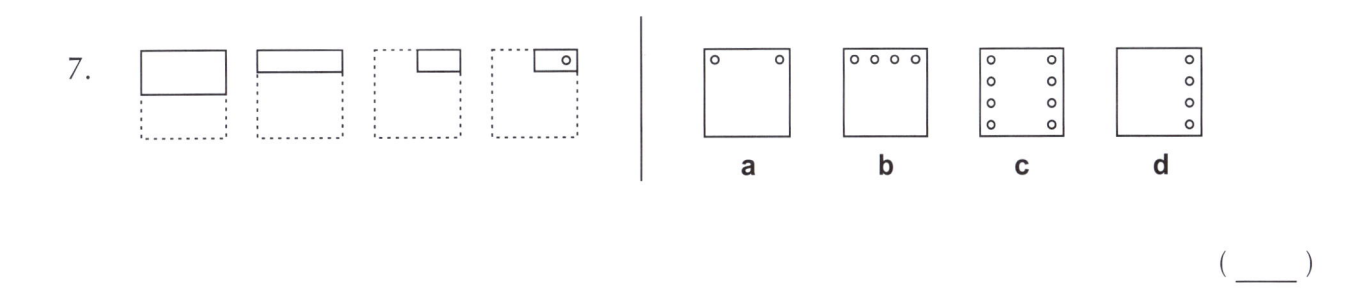

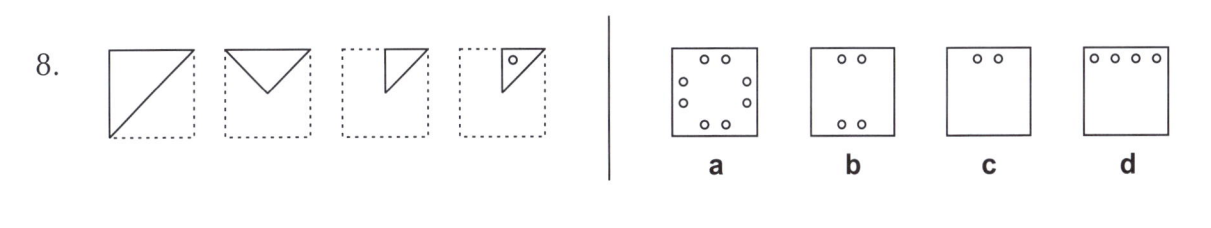

        a   b   c   d

(_a_)

Unfold the figure, one fold at a time:

6.
        a   b   c   d

(___)

7.
        a   b   c   d

(___)

8.
        a   b   c   d

(___)

3D Shapes and Folding

Assessment Test 1

This book contains seven assessment tests, which get harder as you work through them to help you improve your NVR skills.

Allow around 20 minutes to do each test and work as quickly and as carefully as you can.

If you want to attempt each test more than once, you will need to print **multiple-choice answer sheets** for these questions from our website — go to cgpbooks.co.uk/11plus/answer-sheets. If you'd prefer to answer the questions on the page, just follow the instructions in the question.

Section 1 — Complete the Pair

Look at how the first two figures are changed, and then work out which option would look like the third figure if you changed it in the same way.

Example:

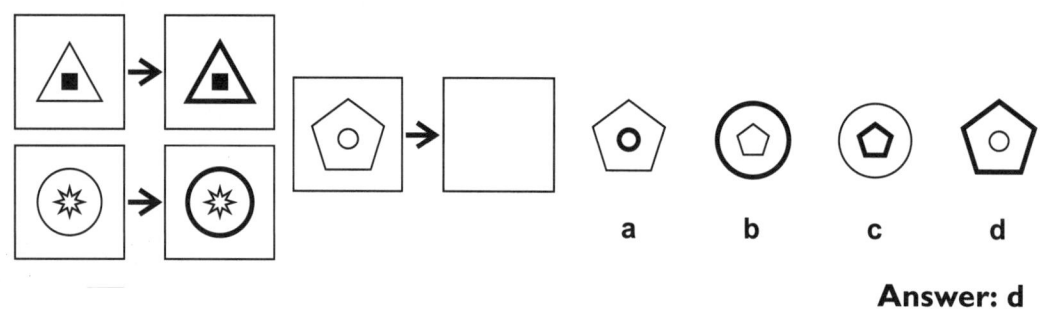

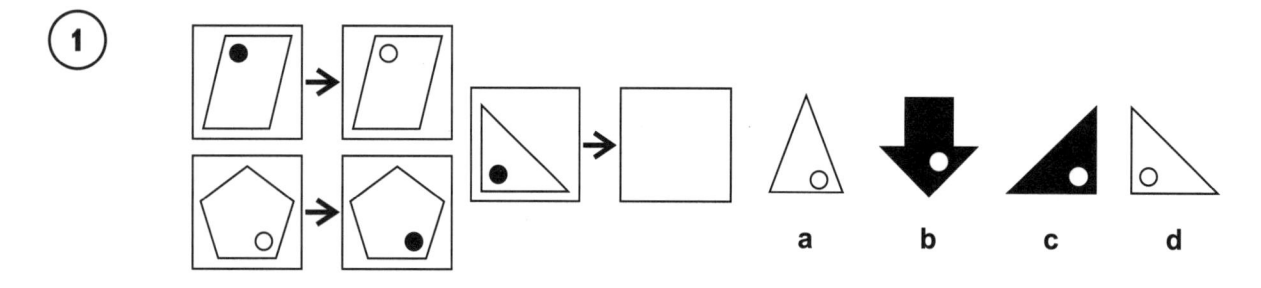

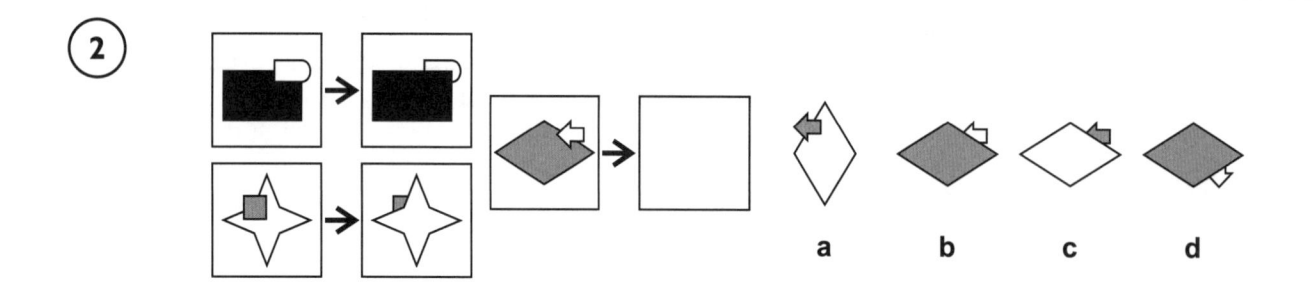

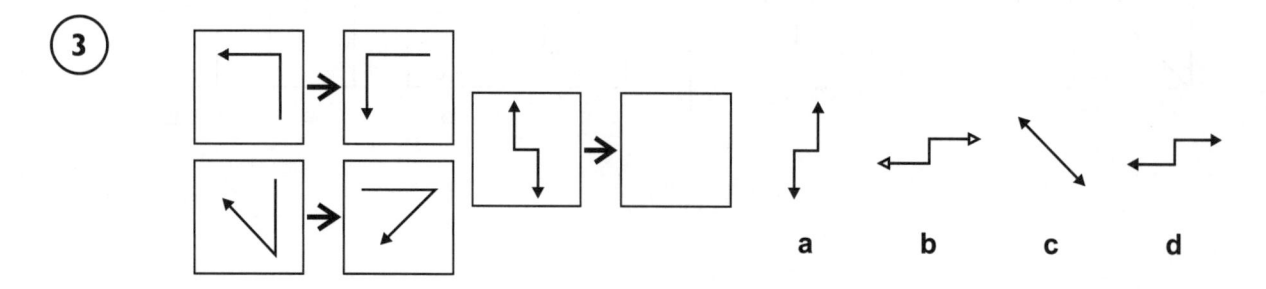

Answer: d

4

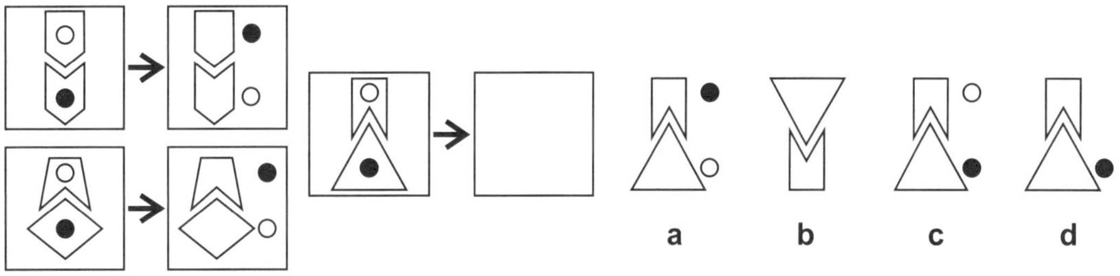

5

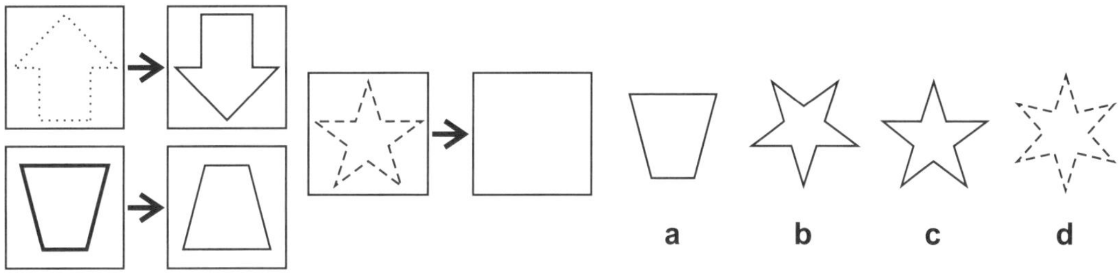

6

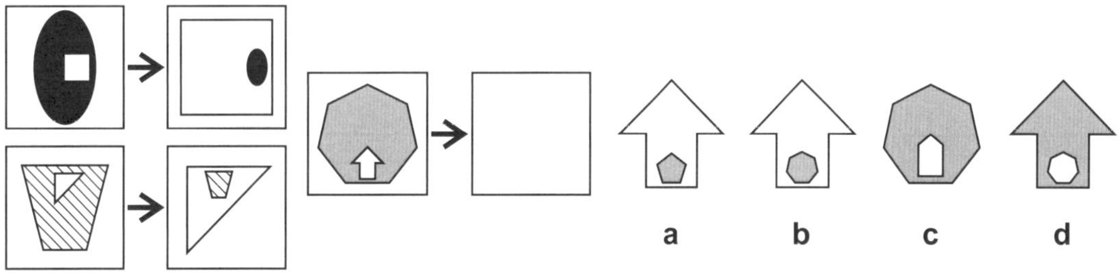

7

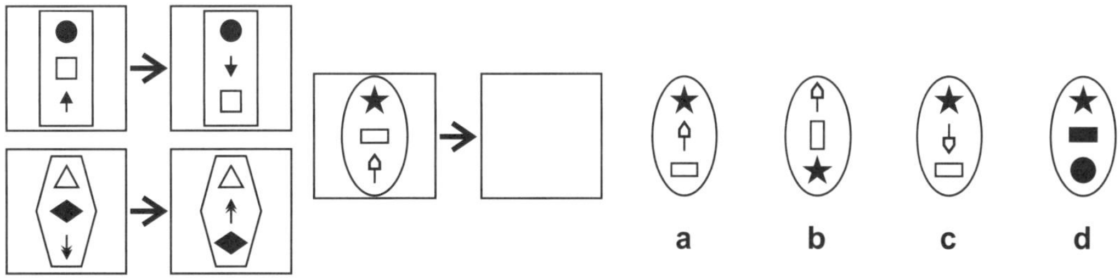

8

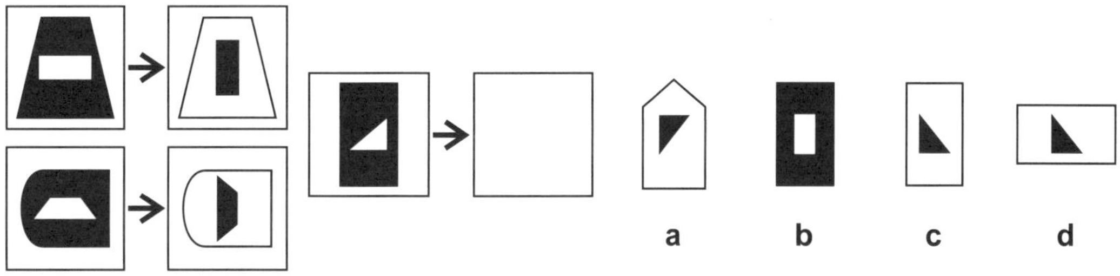

/ 8

Carry on to the next question → →

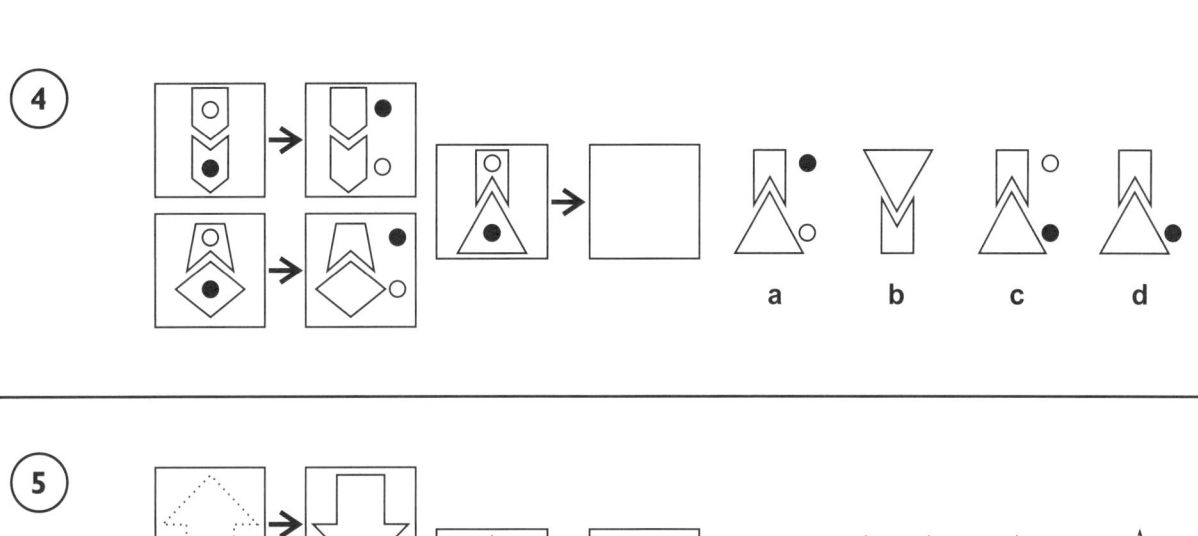

Section 2 — Find the Figure Like the First Two

Work out which option is most like the two figures on the left.

Example:

a b c d

Answer: a

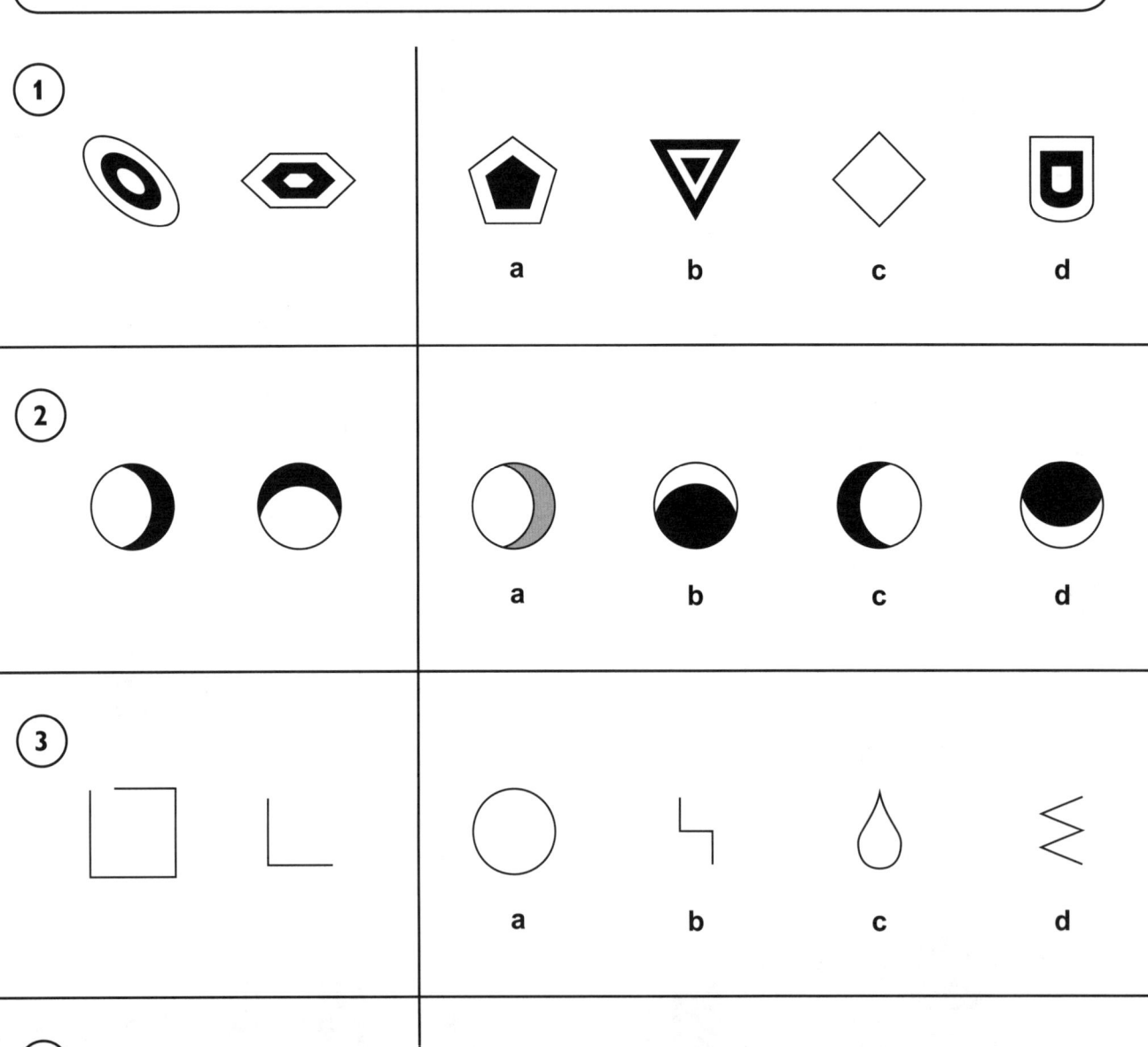

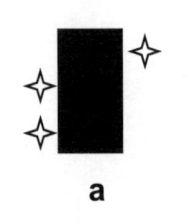

1.

2.

3.

4.

Assessment Test 1

5 ⑤

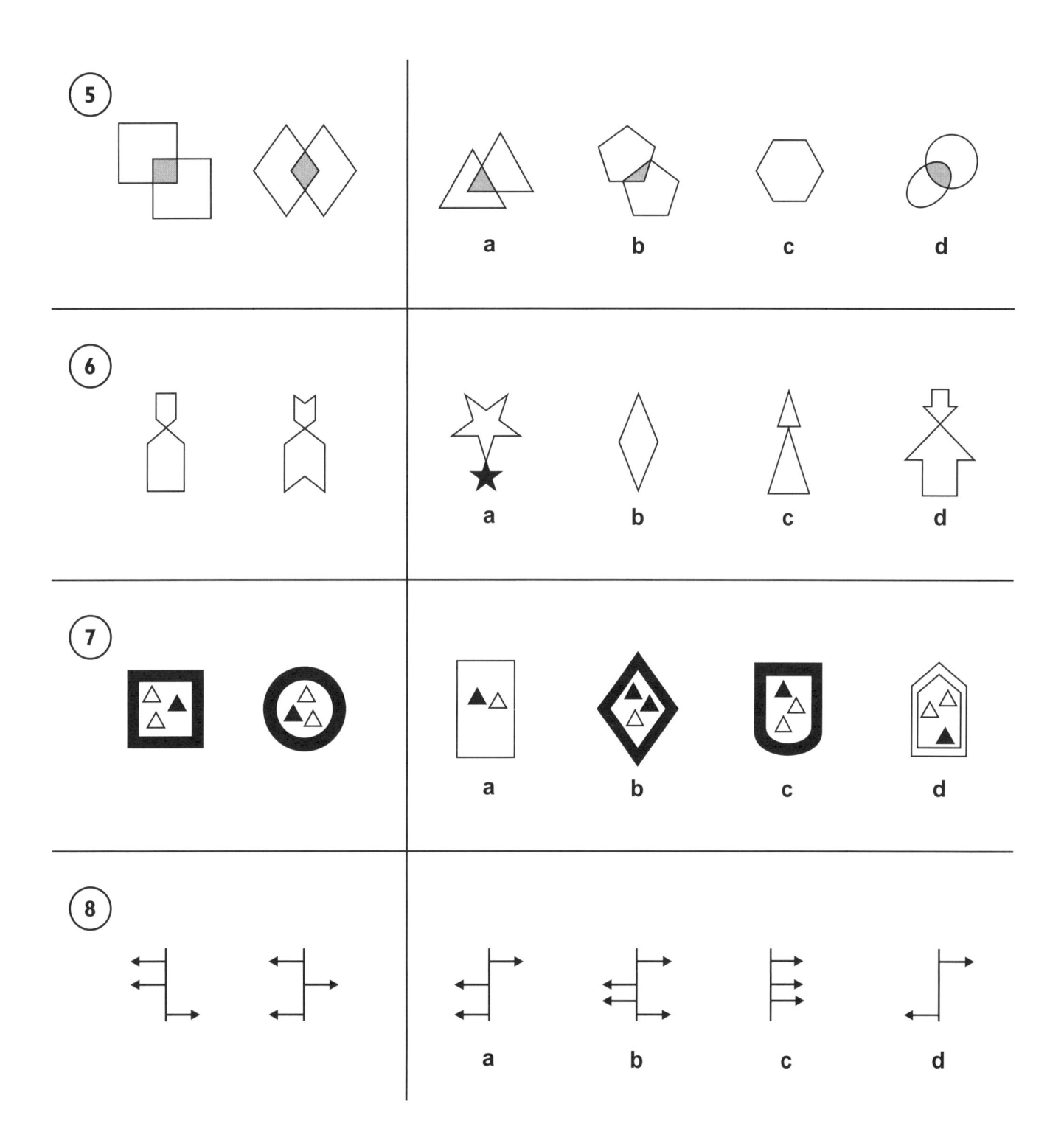

a b c d

6 ⑥

a b c d

7 ⑦

a b c d

8 ⑧

a b c d

/ 8

Carry on to the next question → →

Assessment Test 1

Section 3 — Complete the Hexagonal Grid

Work out which of the options best fits in place of the missing hexagon in the grid.

Example:

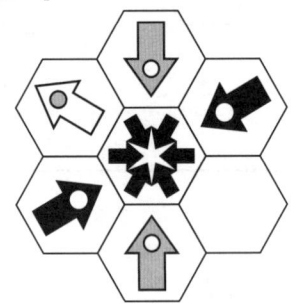

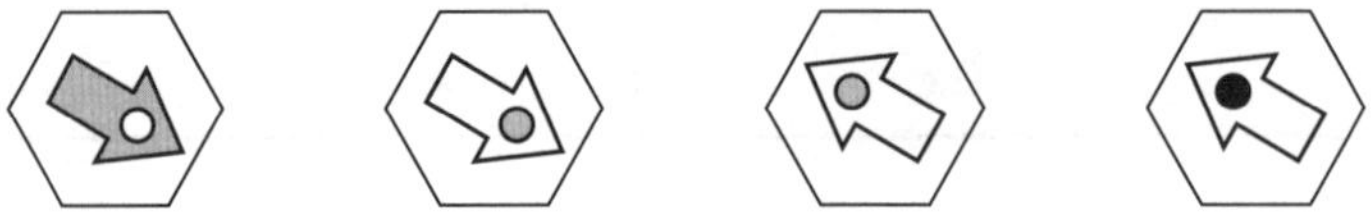

Answer: b

1

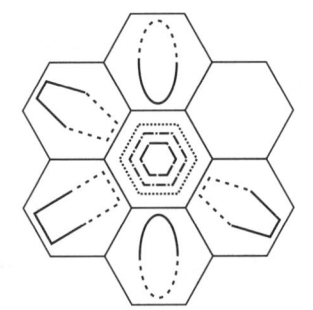

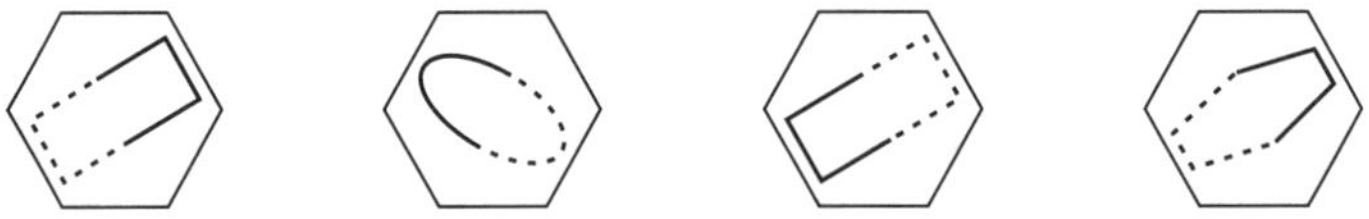

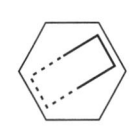

2

3

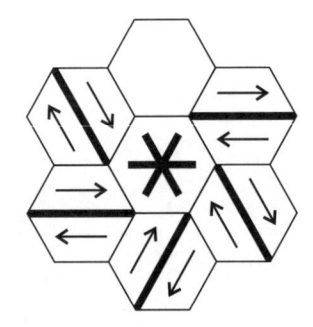

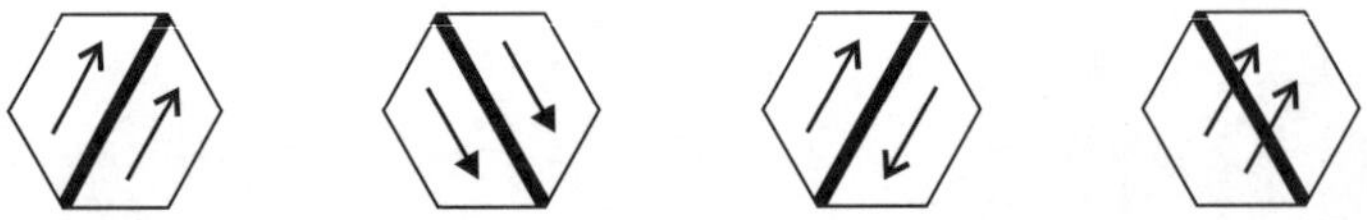

Assessment Test 1

4.

5.

6.

7.

8.

/ 8

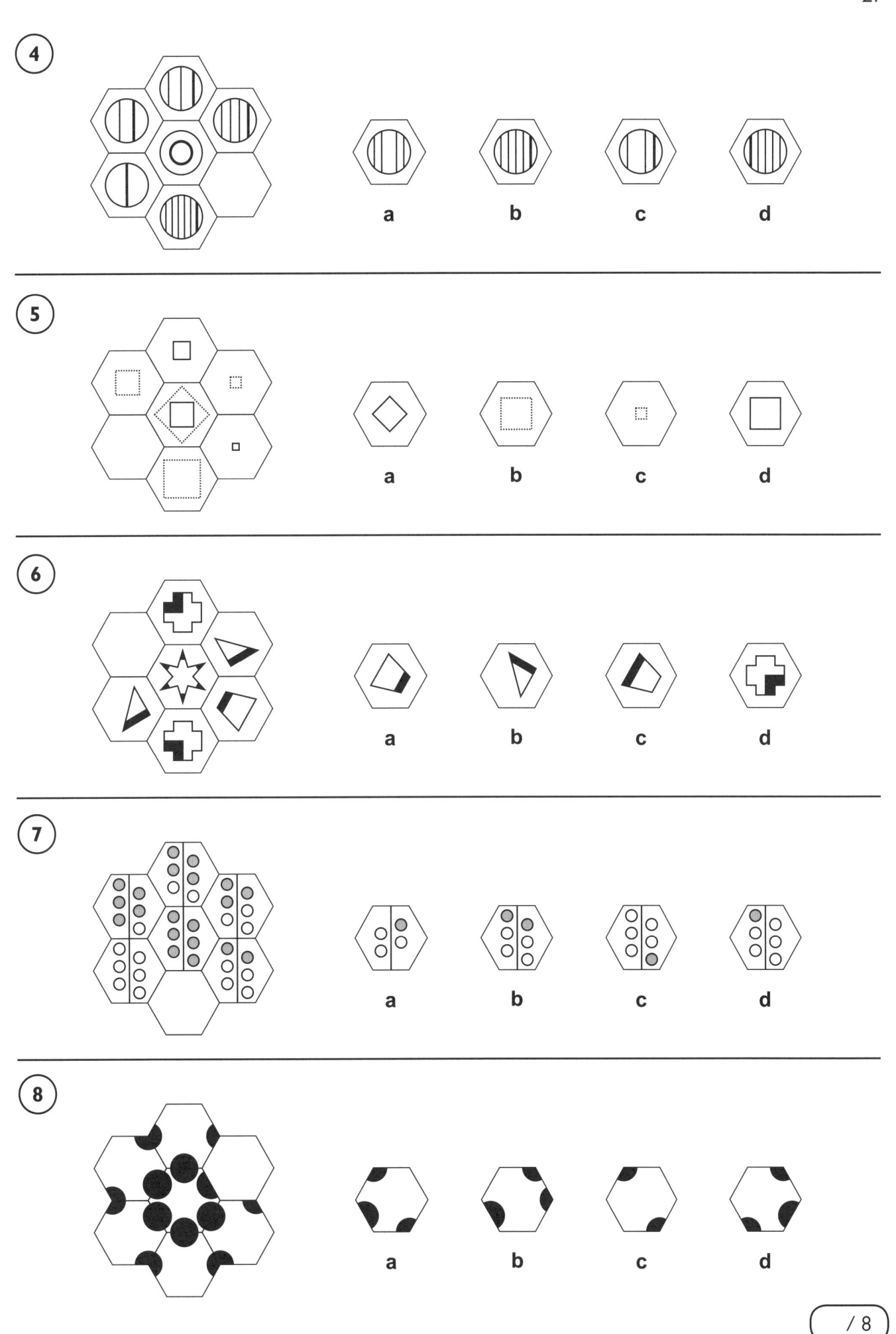

Carry on to the next question → →

Assessment Test 1

Section 4 — Rotate the Figure

Work out which option would look like the figure on the left if it was rotated.

Example:

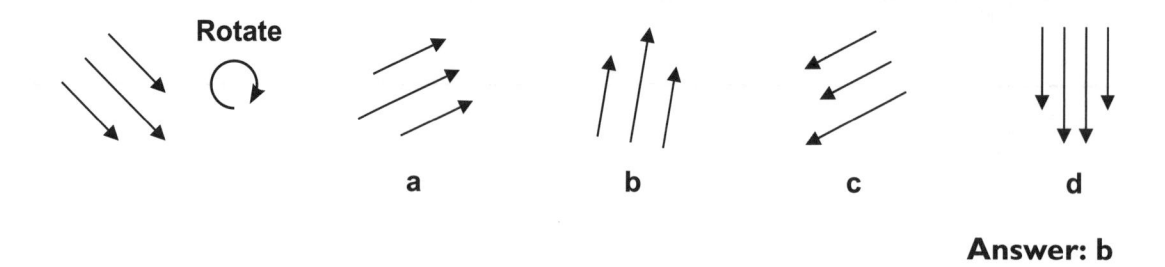

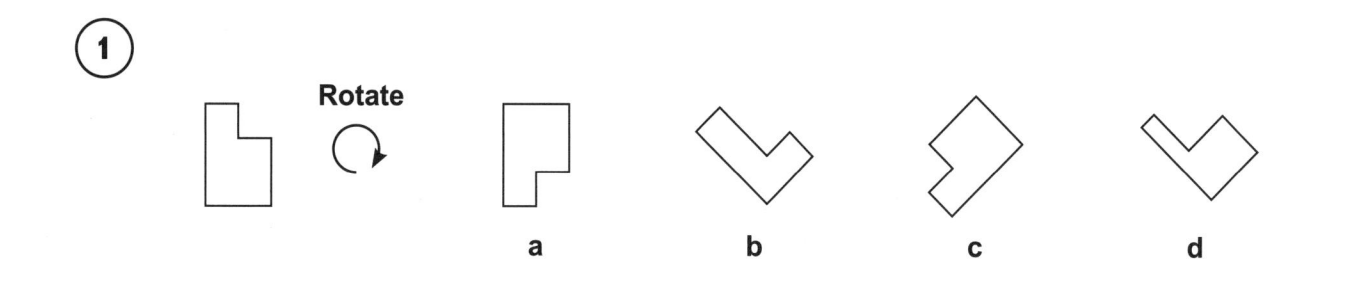

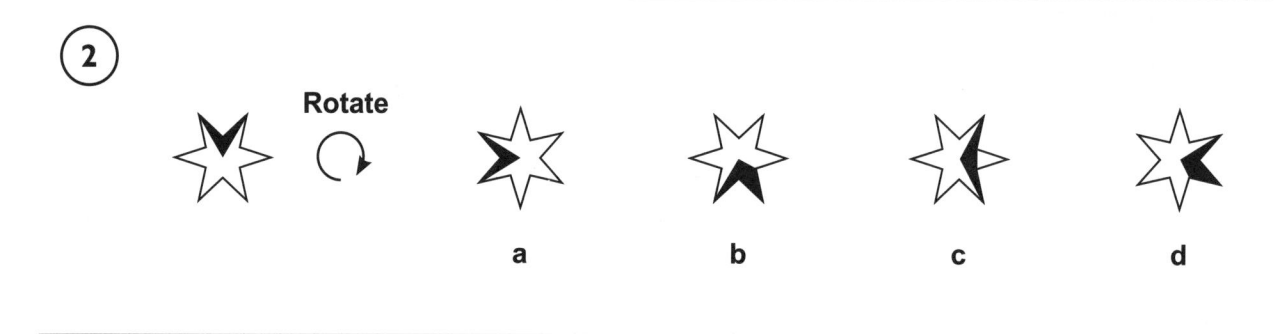

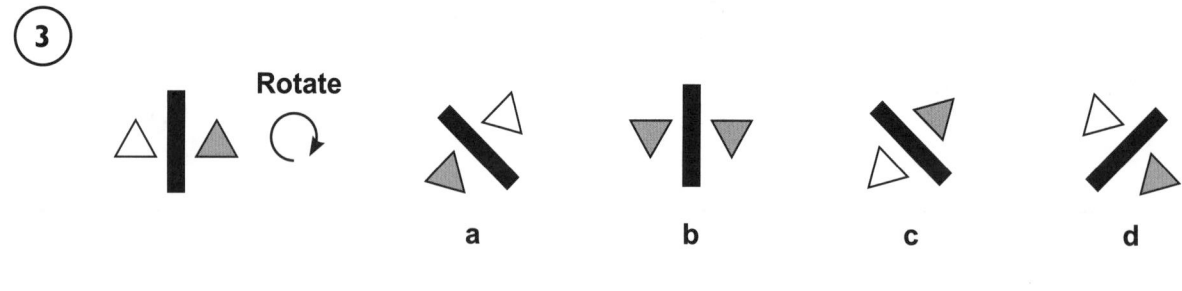

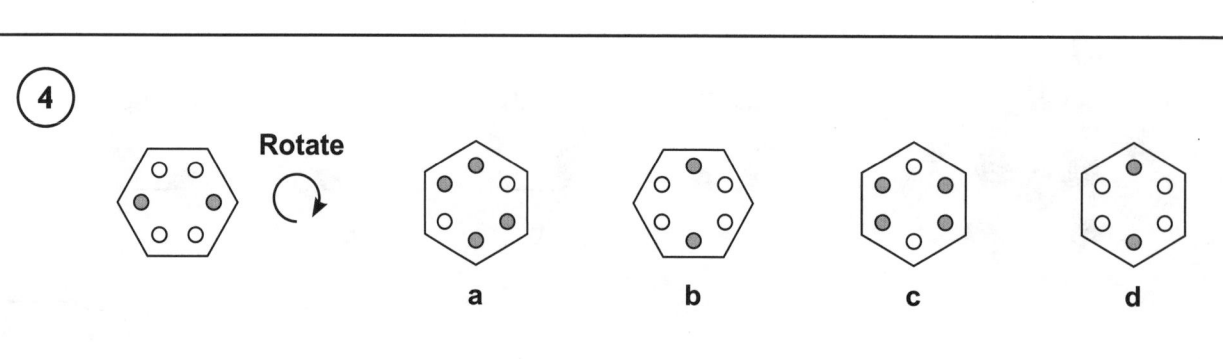

Rotate

a b c d

Answer: b

1 Rotate

a b c d

2 Rotate

a b c d

3 Rotate

a b c d

4 Rotate

a b c d

Assessment Test 1

5 Rotate ↻

a b c d

6 Rotate ↻

a b c d

7 Rotate ↻

a b c d

8 Rotate ↻

a b c d

9 Rotate ↻

a b c d

10 Rotate ↻

a b c d

/ 10

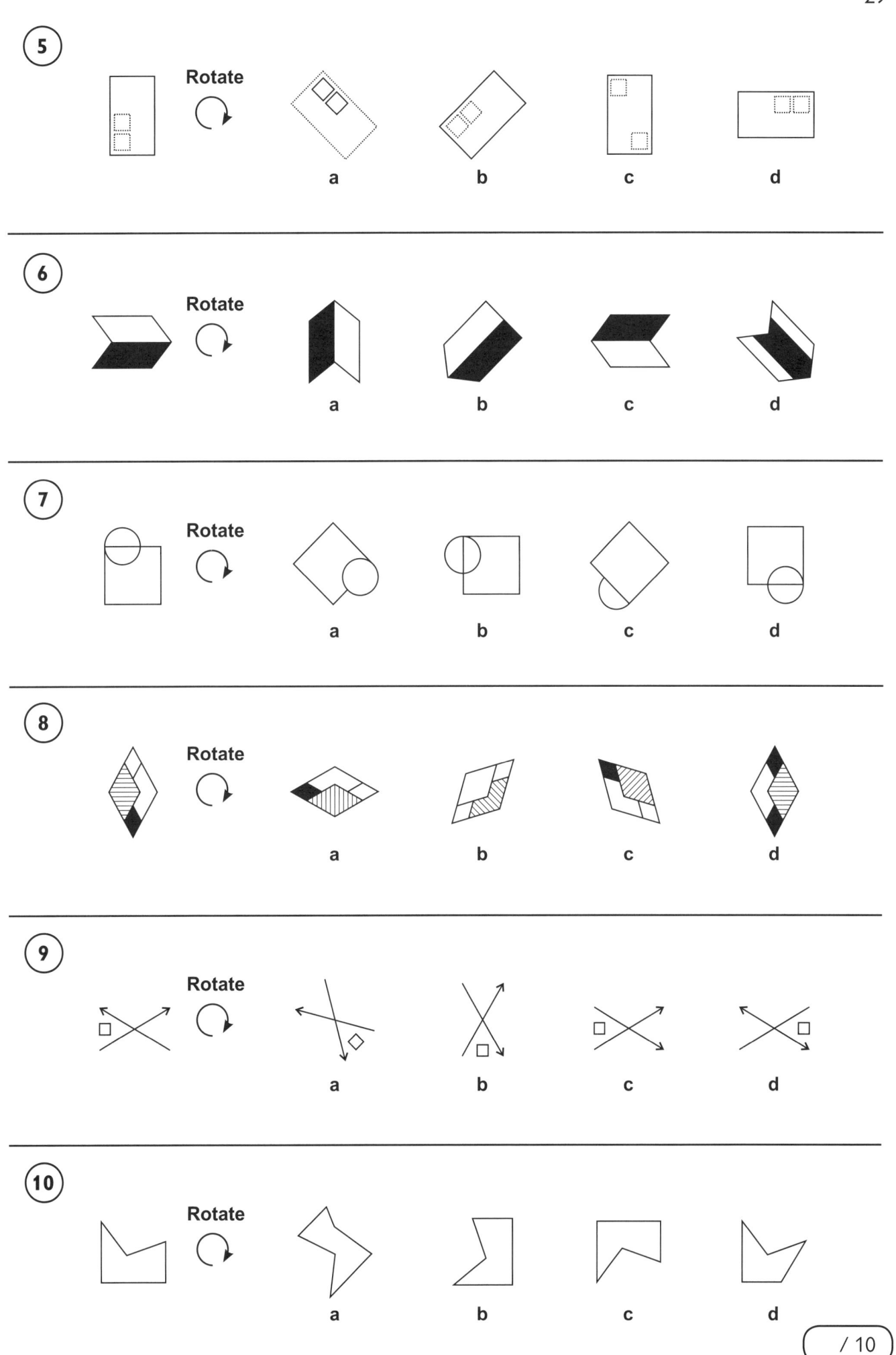

Carry on to the next question → →

Assessment Test 1

Section 5 — Complete the Series

Work out which of the options best fits in place of the missing square in the series.

Example:

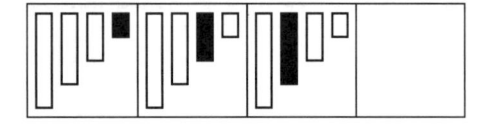

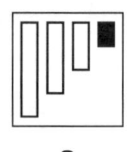

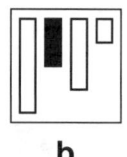

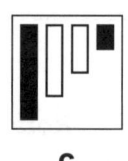

Answer: **d**

1

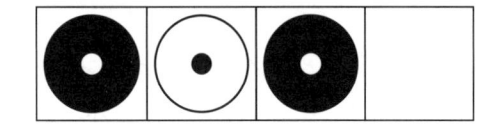

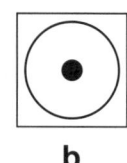

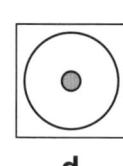

2

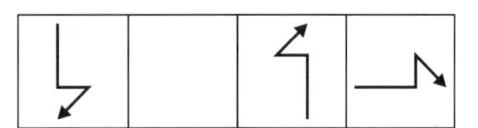

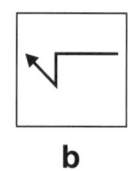

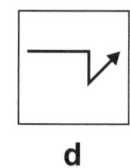

3

4

Assessment Test 1

5
6
7
8
9
10

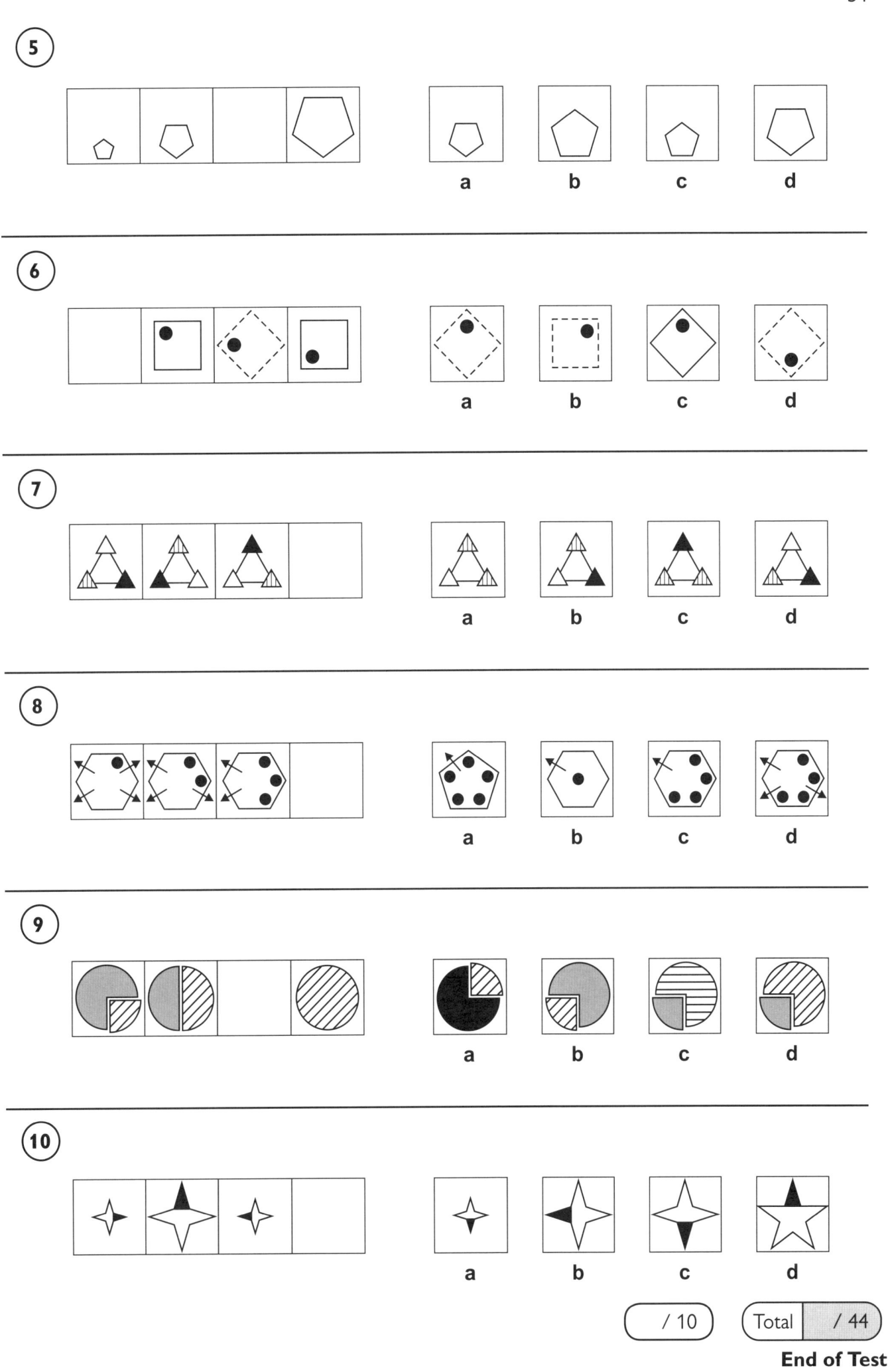

/ 10   Total / 44

End of Test

Assessment Test 1

Assessment Test 2

You can print **multiple-choice answer sheets** for these questions from our website — go to cgpbooks.co.uk/11plus/answer-sheets. If you'd prefer to answer them in standard write-in format, just circle the letter underneath your answer. The test should take around 20 minutes.

Section 1 — Changing Bugs

Look at how the first bug changes to become the second bug.
Then work out which option would look like the third bug if you changed it in the same way.

Example:

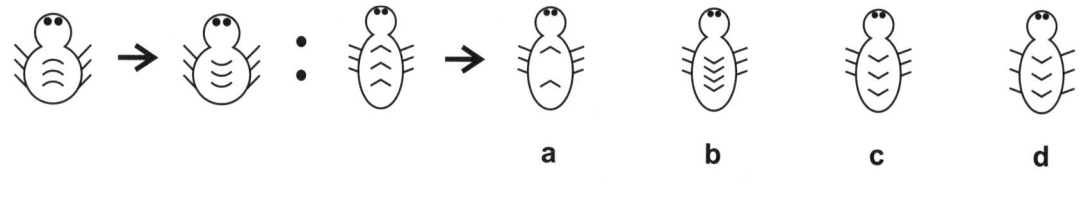

Answer: c

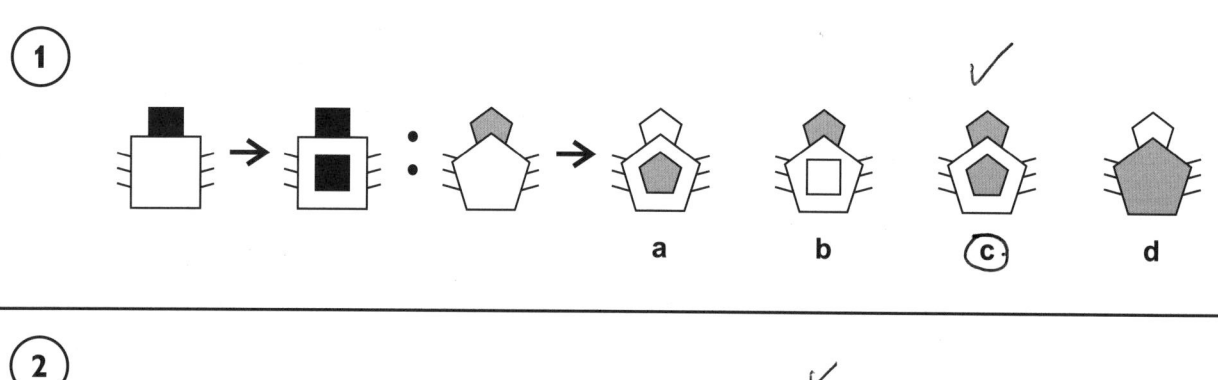

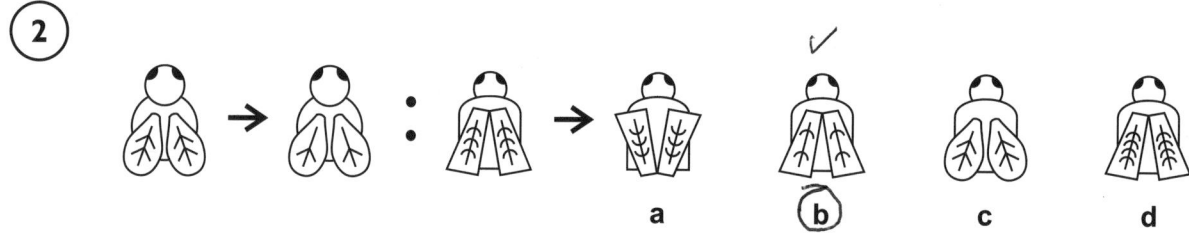

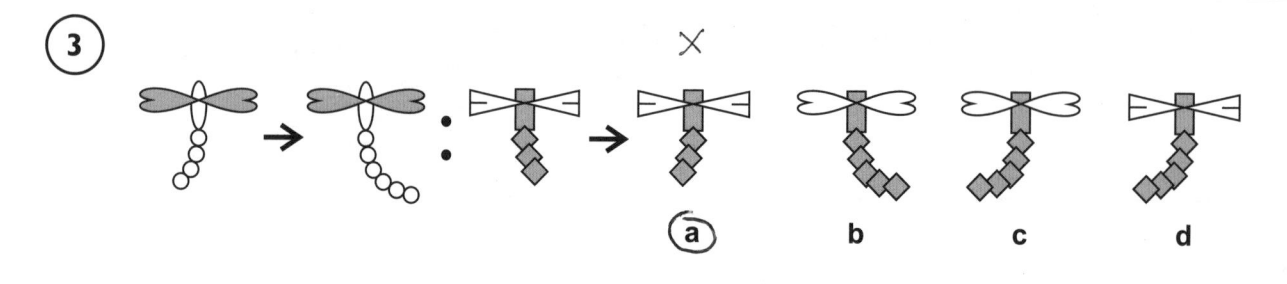

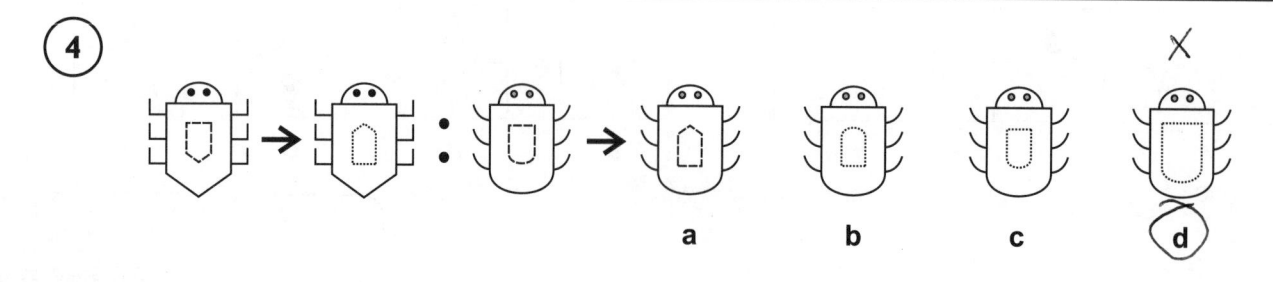

33

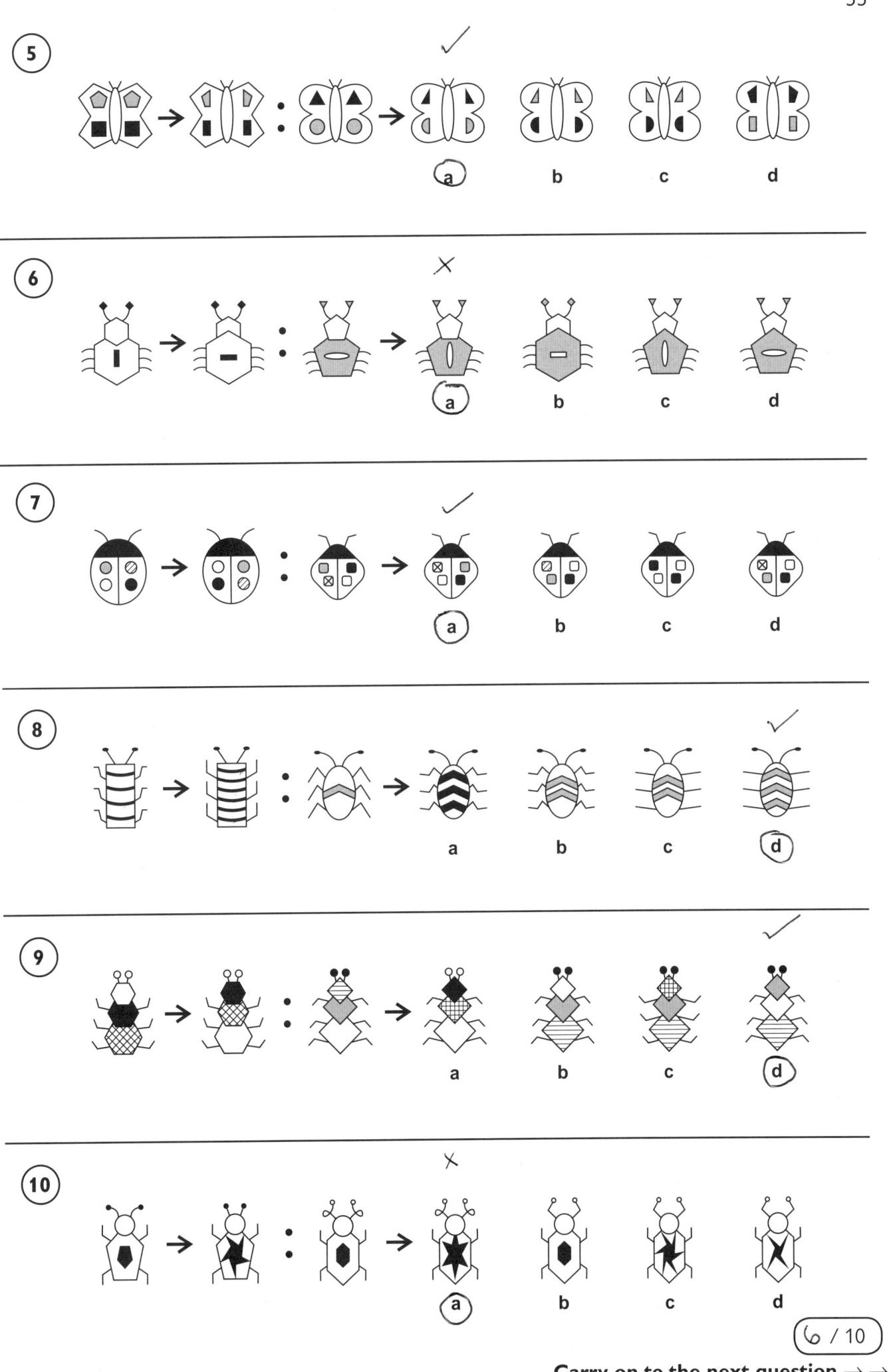

Section 2 — Complete the Square Grid

Work out which of the options best fits in place of the missing square in the grid.

Example:

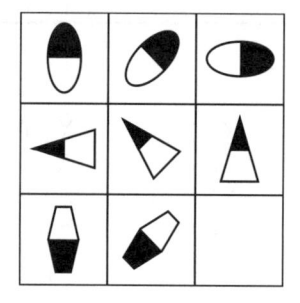

Answer: d

1

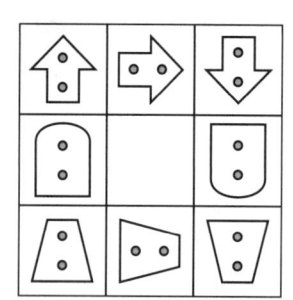

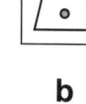

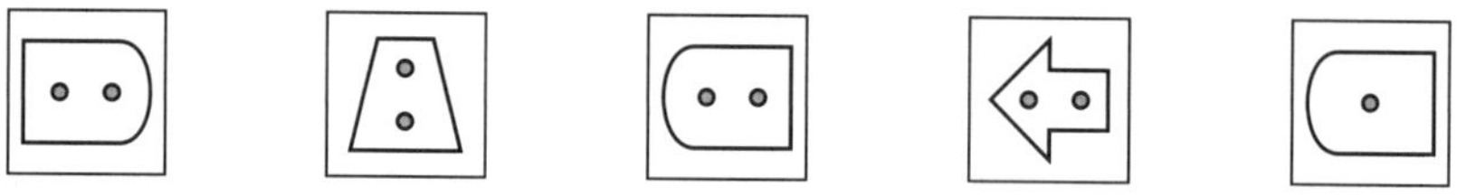

2

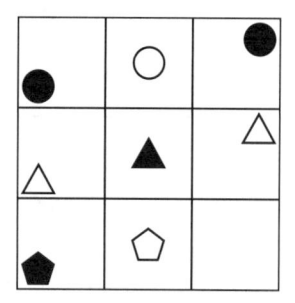

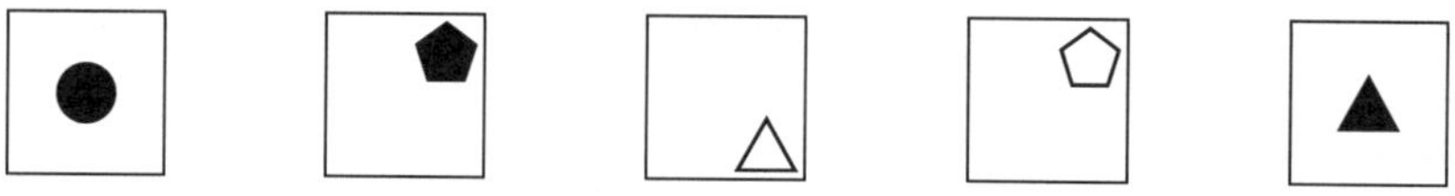

3

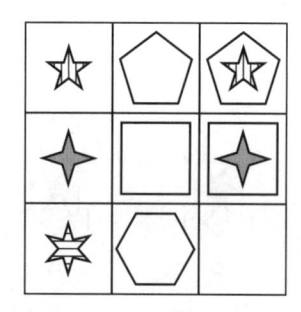

Assessment Test 2

35

④ b ✓

⑤ a ✓

⑥ b ✓

⑦ e ✓

⑧ b ✓

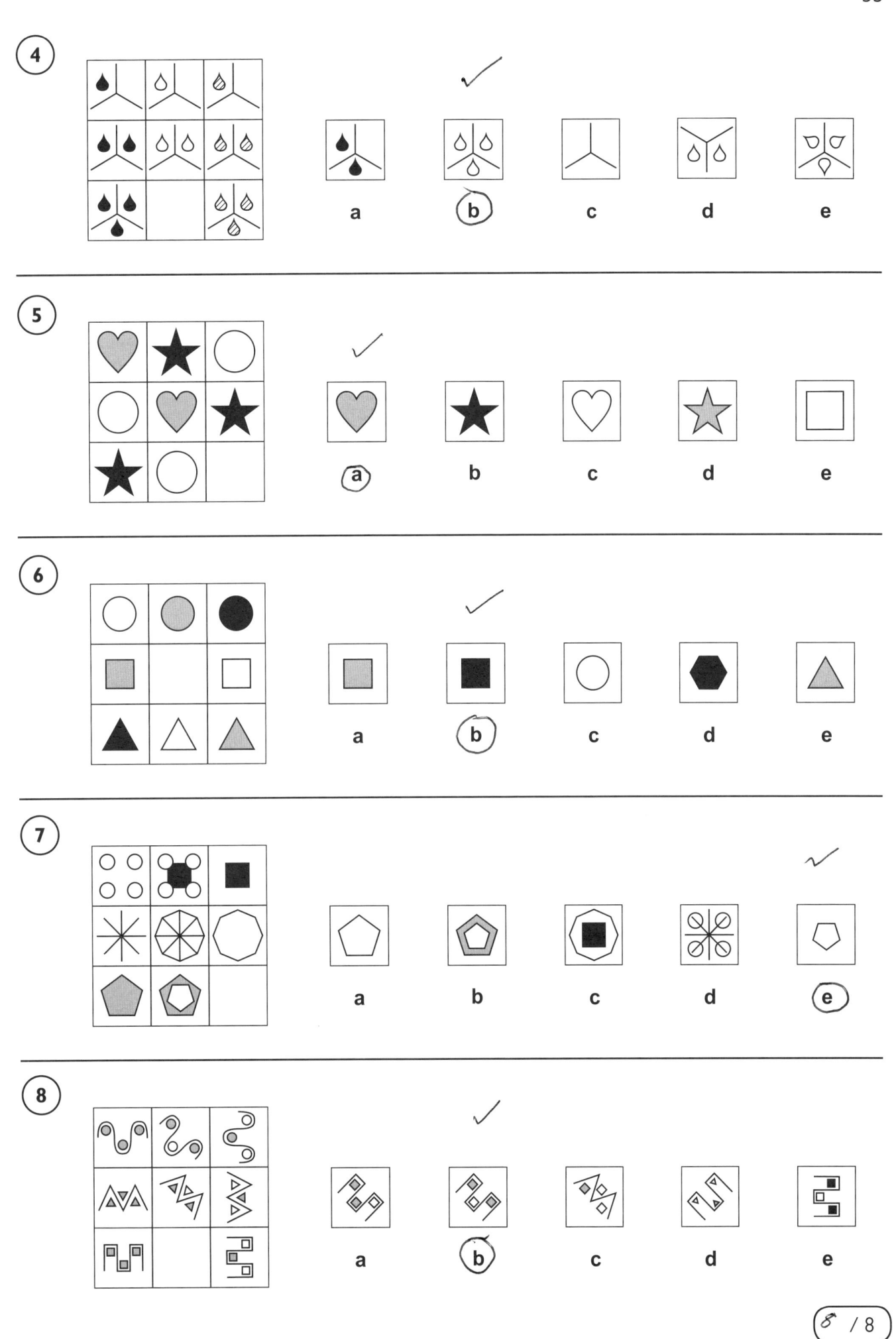

8 / 8

Carry on to the next question → →

Assessment Test 2

Section 3 — Fold Along the Line

Work out which option shows the figure on the left when folded along the dotted line.

Example:

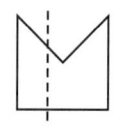

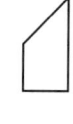

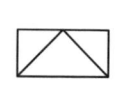

a b c d

Answer: a

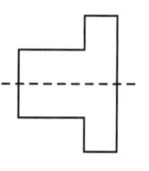

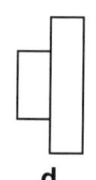

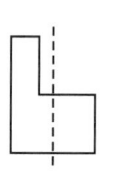

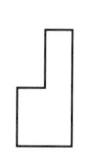

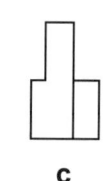

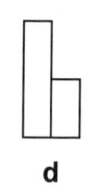

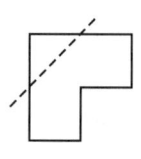

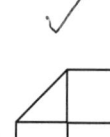

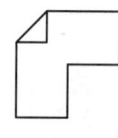

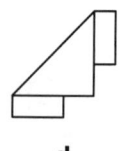

1) a b c ✓ (circled) d

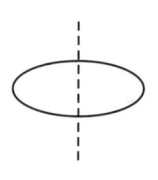

2) a b ✓ (circled) c d

3) a b ✓ (circled) c d

4) a ✓ (circled) b c d

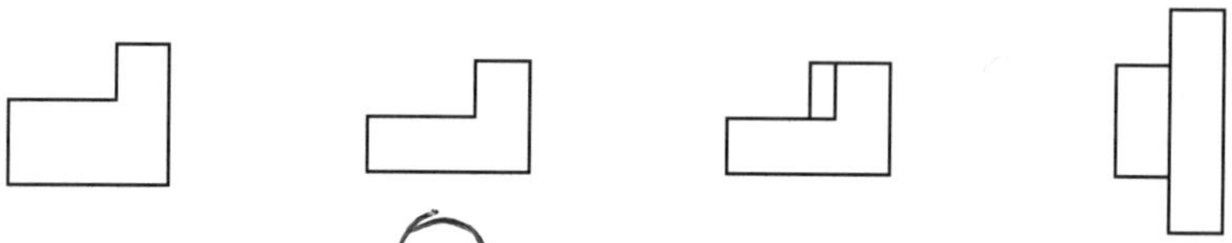

Assessment Test 2

5 a   b   c   d ✓ (circled)

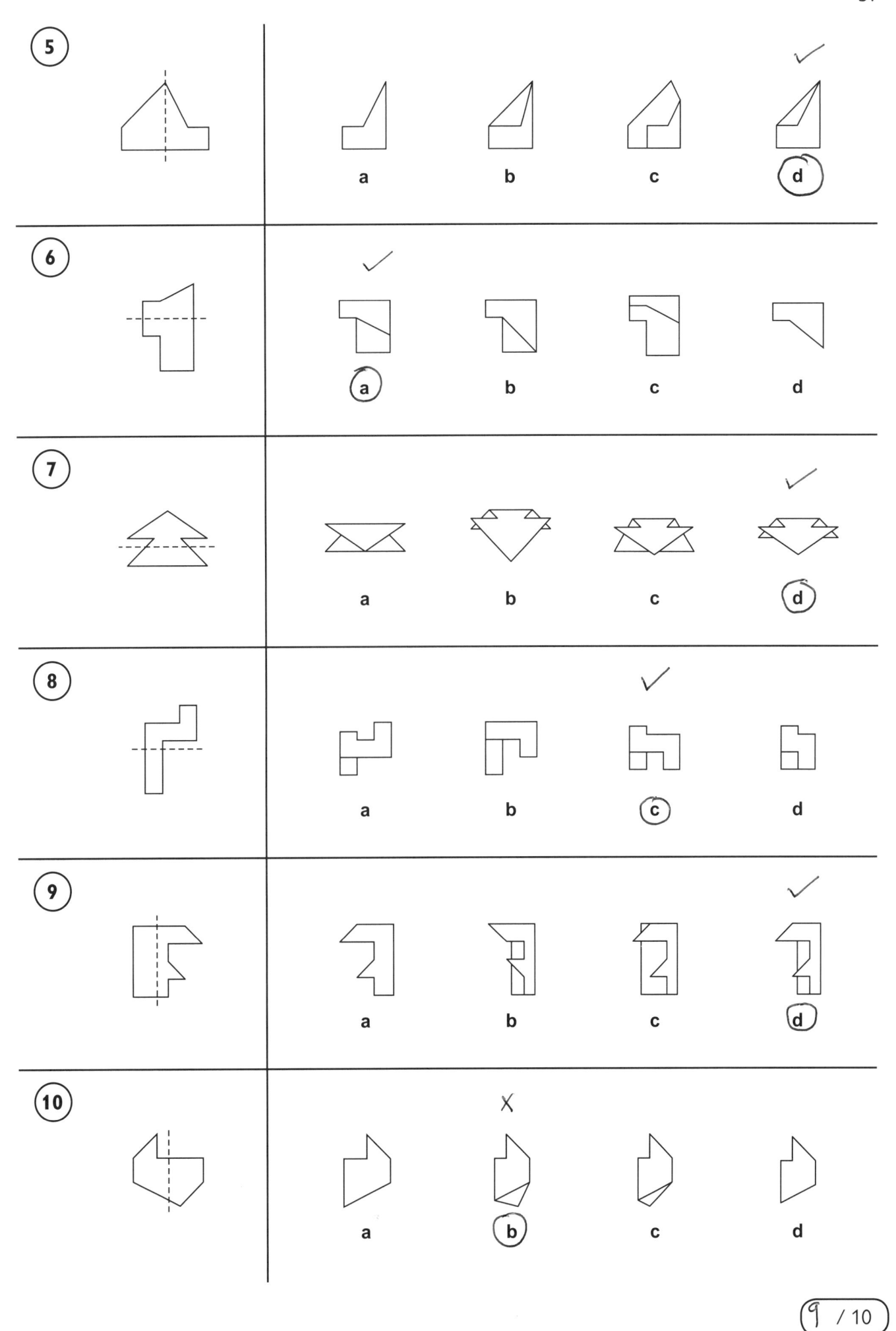

6 a ✓ (circled)   b   c   d

7 a   b   c   d ✓ (circled)

8 a   b   c ✓ (circled)   d

9 a   b   c   d ✓ (circled)

10 a   b ✗ (circled)   c   d

9 / 10

Carry on to the next question → →

Assessment Test 2

Section 4 — 3D Building Blocks

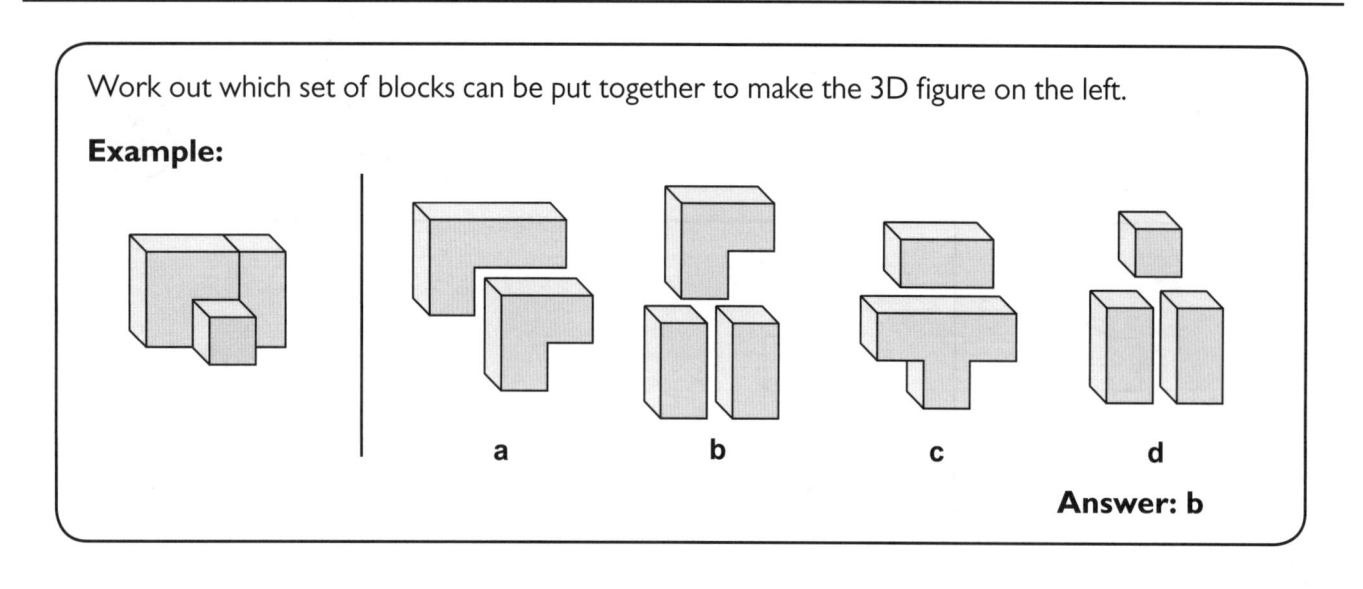

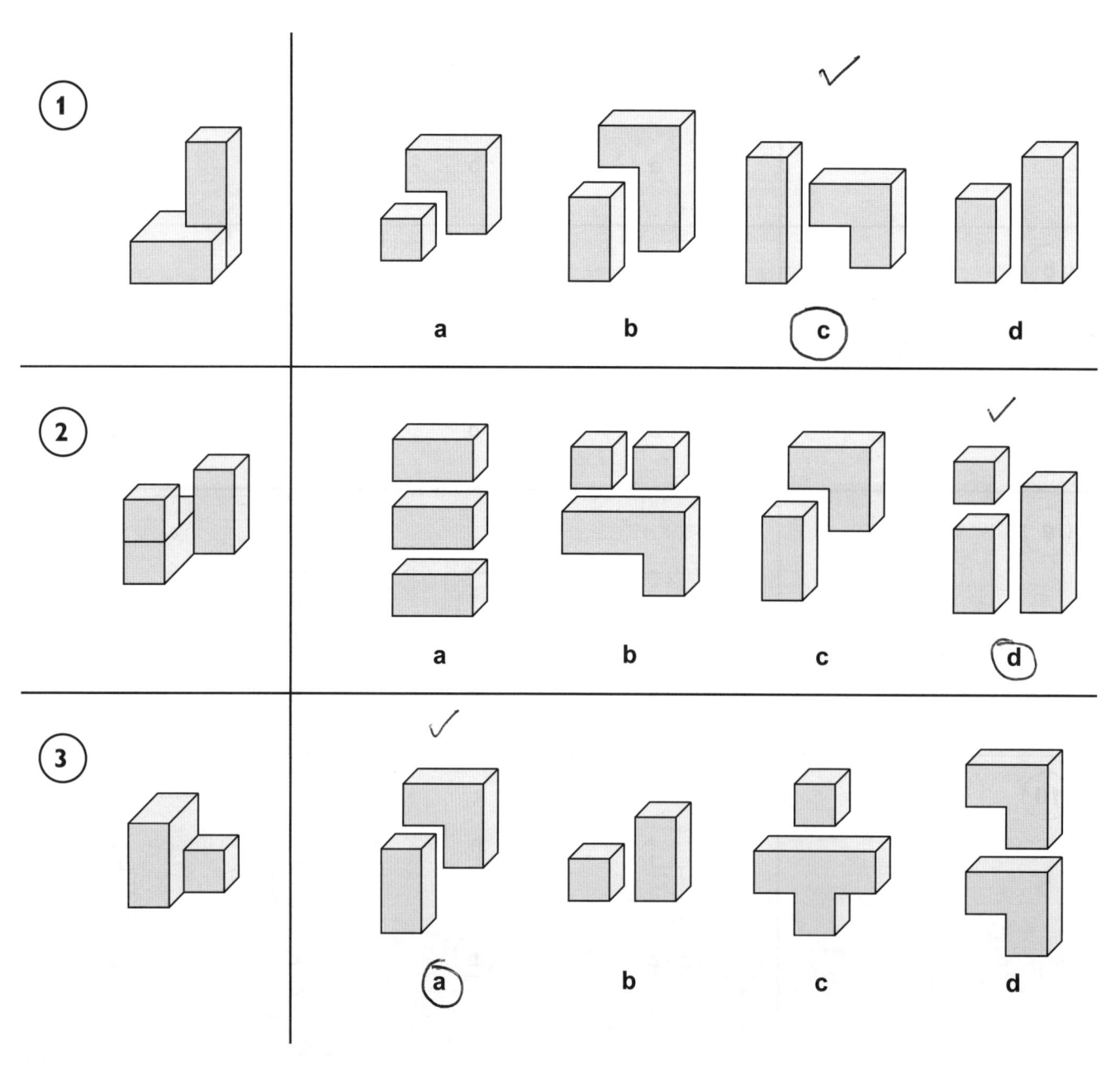

Work out which set of blocks can be put together to make the 3D figure on the left.

Example:

	a	b	c	d

Answer: b

1. a b c ✓(circled) d

2. a b c d ✓(circled)

3. a ✓(circled) b c d

Assessment Test 2

④

a b ⓒ ✓ d

⑤

ⓐ ✓ b c d

⑥

a ⓑ ✓ c d

⑦

ⓐ ✓ b c d

⑧

a b c ⓓ ✓

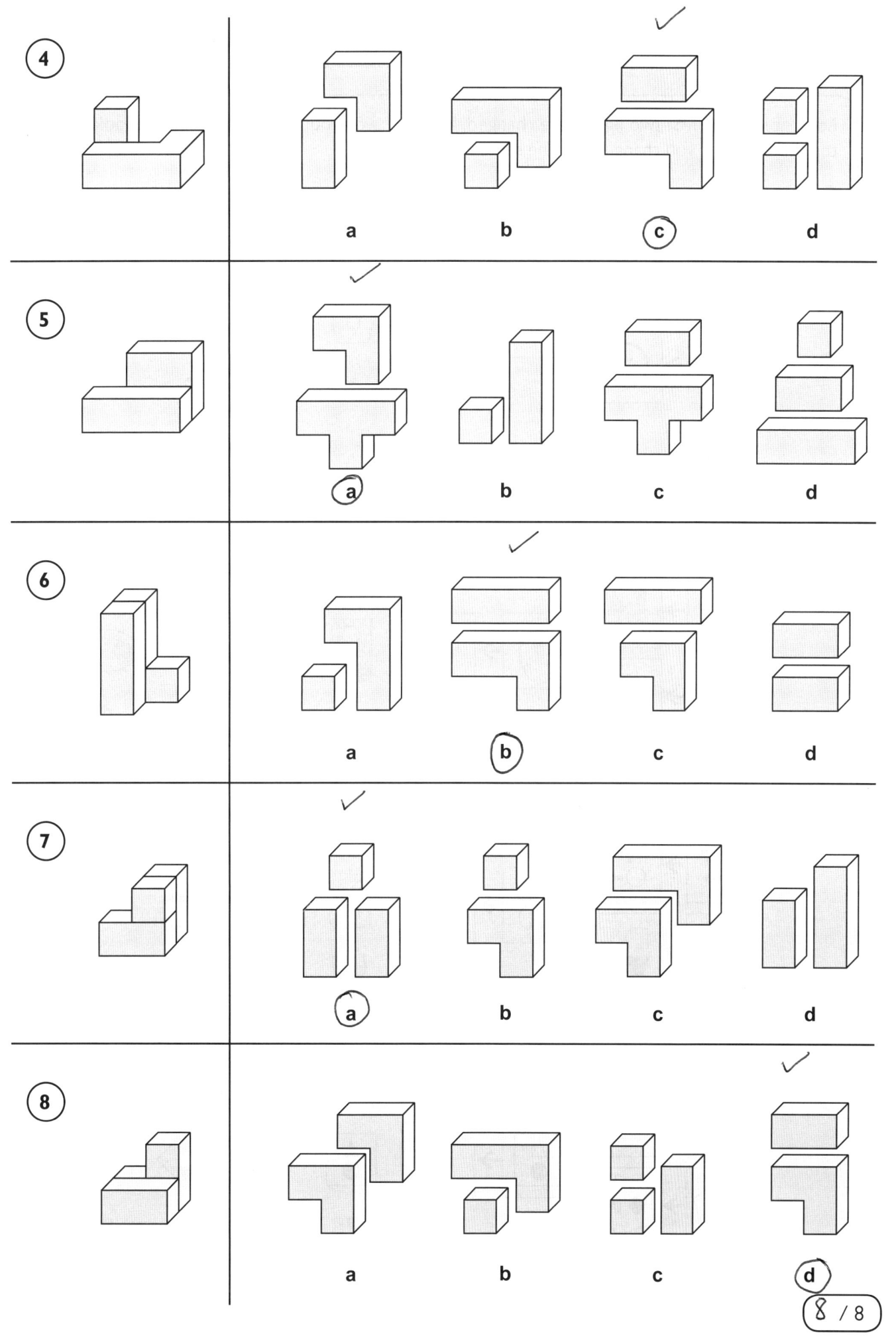

8 / 8

Carry on to the next question → →

Assessment Test 2

Section 5 — Complete the Pair

Look at how the first two figures are changed, and then work out which option would look like the third figure if you changed it in the same way.

Example:

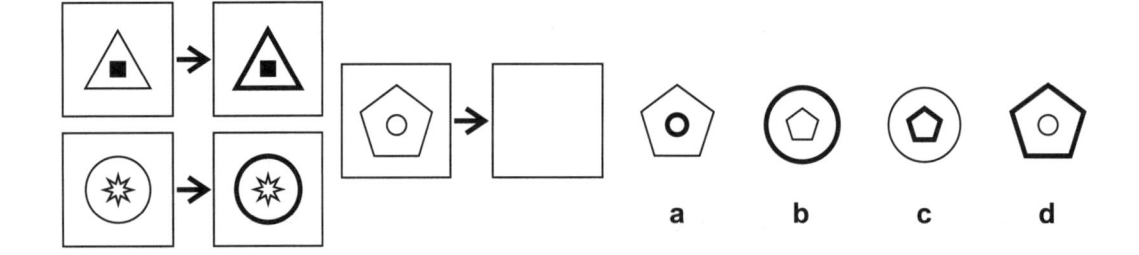

Answer: d

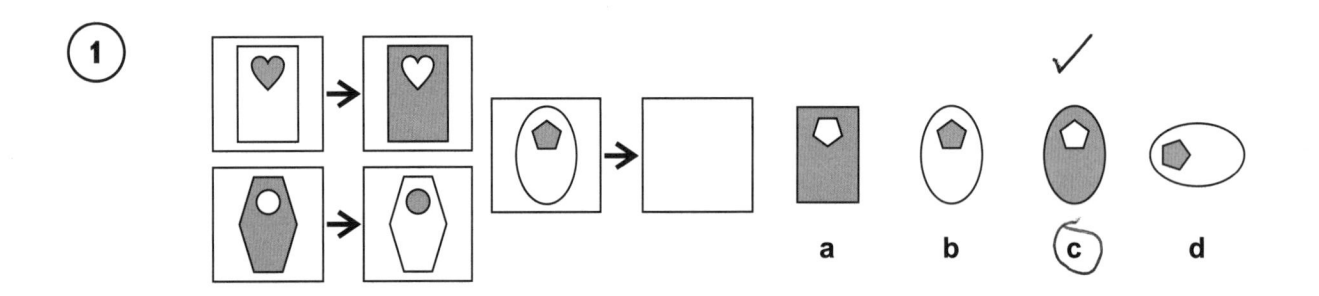

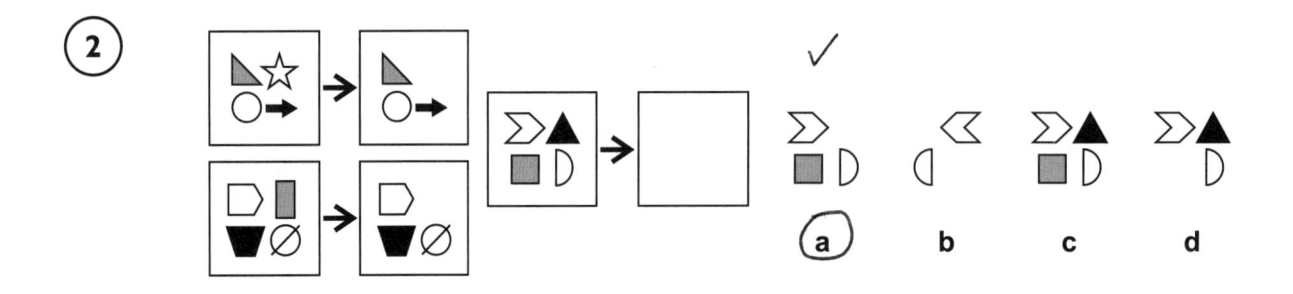

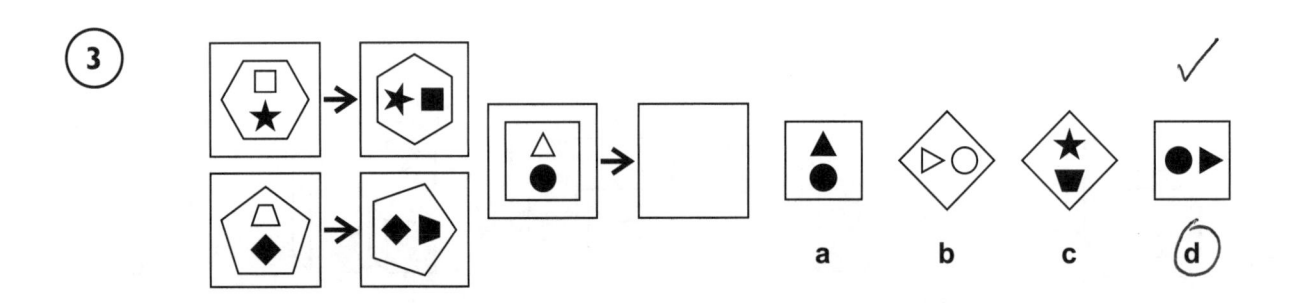

1. ✓ c

2. ✓ a

3. ✓ d

Assessment Test 2

41

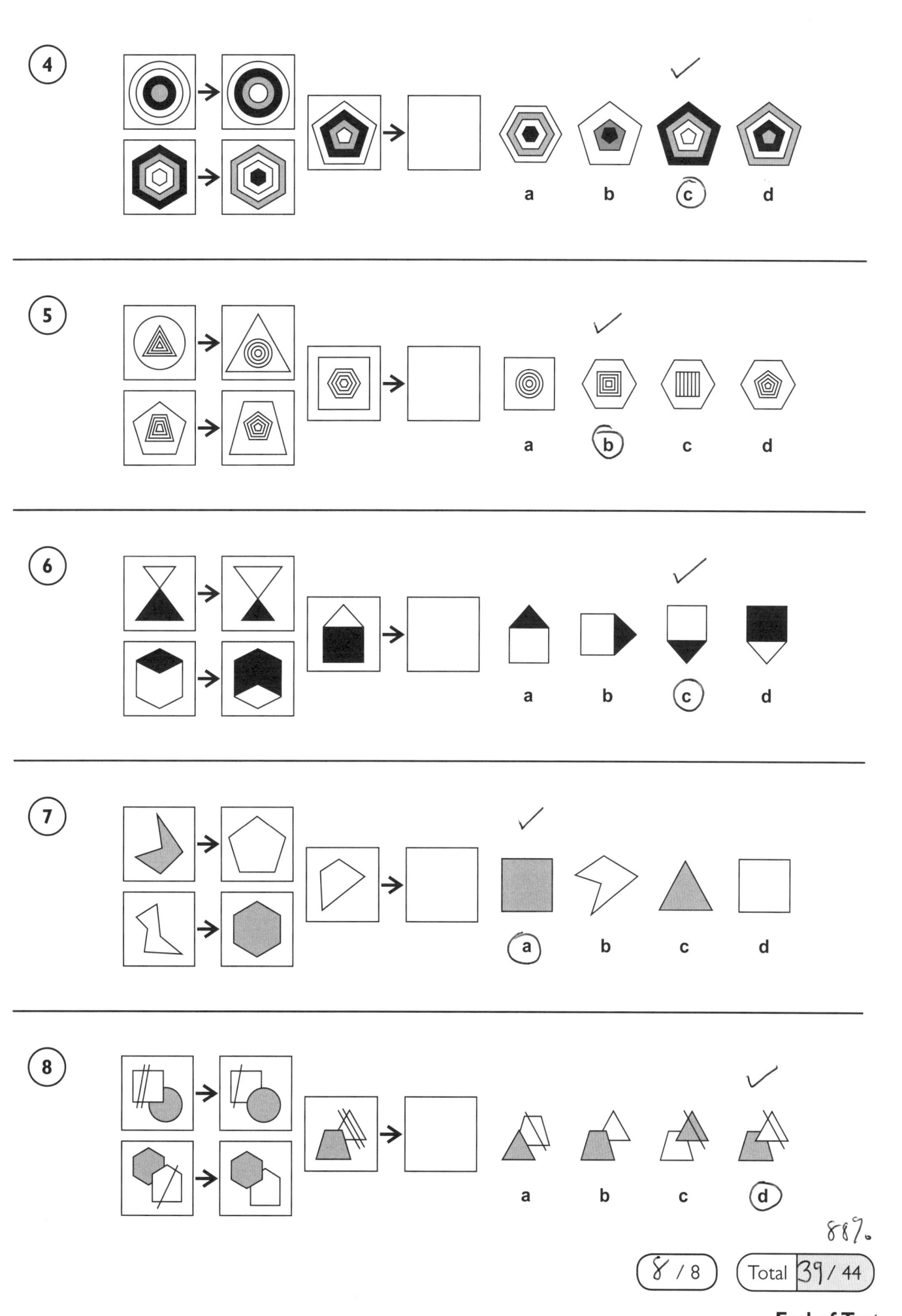

End of Test

Assessment Test 2

Assessment Test 3

You can print **multiple-choice answer sheets** for these questions from our website — go to cgpbooks.co.uk/11plus/answer-sheets. If you'd prefer to answer them in standard write-in format, just circle the letter underneath your answer. The test should take around 20 minutes.

Section 1 — Complete the Series

Work out which of the options best fits in place of the missing square in the series.

Example:

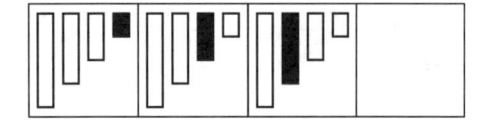

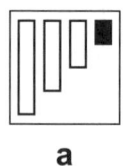

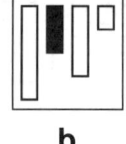

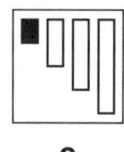

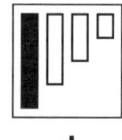

Answer: d

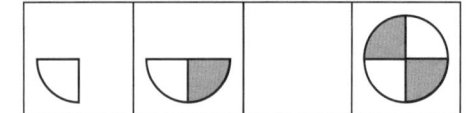

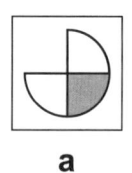

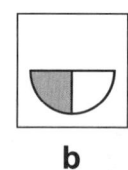

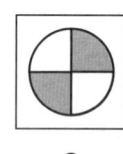

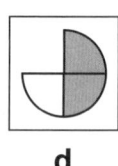

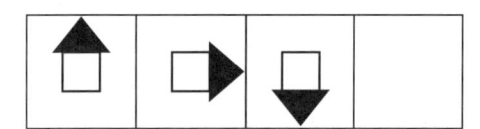

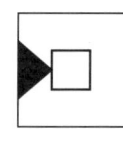

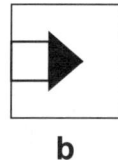

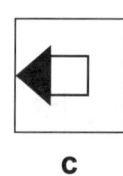

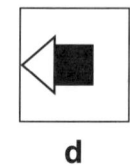

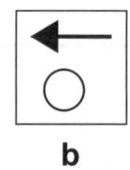

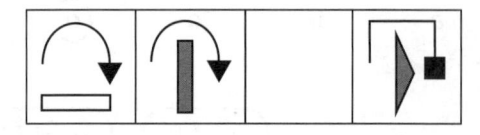

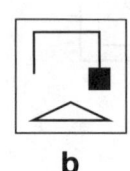

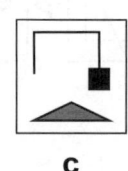

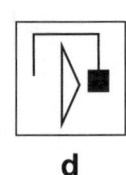

5.

6.

7.

8.

9.

10.

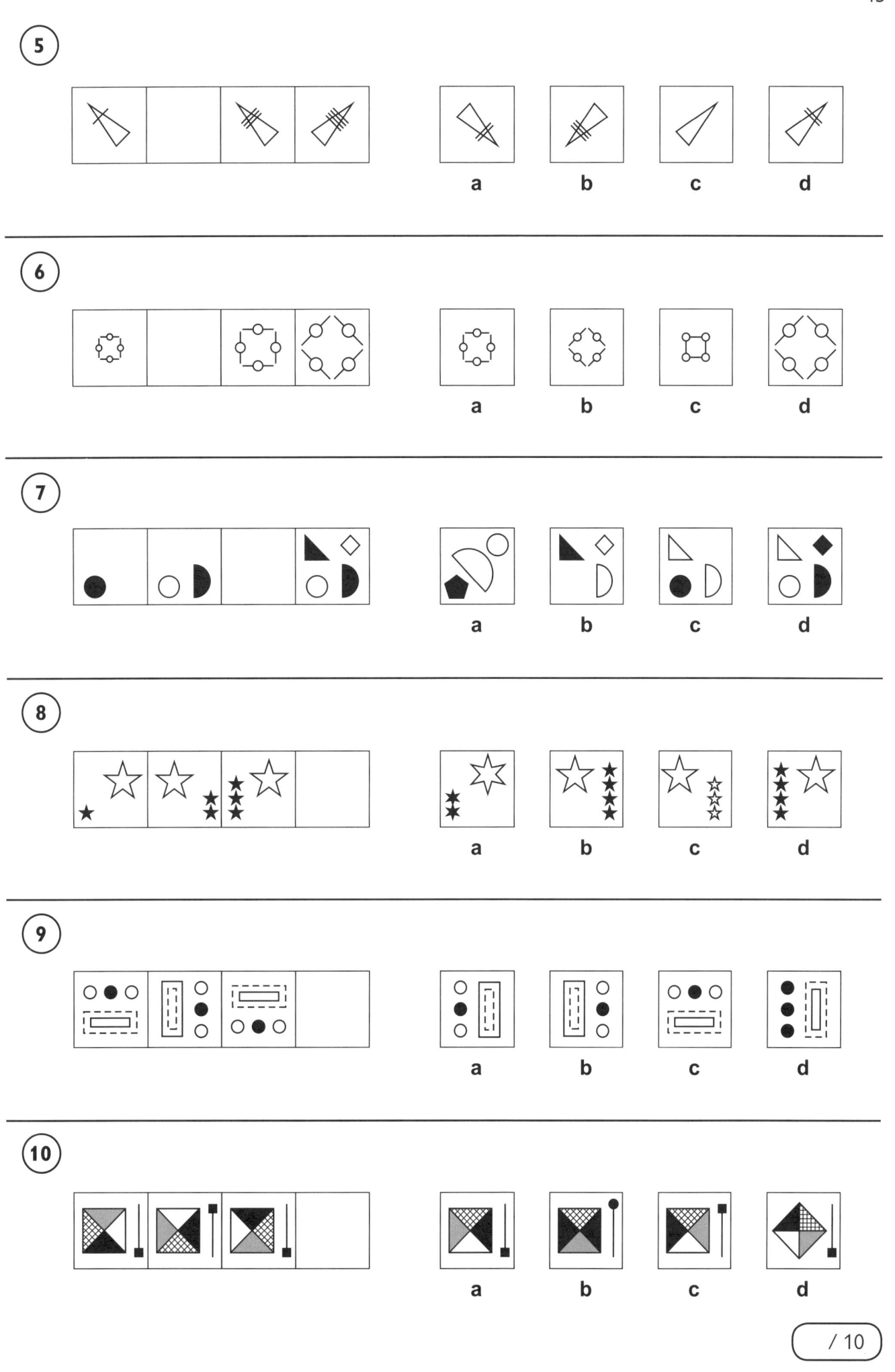

Carry on to the next question → →

Assessment Test 3

Section 2 — Find the Figure Like the First Three

Work out which option is most like the three figures on the left.

Example:

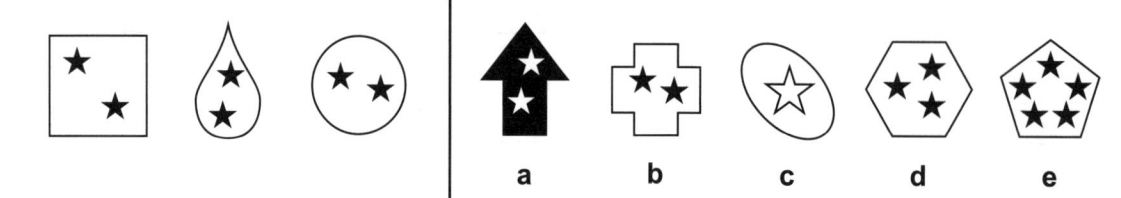

Answer: **b**

1

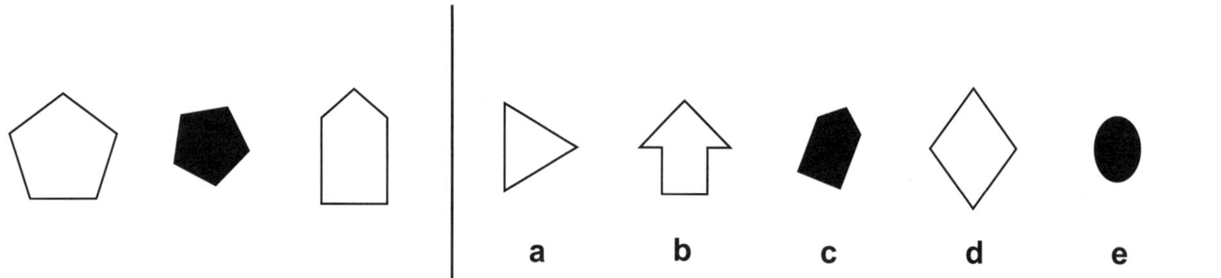

a b c d e

2

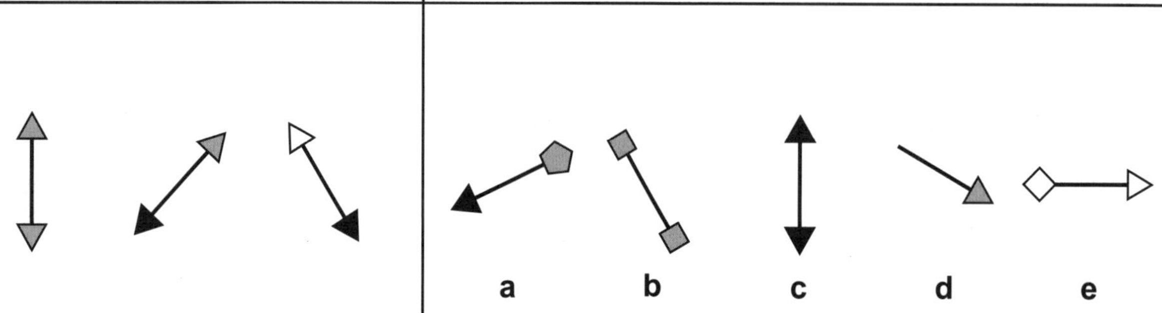

a b c d e

3

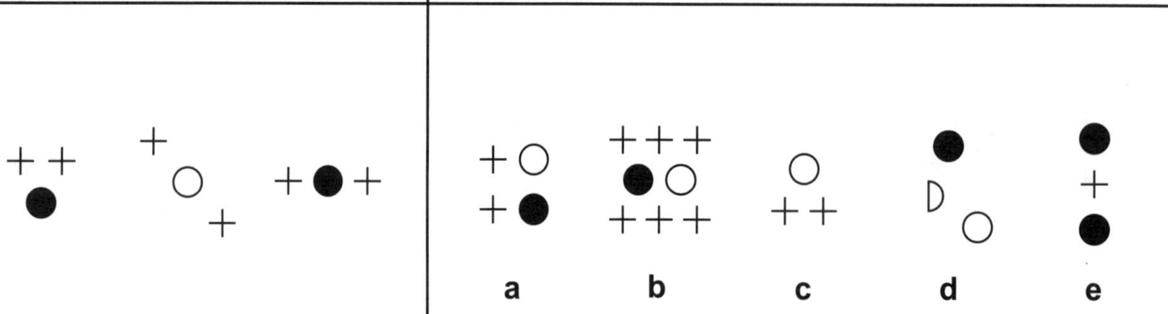

a b c d e

4

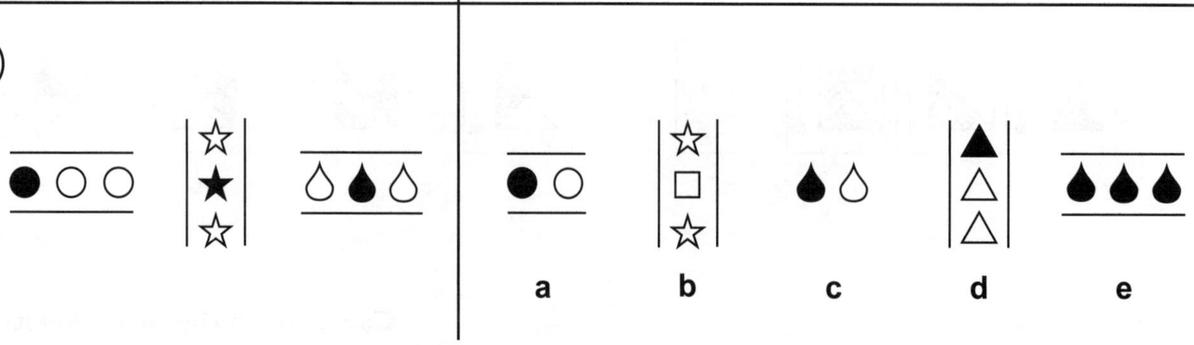

a b c d e

Assessment Test 3

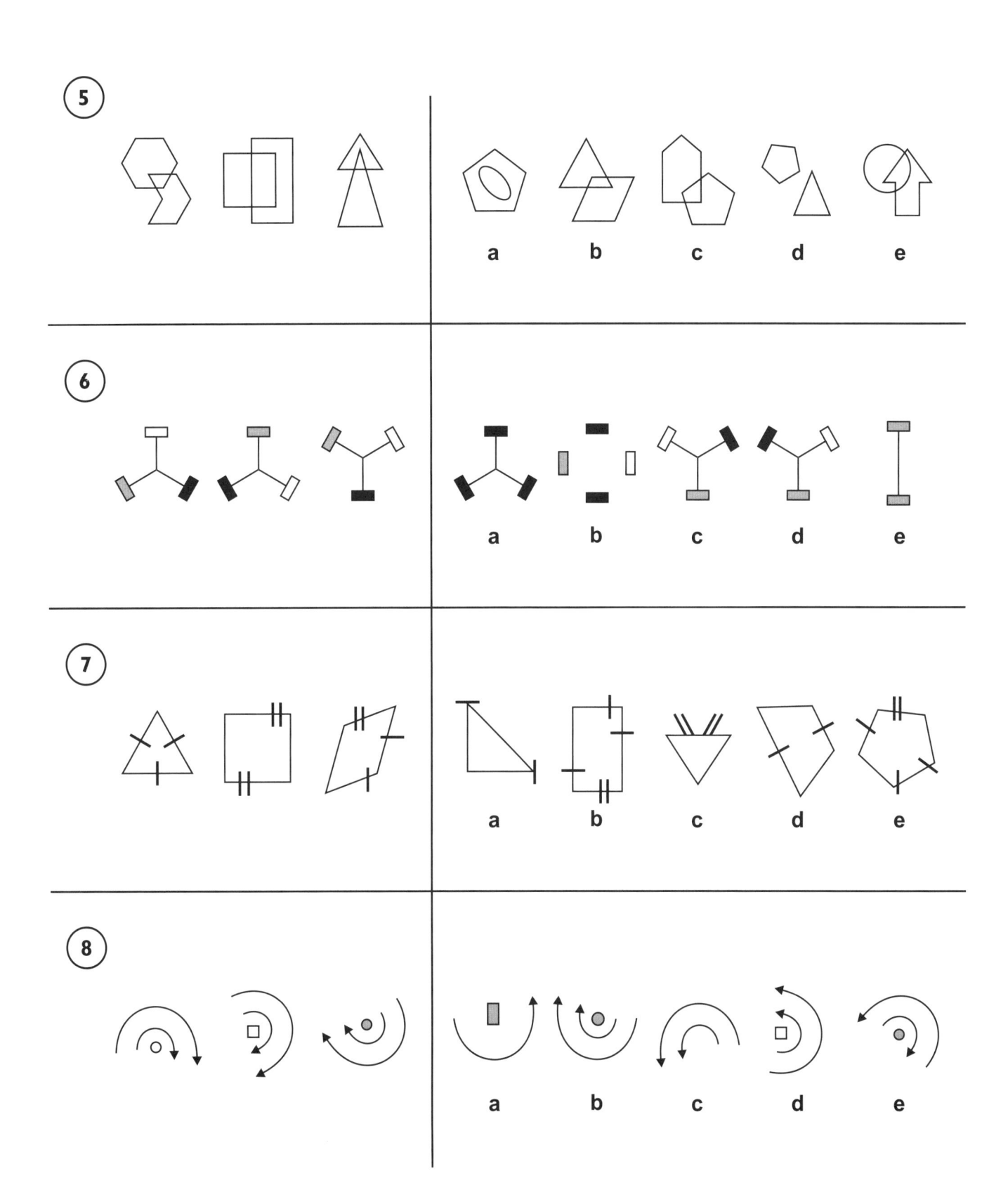

5

a b c d e

6

a b c d e

7

a b c d e

8

a b c d e

/ 8

Carry on to the next question → →

Assessment Test 3

Section 3 — Rotate the Figure

Work out which option would look like the figure on the left if it was rotated.

Example:

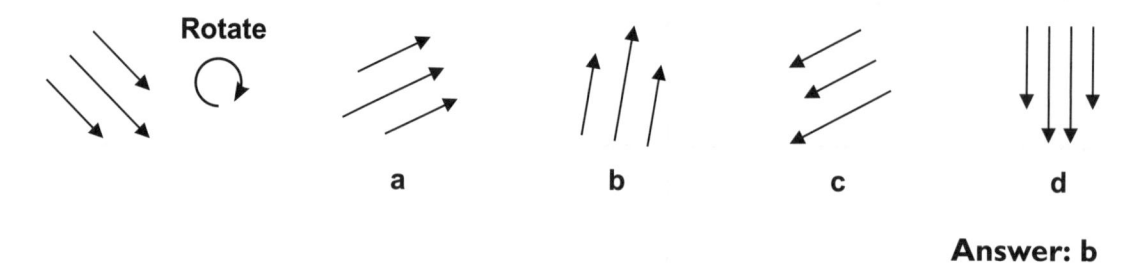

a b c d

Answer: b

1.

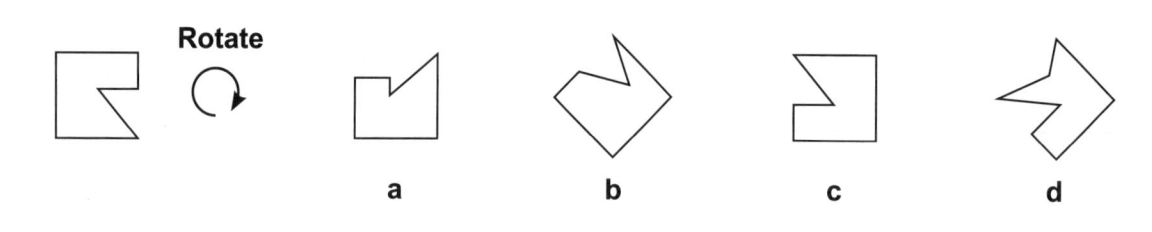

a b c d

2.

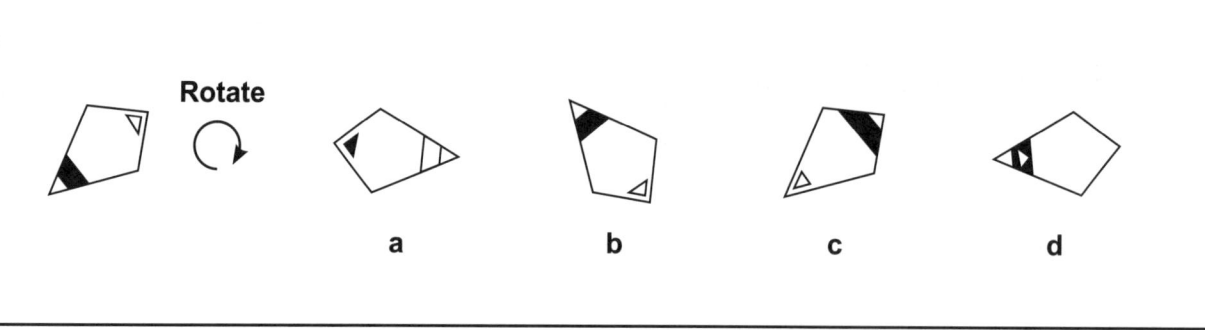

a b c d

3.

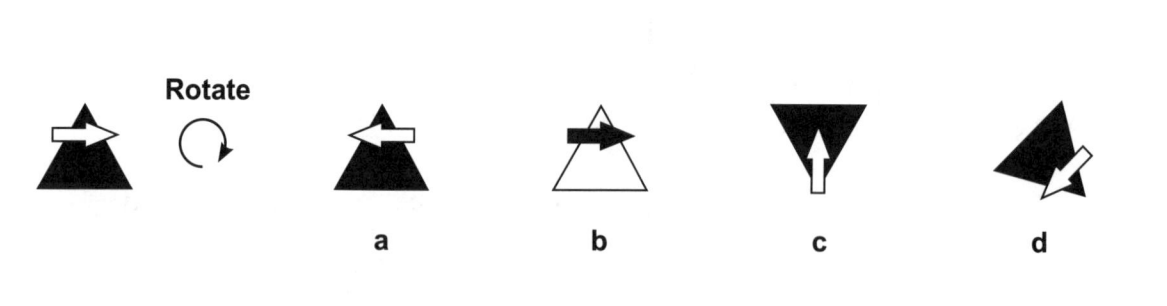

a b c d

4.

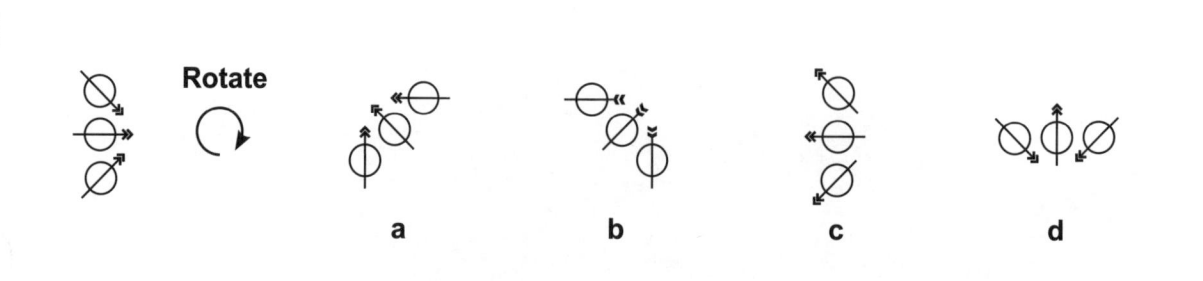

a b c d

Assessment Test 3

5
Rotate

a b c d

6
Rotate

a b c d

7
Rotate

a b c d

8
Rotate

a b c d

9
Rotate

a b c d

10
Rotate

a b c d

/ 10

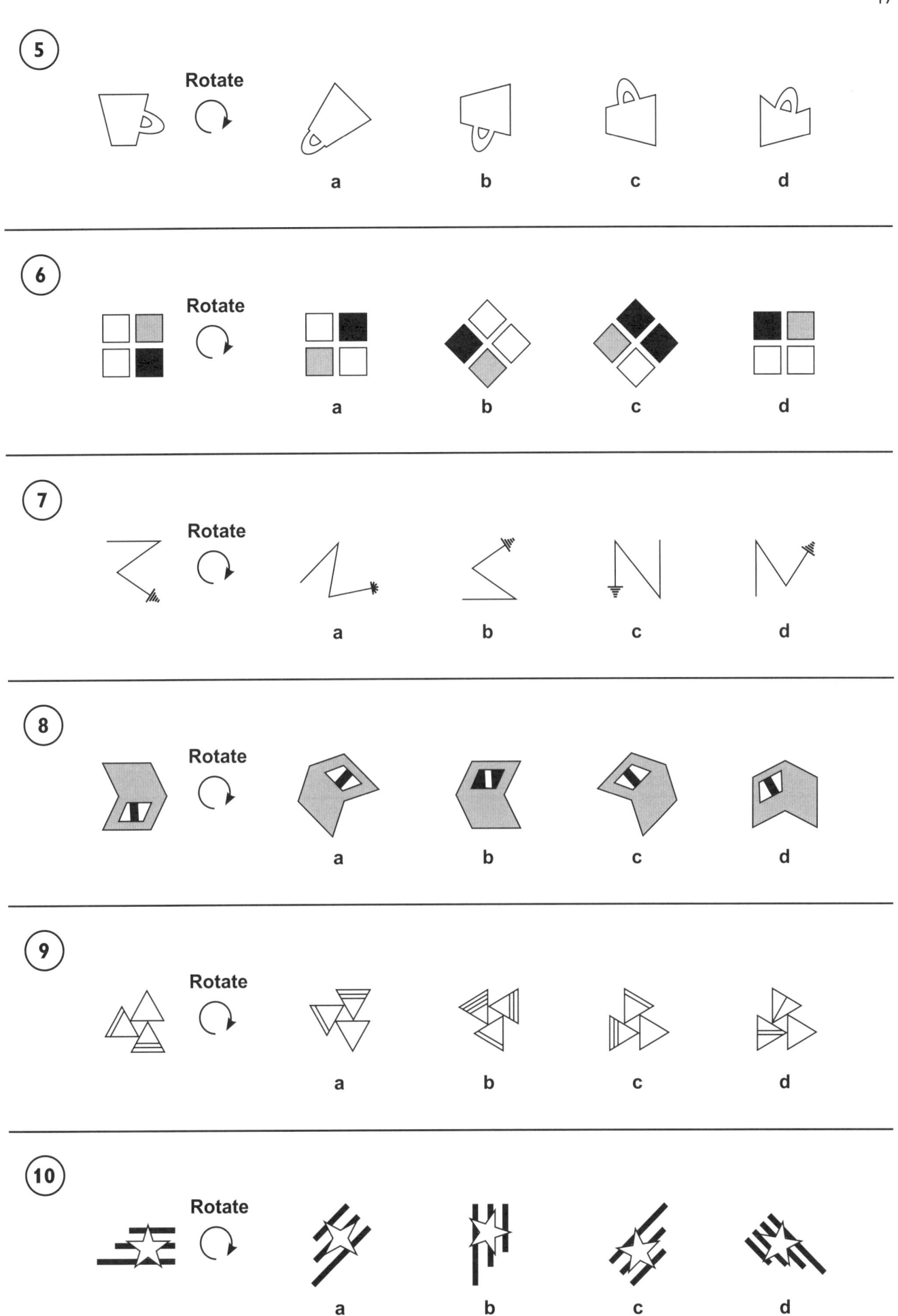

Carry on to the next question → →

Assessment Test 3

Section 4 — 2D Views of 3D Shapes

Work out which option is a top-down 2D view of the 3D figure on the left.

Example:

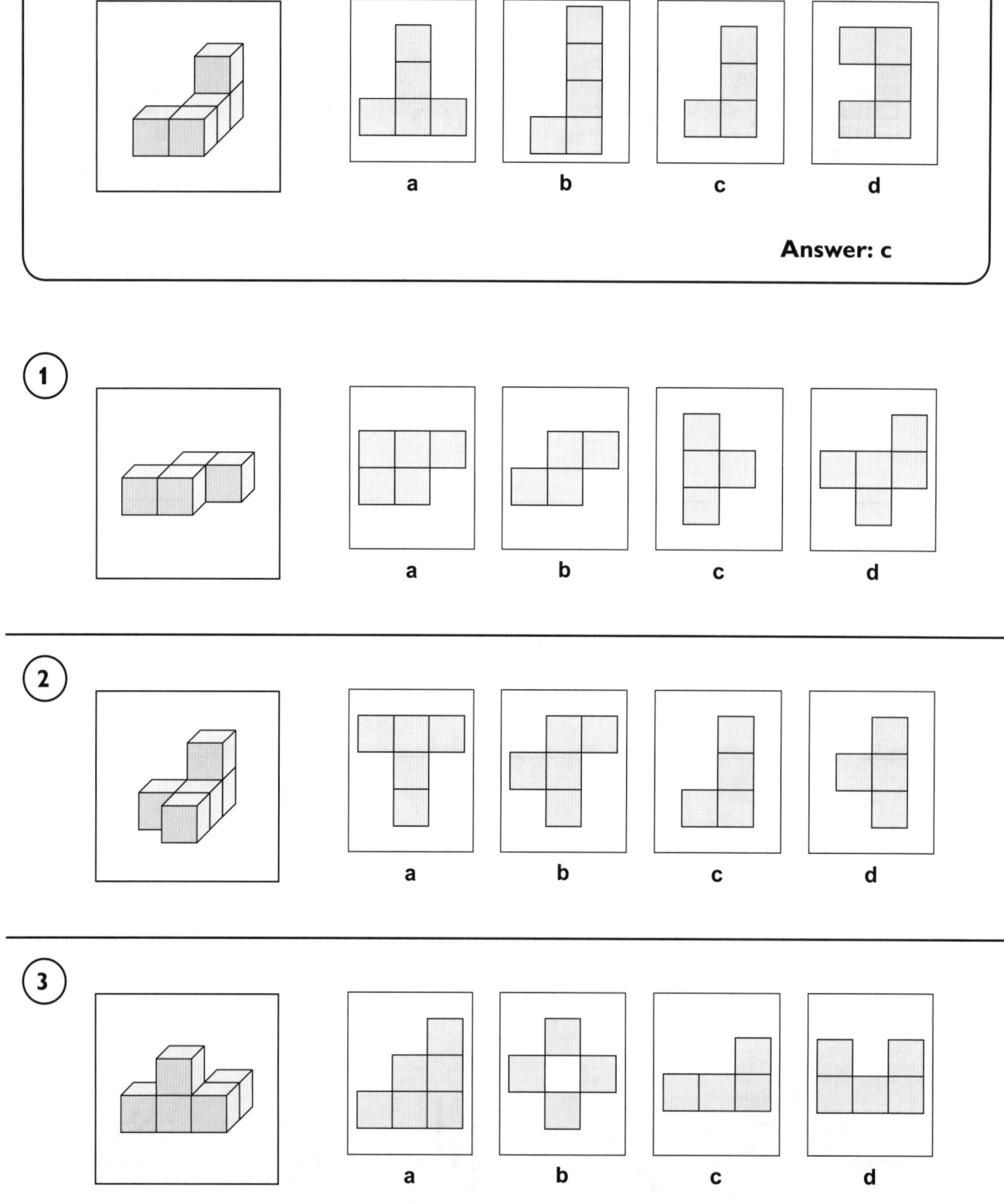

a b c d

Answer: c

1

a b c d

2

a b c d

3

a b c d

Assessment Test 3

4   a   b   c   d

5   a   b   c   d

6   a   b   c   d

7   a   b   c   d

8   a   b   c   d

/ 8

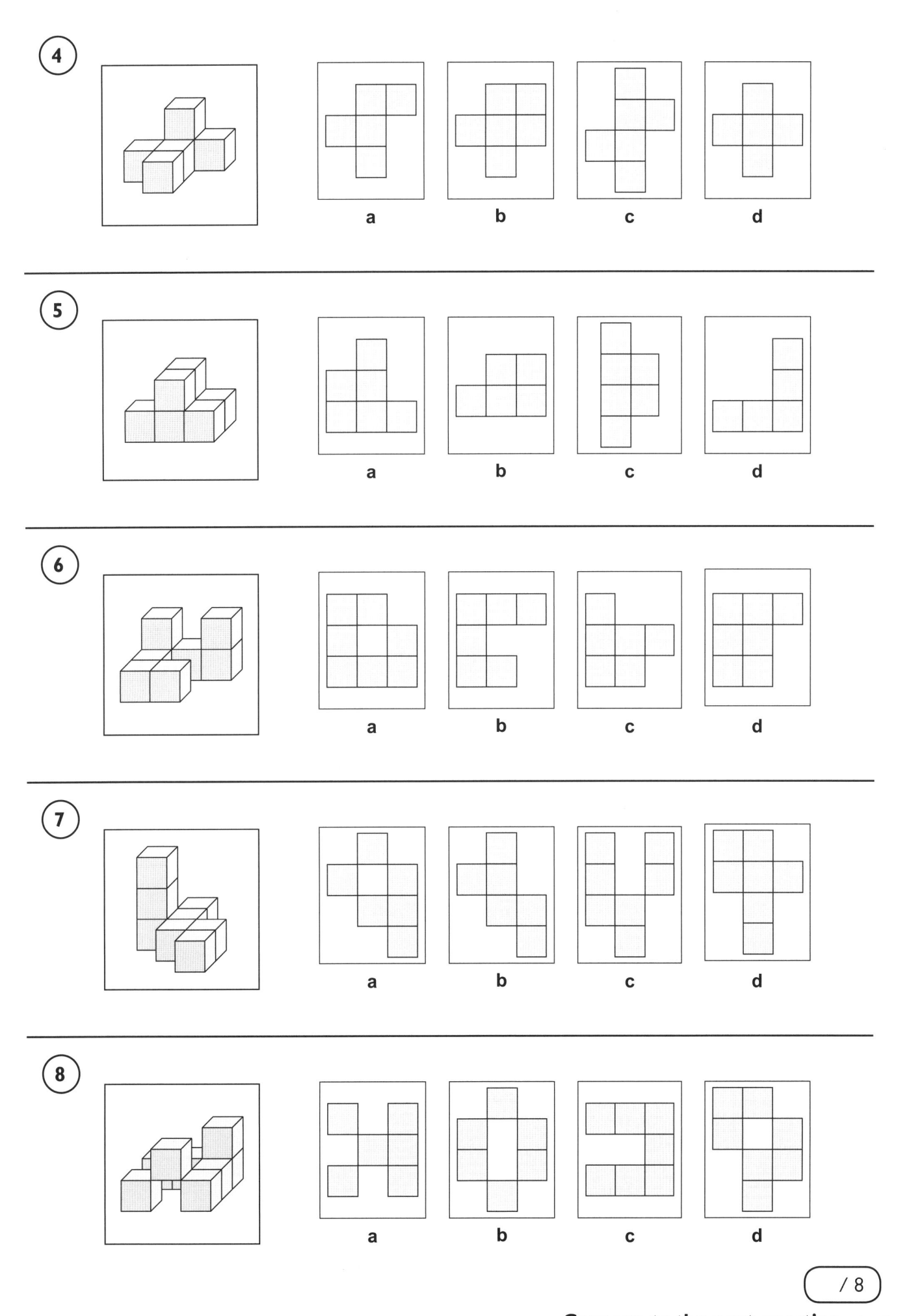

Carry on to the next question → →

Assessment Test 3

Section 5 — Odd One Out

Find the figure in each row that is most unlike the other figures.

Example:

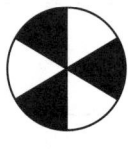

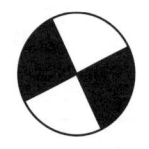

a b c d e

Answer: a

1. a b c d e

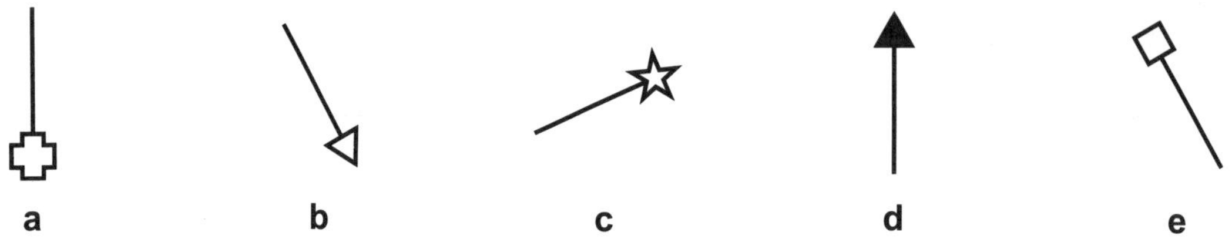

2. a b c d e

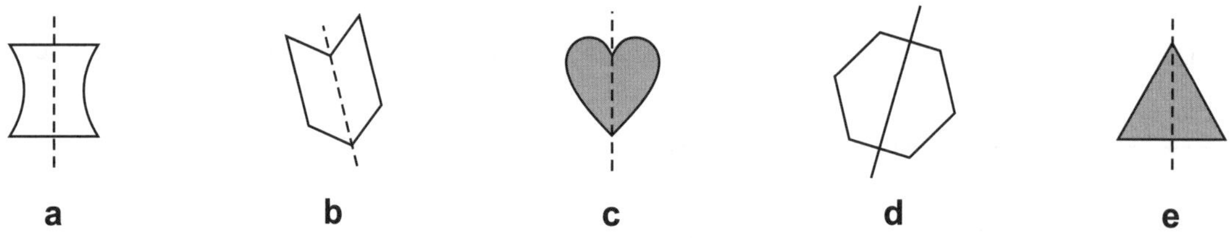

3. a b c d e

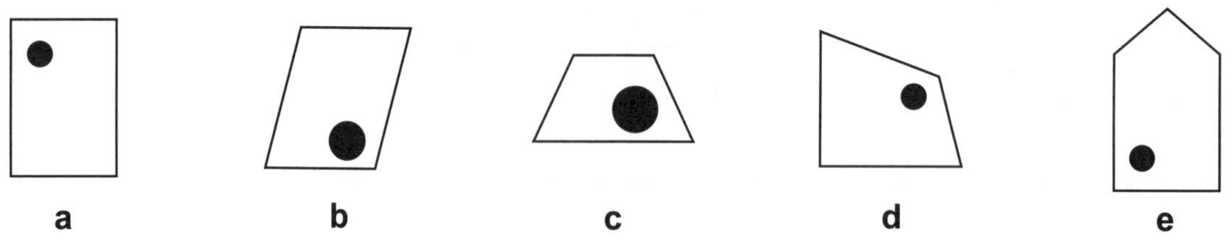

4. a b c d e

Assessment Test 3

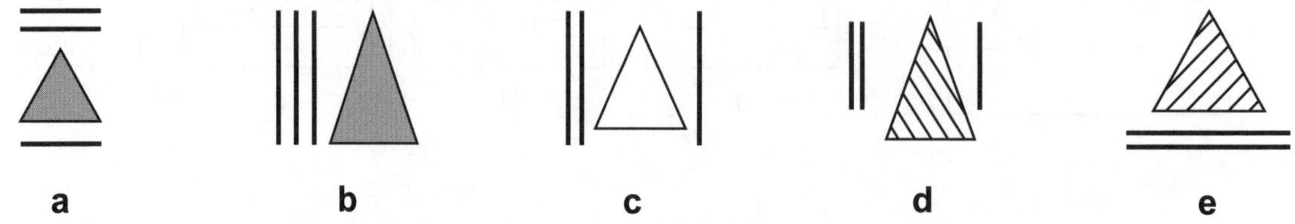

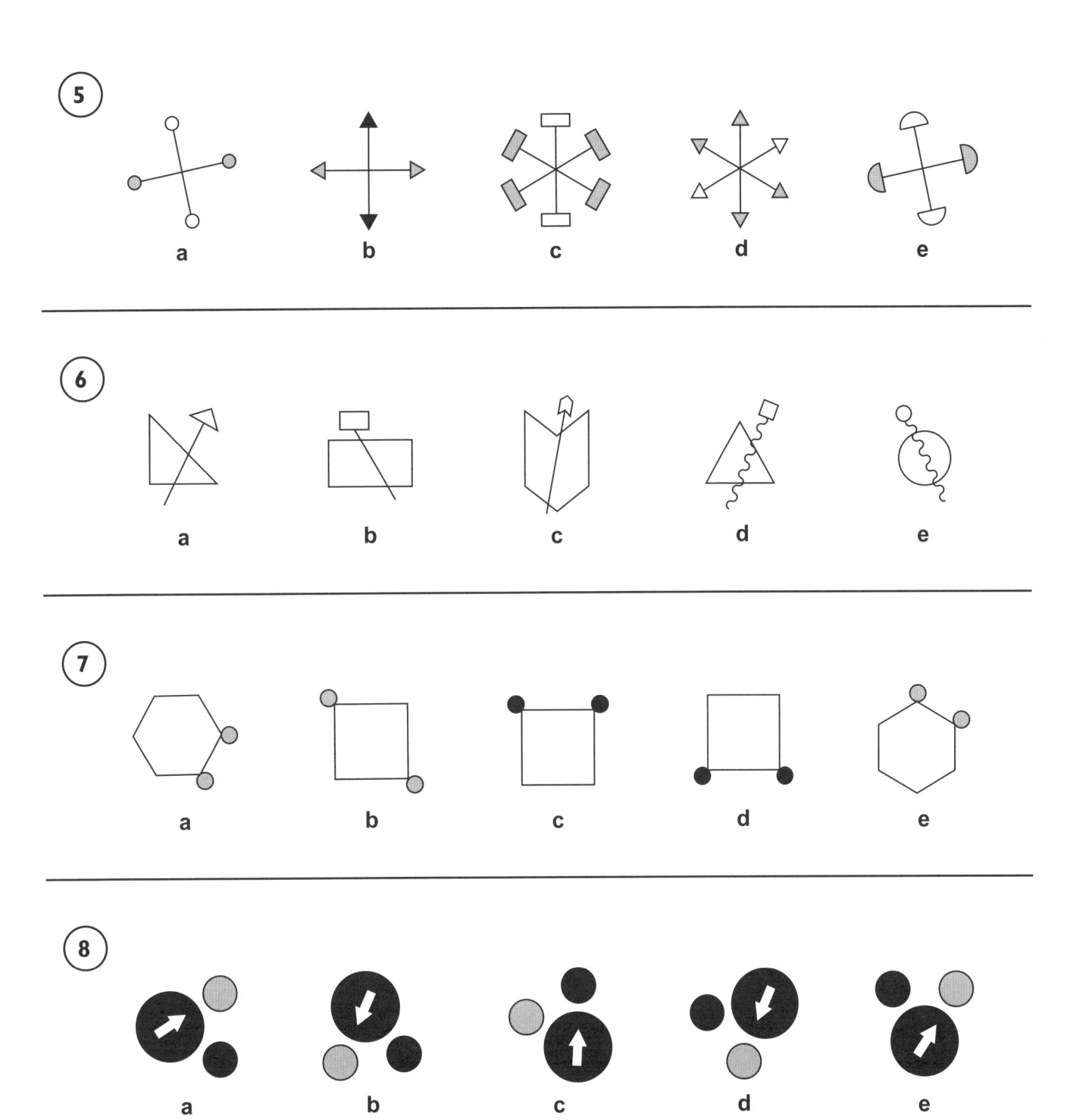

End of Test

Assessment Test 3

Assessment Test 4

You can print **multiple-choice answer sheets** for these questions from our website — go to cgpbooks.co.uk/11plus/answer-sheets. If you'd prefer to answer them in standard write-in format, just circle the letter underneath your answer. The test should take around 20 minutes.

Section 1 — Complete the Hexagonal Grid

Work out which of the options best fits in place of the missing hexagon in the grid.

Example:

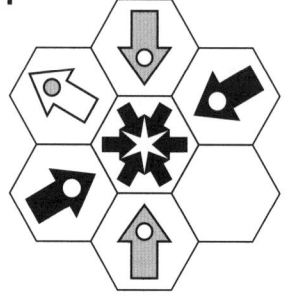

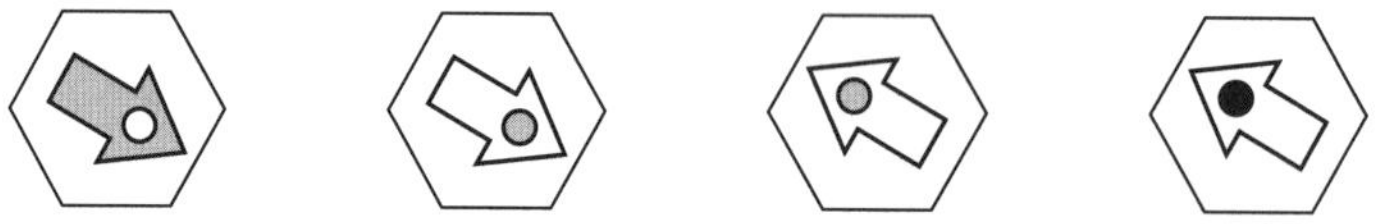

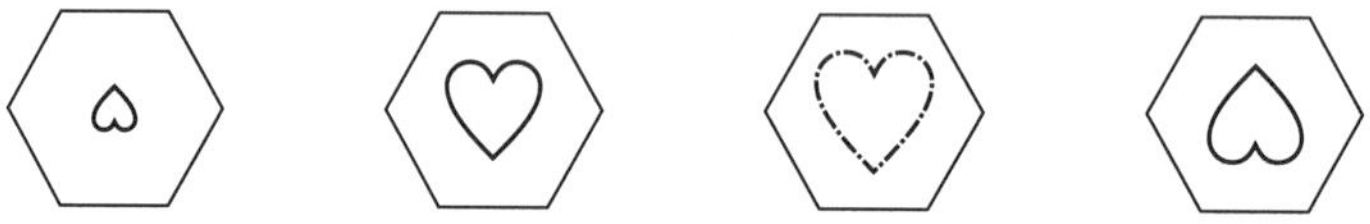

Answer: b

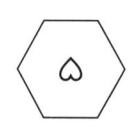

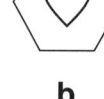

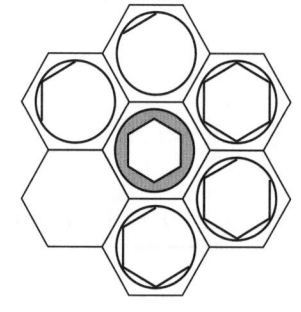

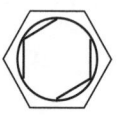

4

5

6

7

8

/ 8

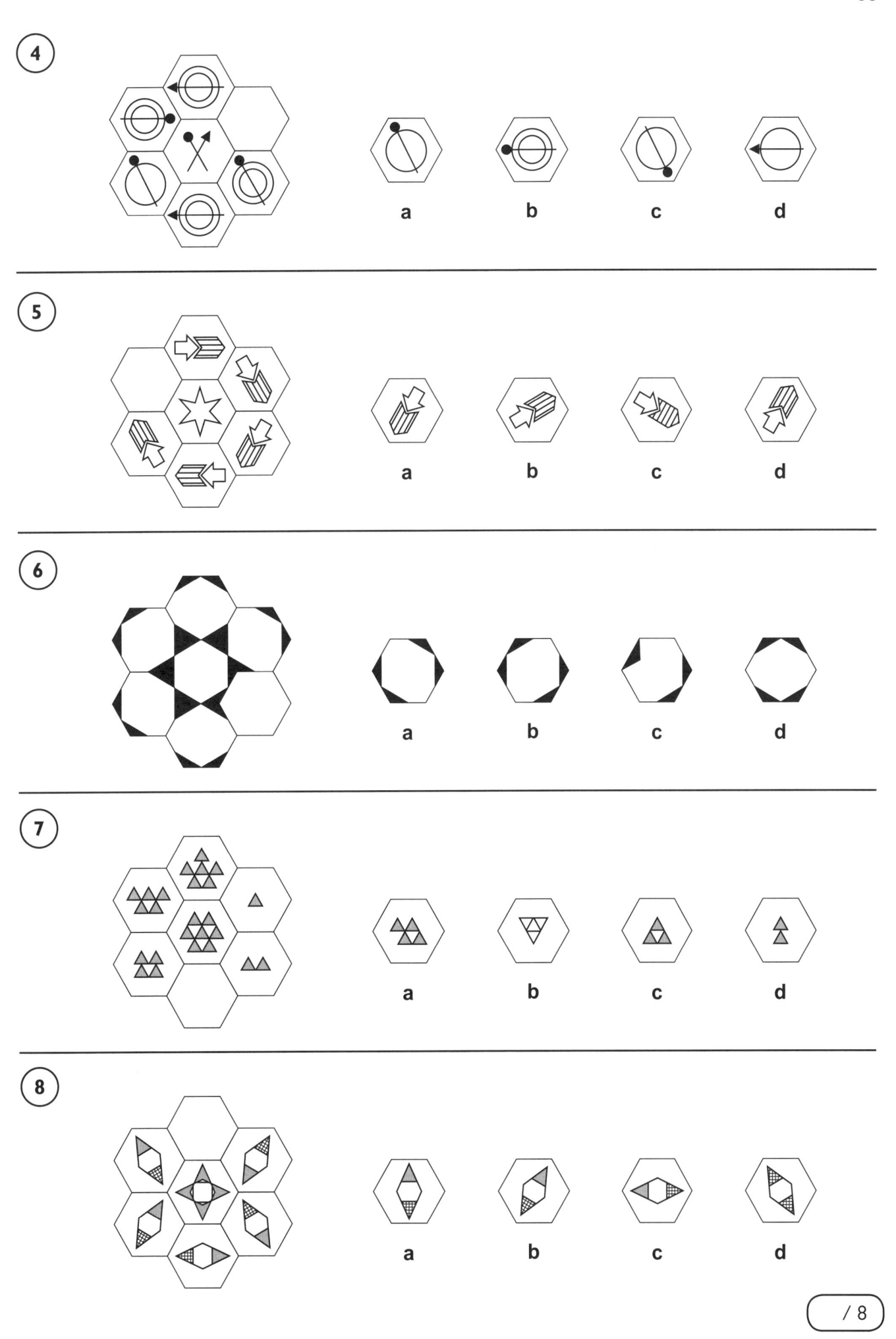

Carry on to the next question → →

Assessment Test 4

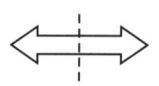

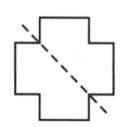

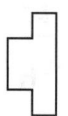

Section 2 — Fold Along the Line

Work out which option shows the figure on the left when folded along the dotted line.

Example:

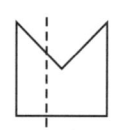

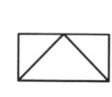

    a   b   c   d

Answer: a

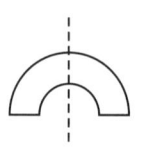

1
    a   b   c   d

2
    a   b   c   d

3
    a   b   c   d

4
    a   b   c   d

Assessment Test 4

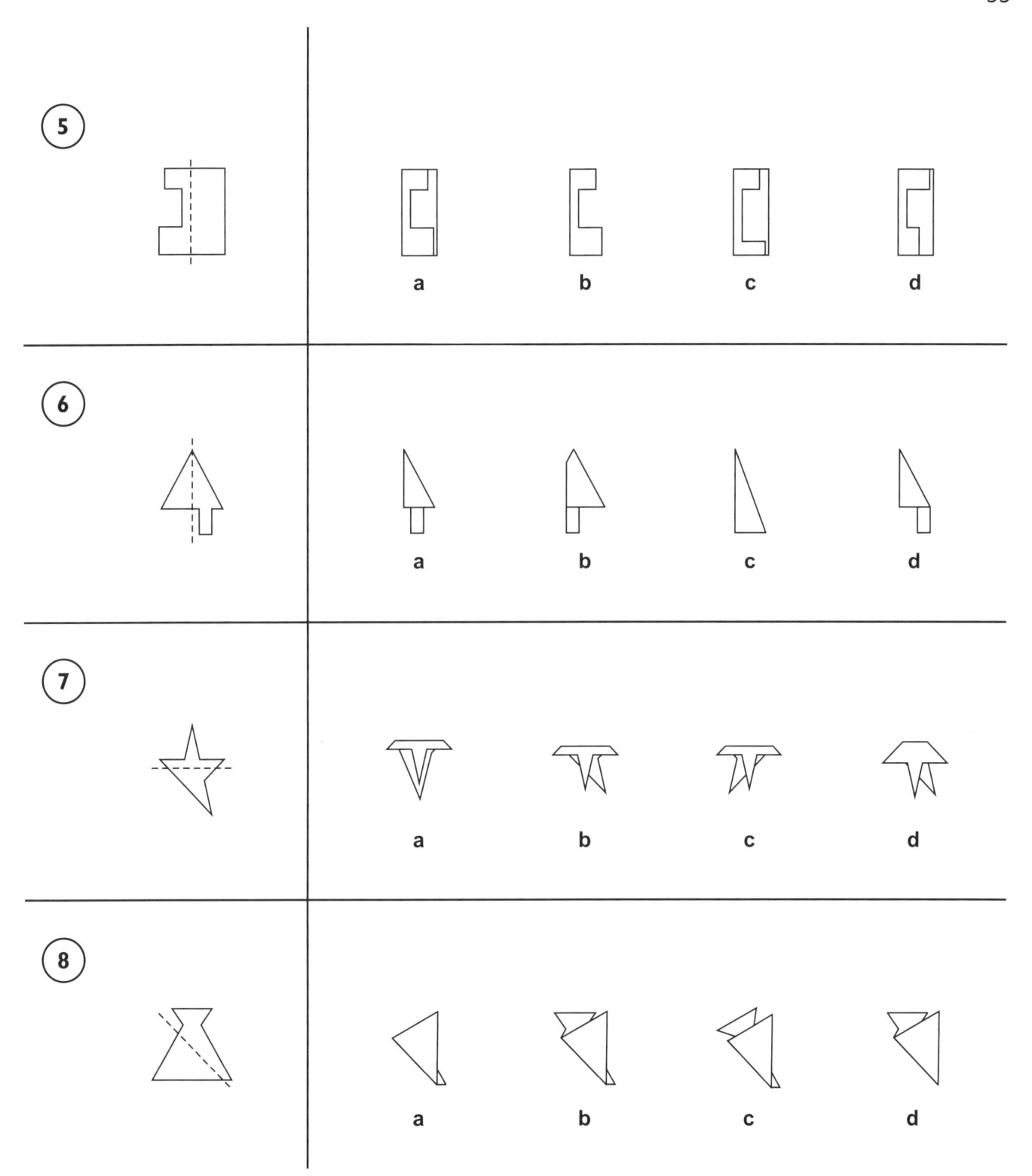

5

a b c d

6

a b c d

7

a b c d

8

a b c d

/ 8

Carry on to the next question → →

Assessment Test 4

Section 3 — Reflect the Figure

Work out which option would look like the figure on the left if it was reflected over the line.

Example:

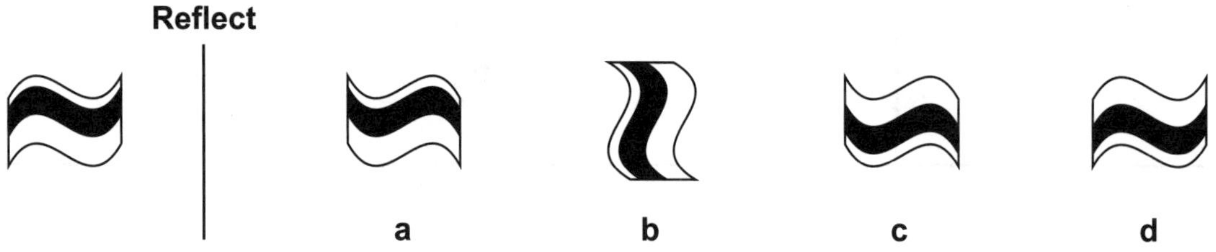

Reflect

a b c d

Answer: a

1 Reflect

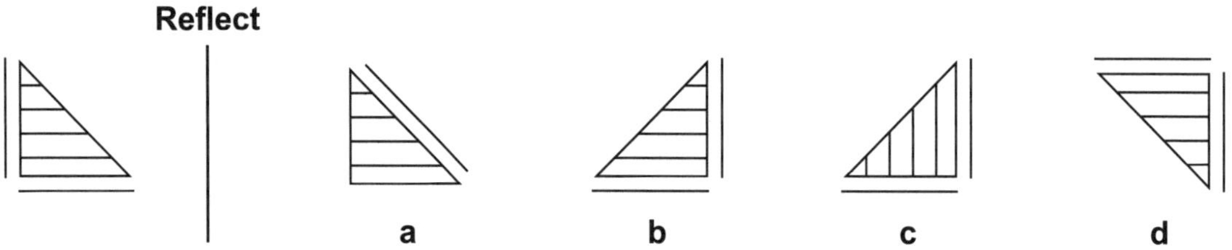

a b c d

2 Reflect

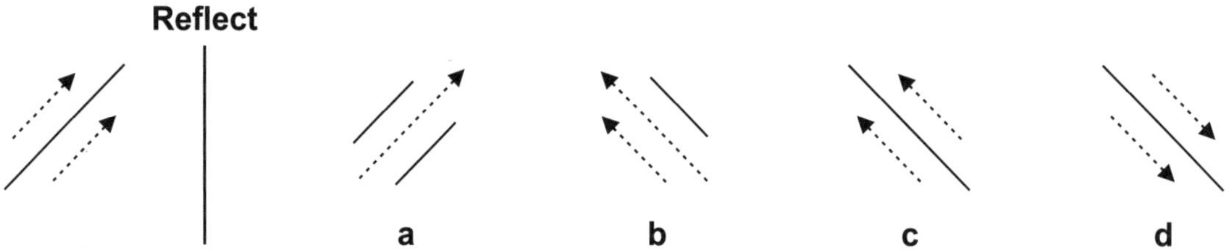

a b c d

3 Reflect

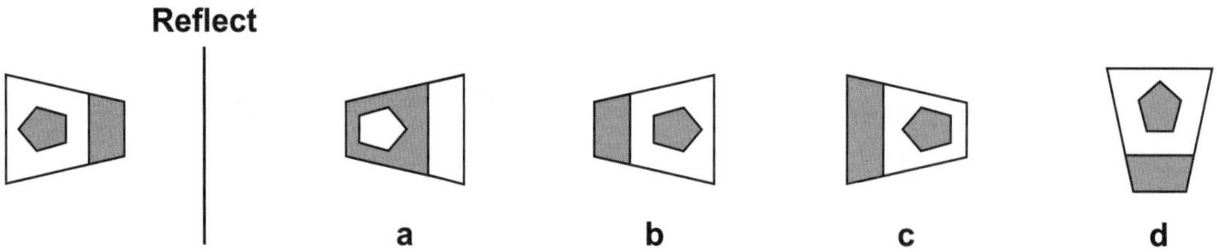

a b c d

4 Reflect

a b c d

Assessment Test 4

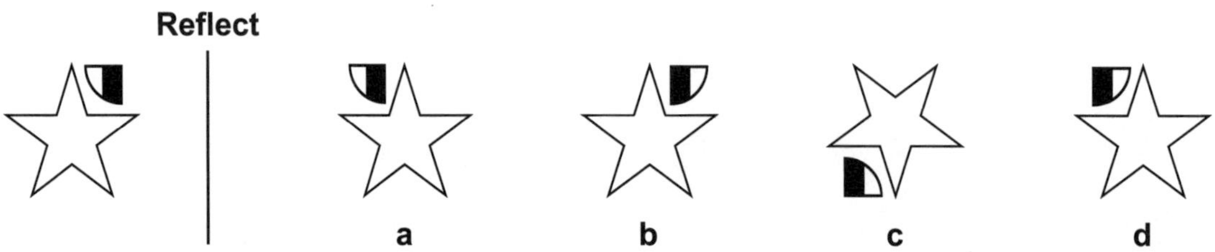

5 Reflect — a b c d

6 Reflect — a b c d

7 Reflect — a b c d

8 Reflect — a b c d

9 Reflect — a b c d

10 Reflect — a b c d

/ 10

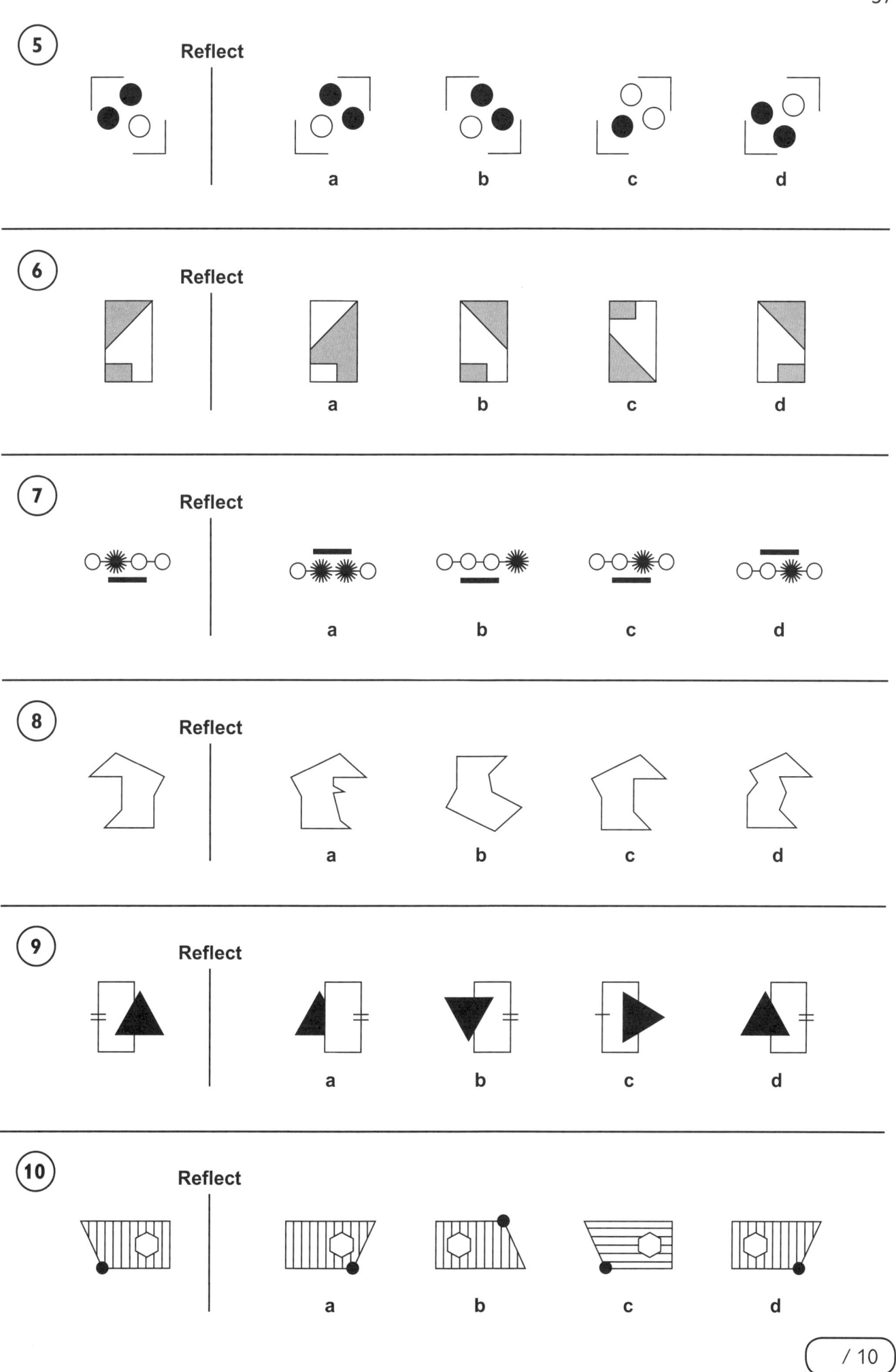

Carry on to the next question → →

Assessment Test 4

Section 4 — Cubes and Nets

Work out which of the four cubes can be made from the net.

Example:

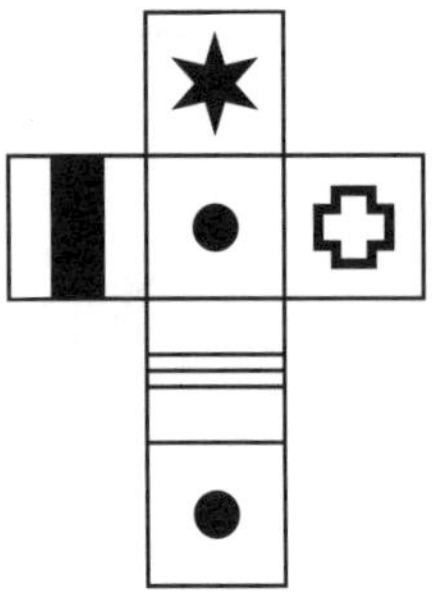

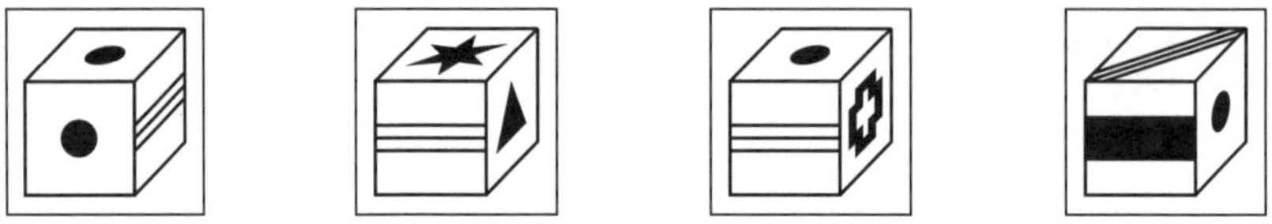

a b c d

Answer: c

1

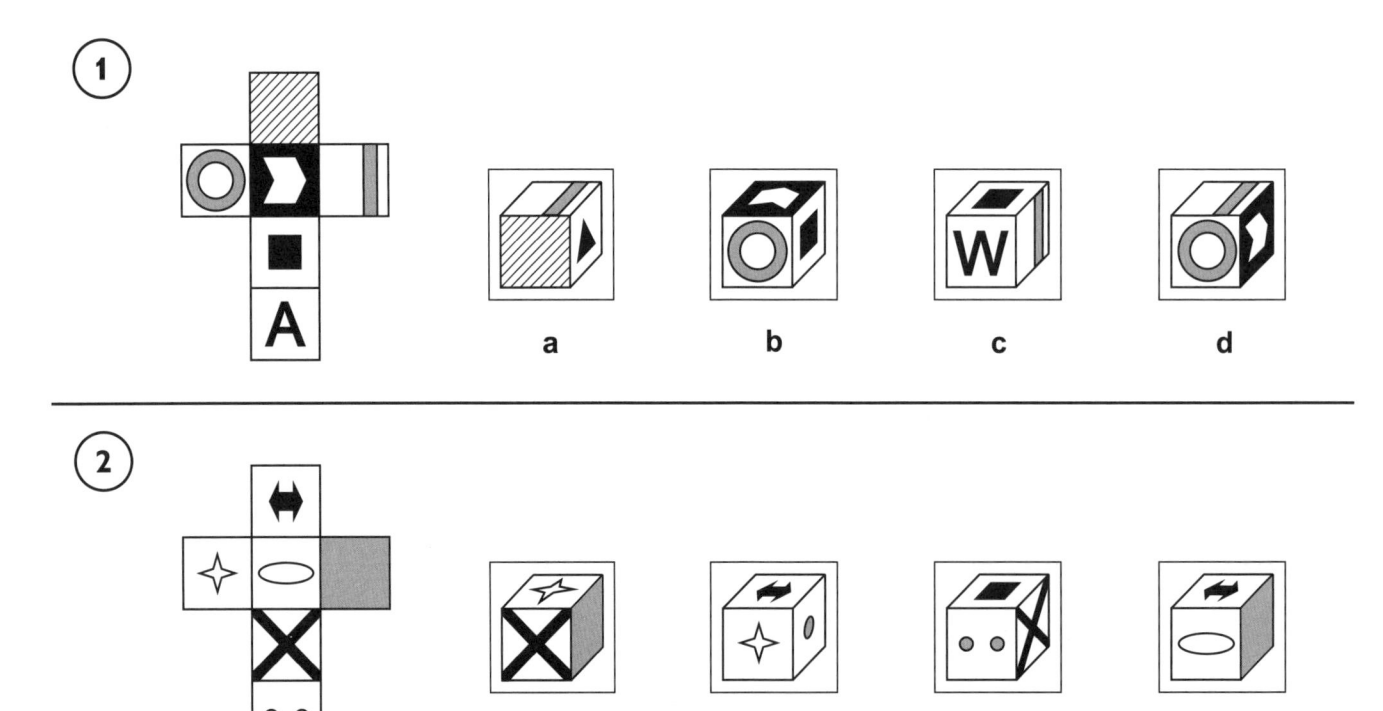

a b c d

2

a b c d

3

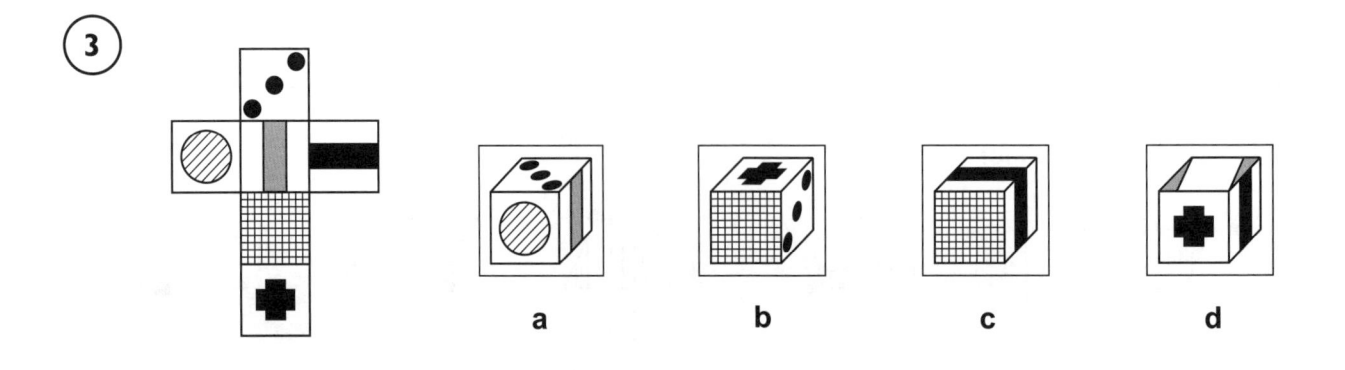

a b c d

Assessment Test 4

Carry on to the next question → →

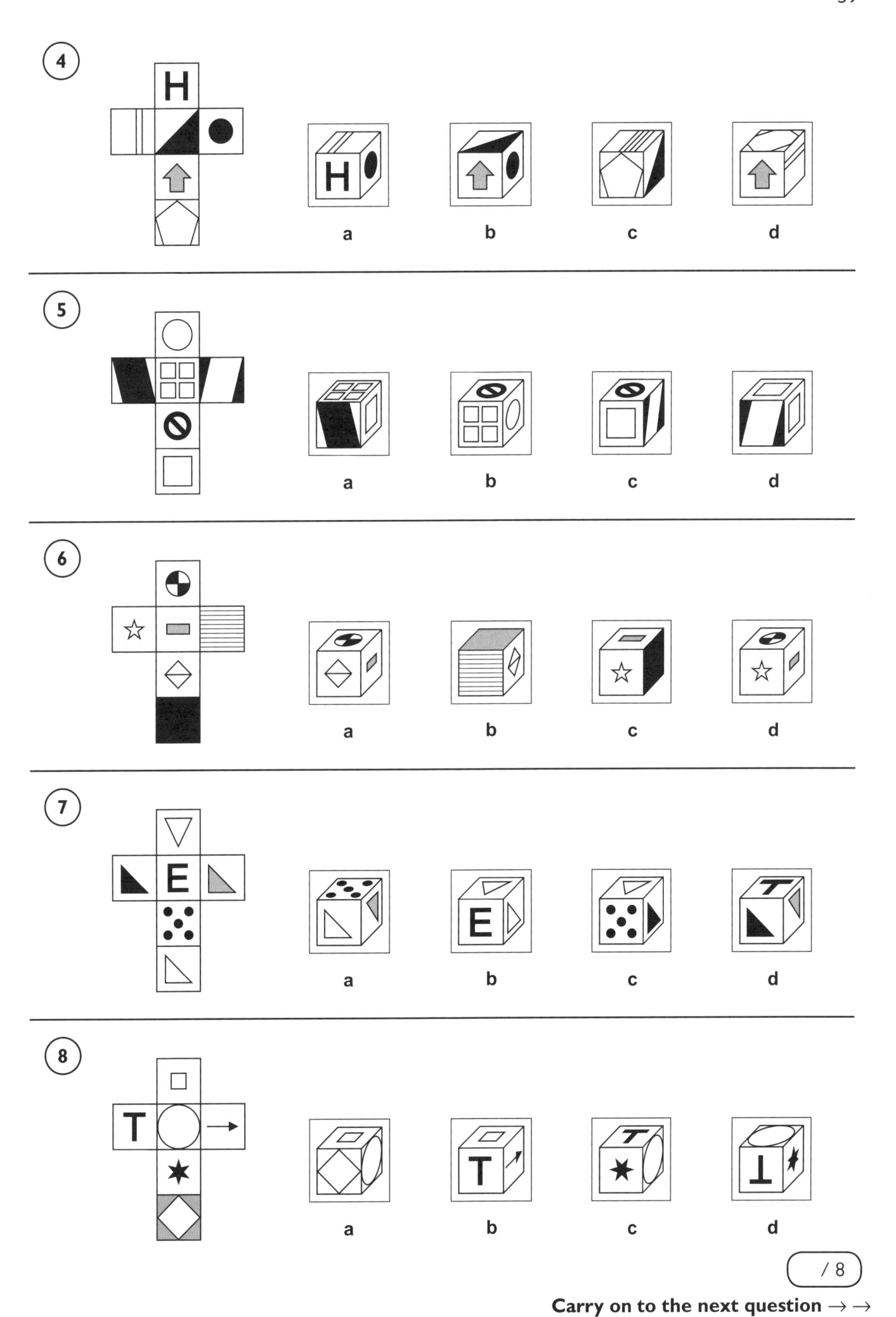

Assessment Test 4

Section 5 — 3D Rotation

Work out which 3D figure in the grey box has been rotated to make the new 3D figure.

Example:

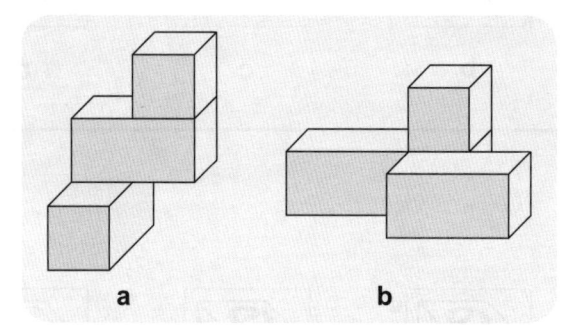

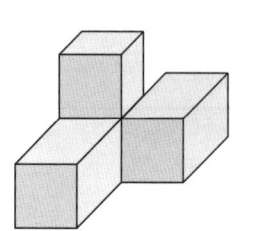

Answer: b

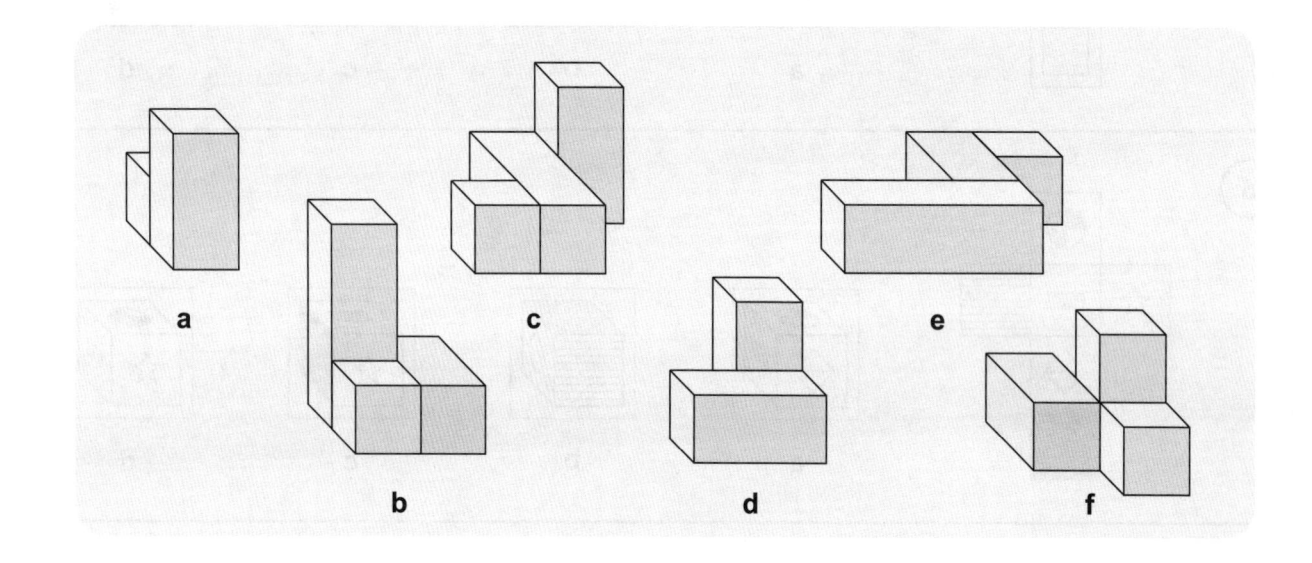

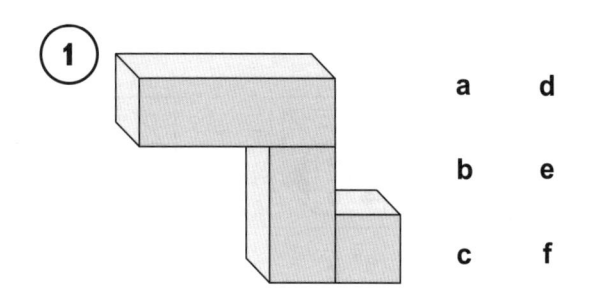

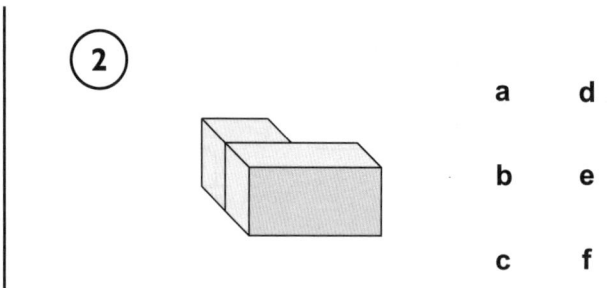

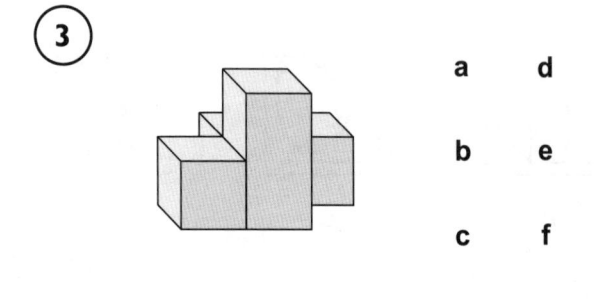

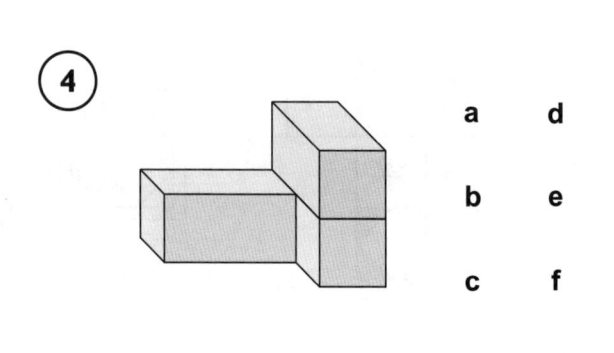

1. a d
   b e
   c f

2. a d
   b e
   c f

3. a d
   b e
   c f

4. a d
   b e
   c f

Assessment Test 4

a

b

c

d

e

f

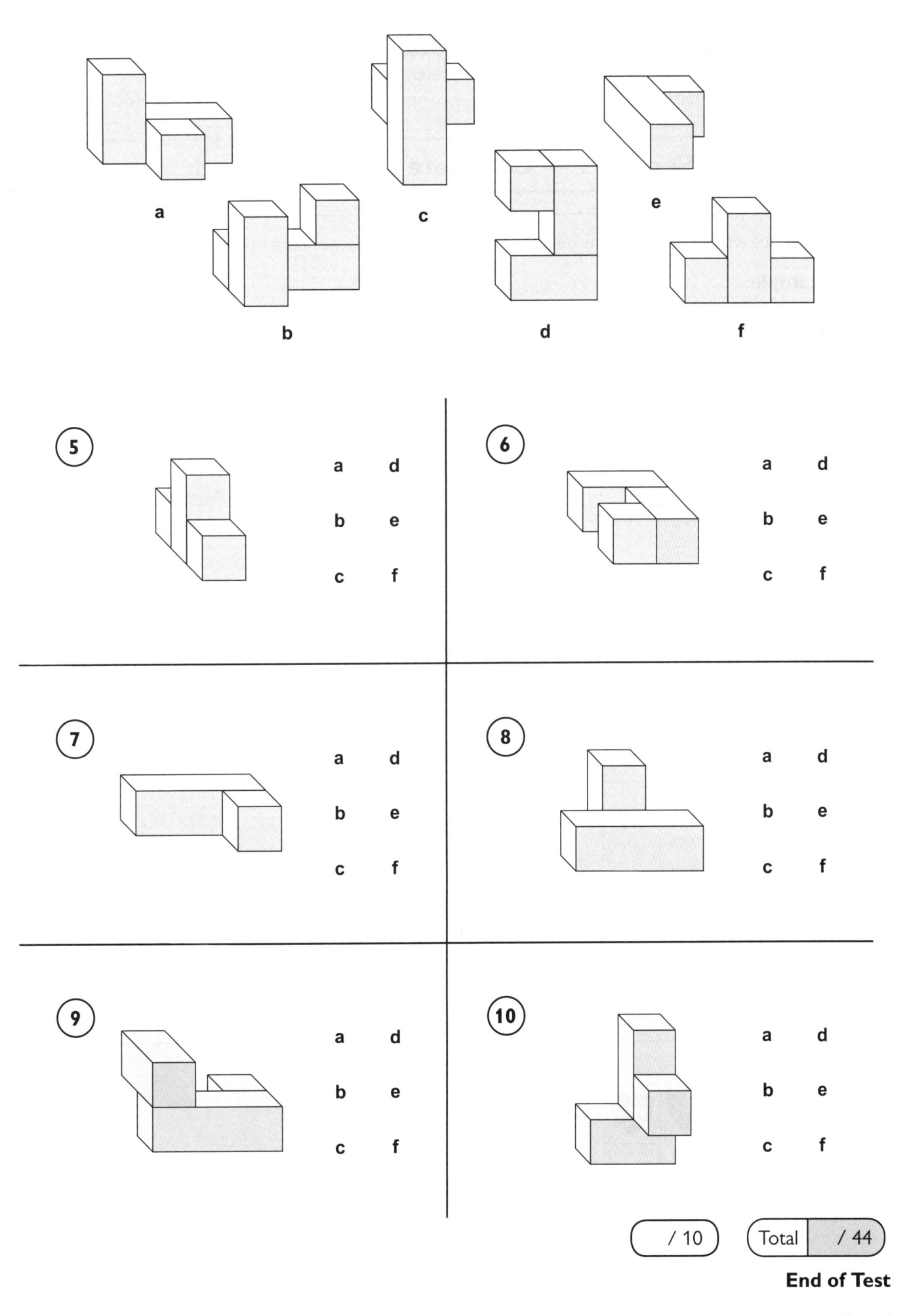

5
a	d
b	e
c	f

6
a	d
b	e
c	f

7
a	d
b	e
c	f

8
a	d
b	e
c	f

9
a	d
b	e
c	f

10
a	d
b	e
c	f

/ 10   Total / 44

End of Test

Assessment Test 4

Assessment Test 5

You can print **multiple-choice answer sheets** for these questions from our website — go to cgpbooks.co.uk/11plus/answer-sheets. If you'd prefer to answer them in standard write-in format, just circle the letter underneath your answer. The test should take around 20 minutes.

Section 1 — Complete the Square Grid

Work out which of the options best fits in place of the missing square in the grid.

Example:

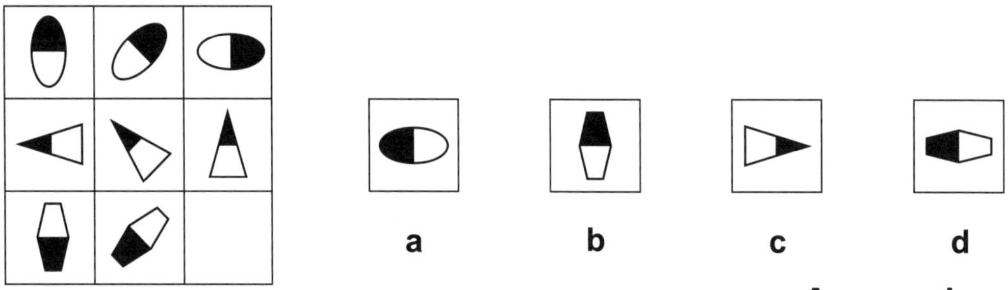

Answer: d

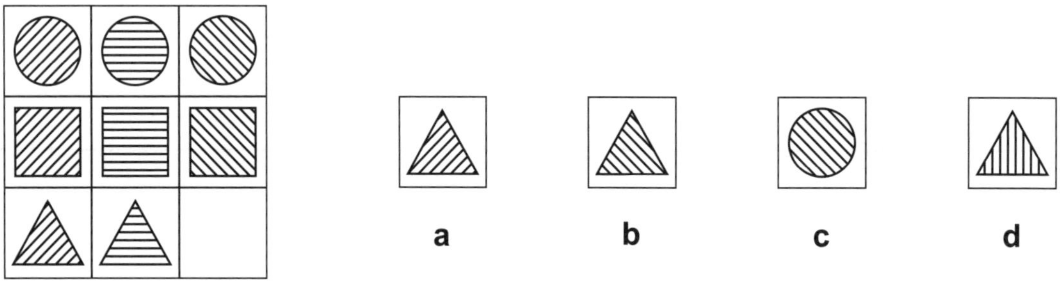

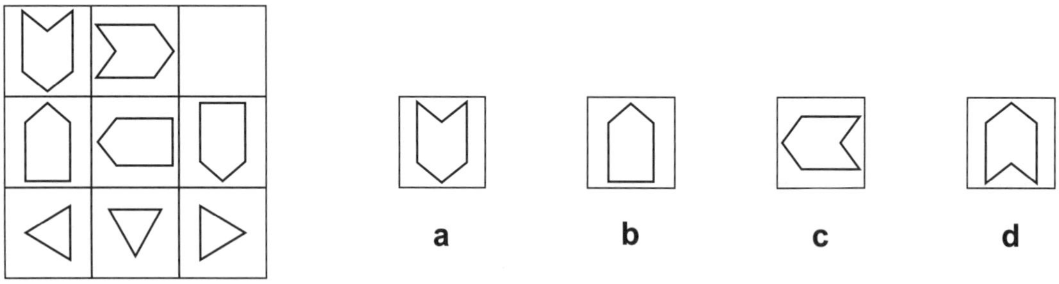

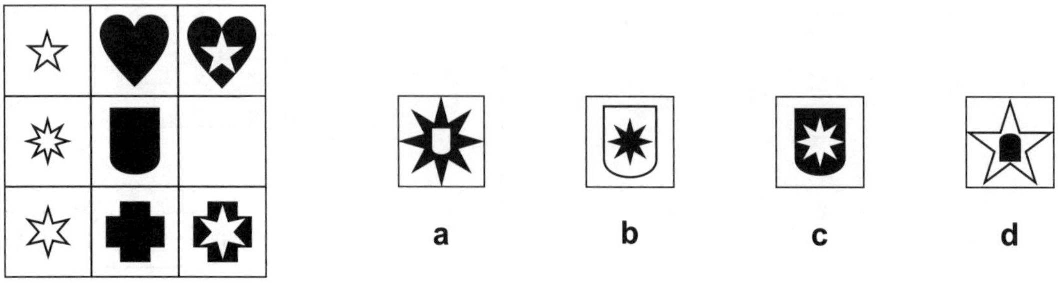

(4)

(5)

(6)

(7)

(8)

/ 8

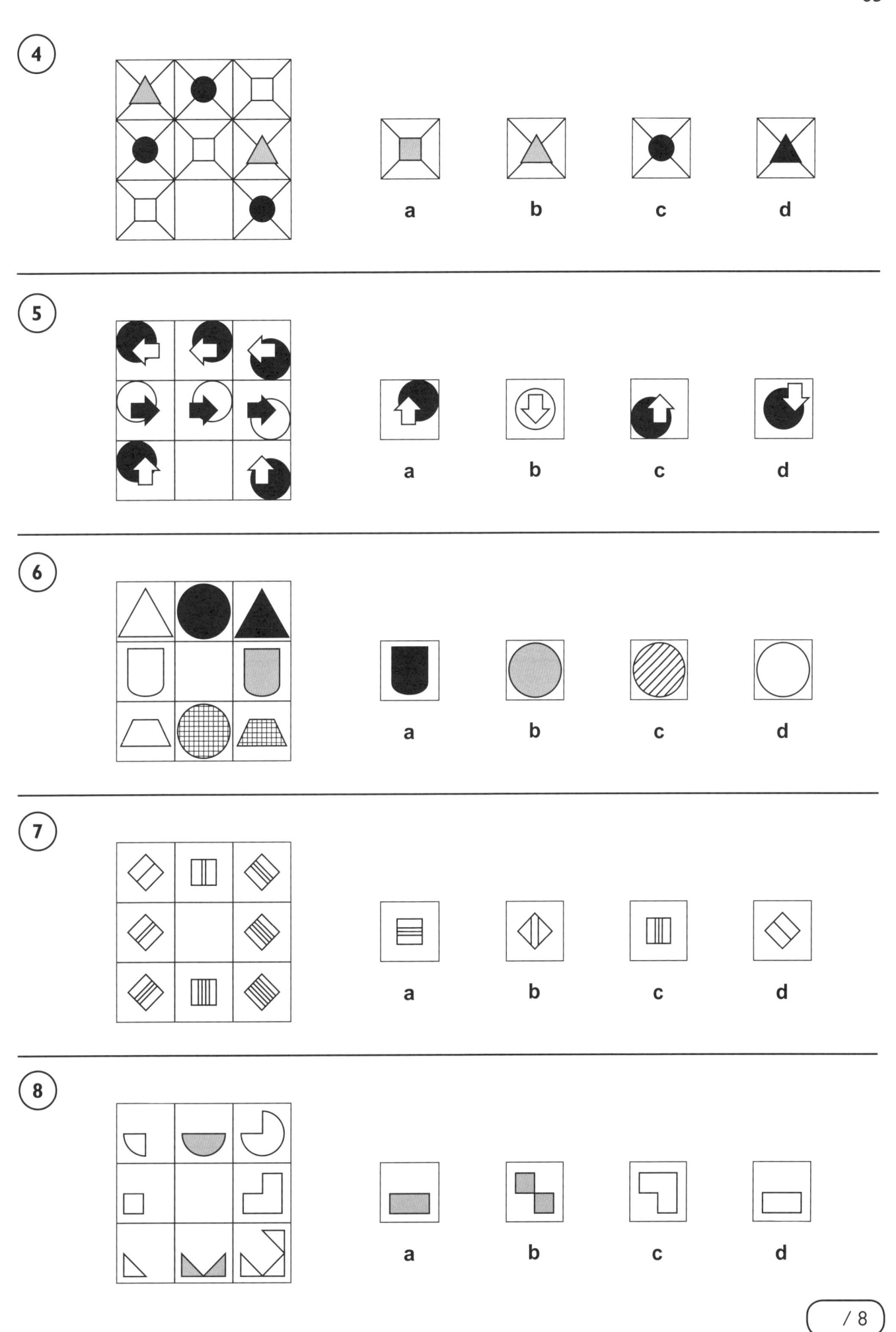

Carry on to the next question → →

Assessment Test 5

Section 2 — Find the Figure Like the First Two

Work out which option is most like the two figures on the left.

Example:

a b c d

Answer: a

1

a b c d

2

a b c d

3

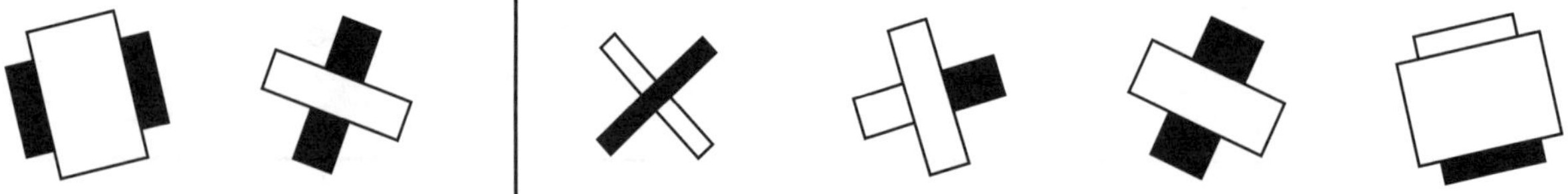

a b c d

4

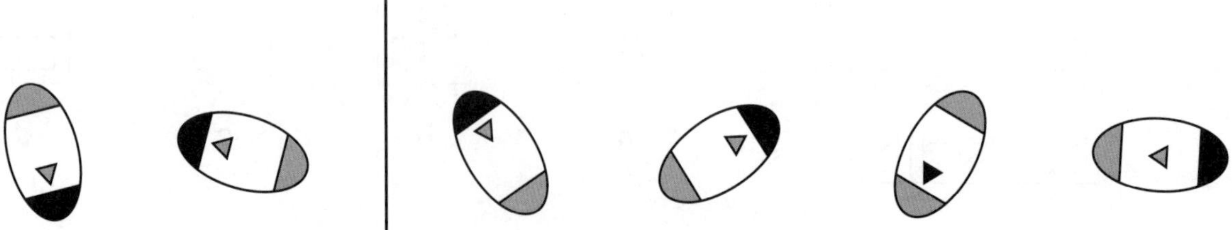

a b c d

Assessment Test 5

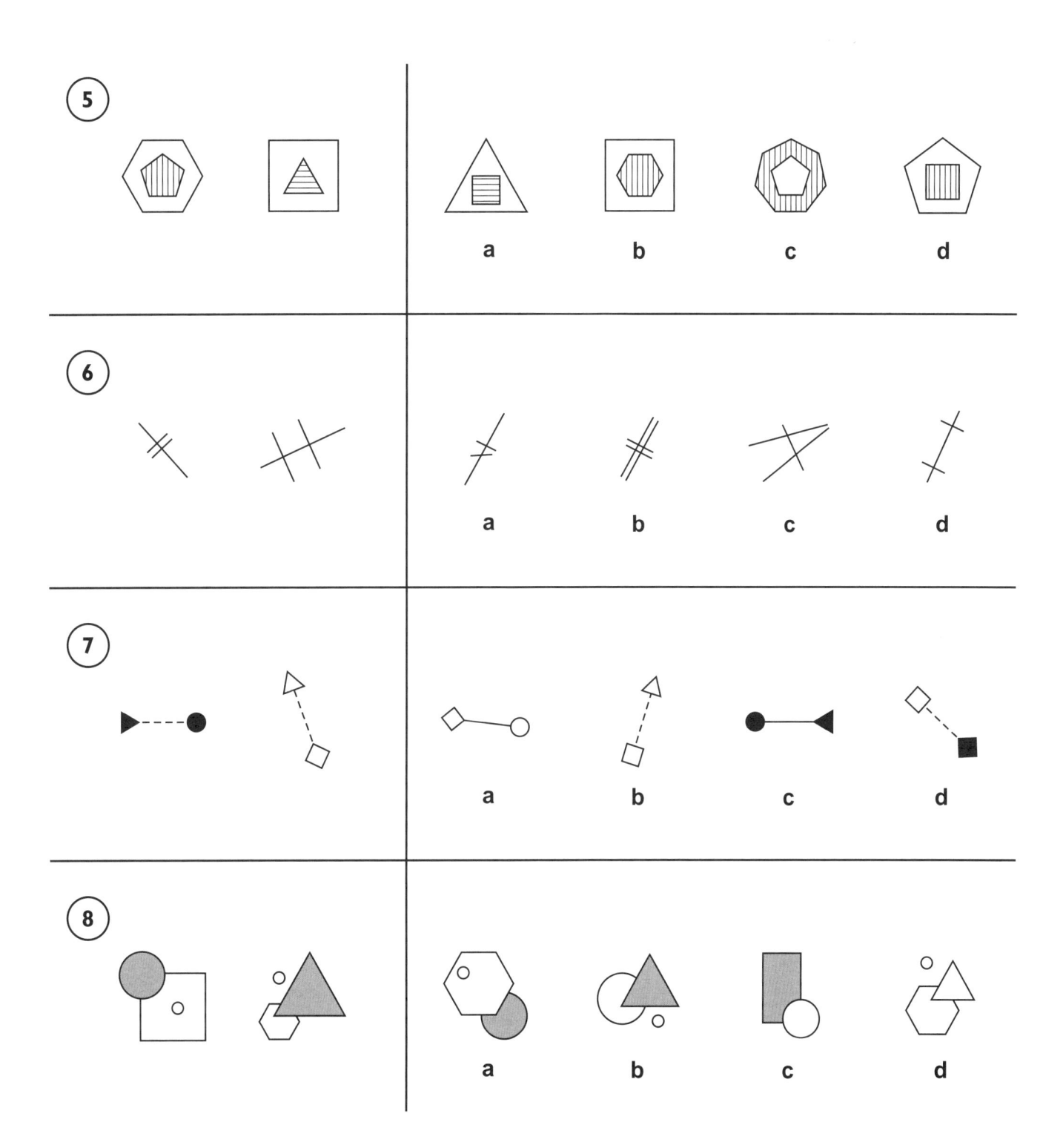

5

a b c d

6

a b c d

7

a b c d

8

a b c d

/ 8

Carry on to the next question → →

Assessment Test 5

Section 3 — Complete the Pair

Look at how the first two figures are changed, and then work out which option would look like the third figure if you changed it in the same way.

Example:

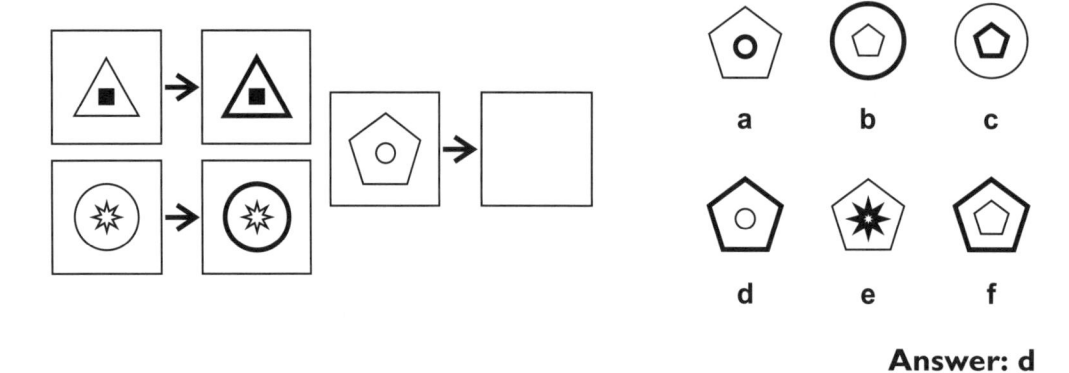

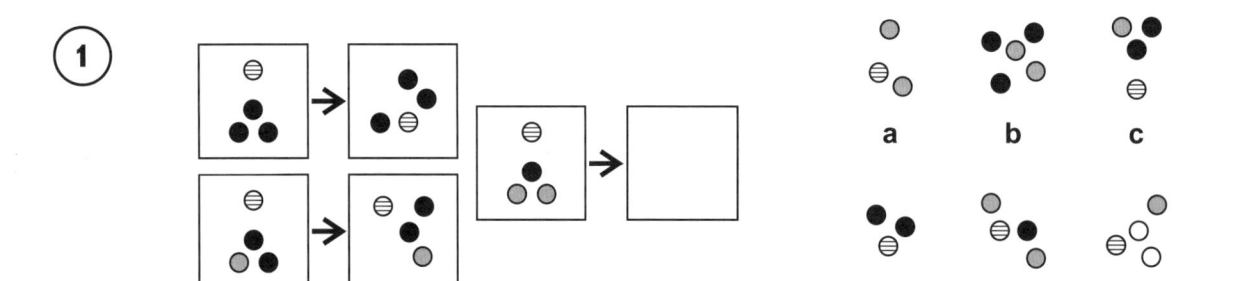

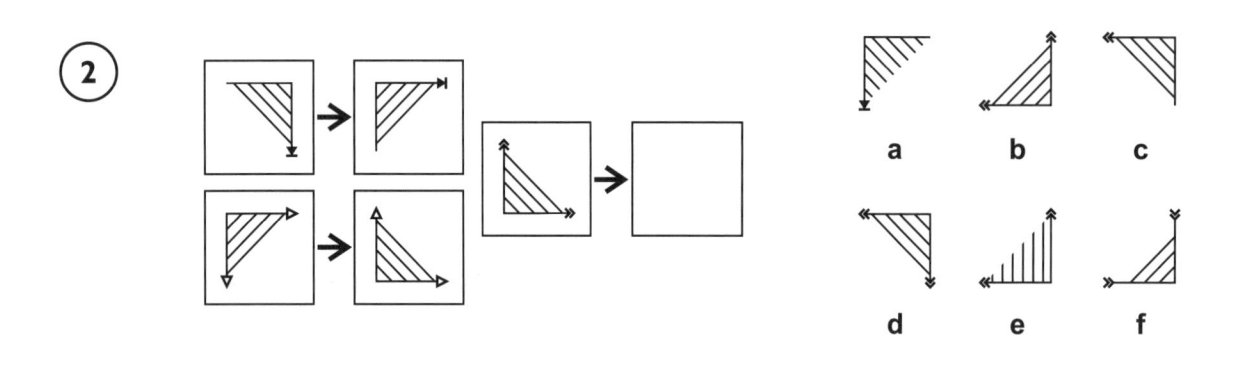

Answer: d

Assessment Test 5

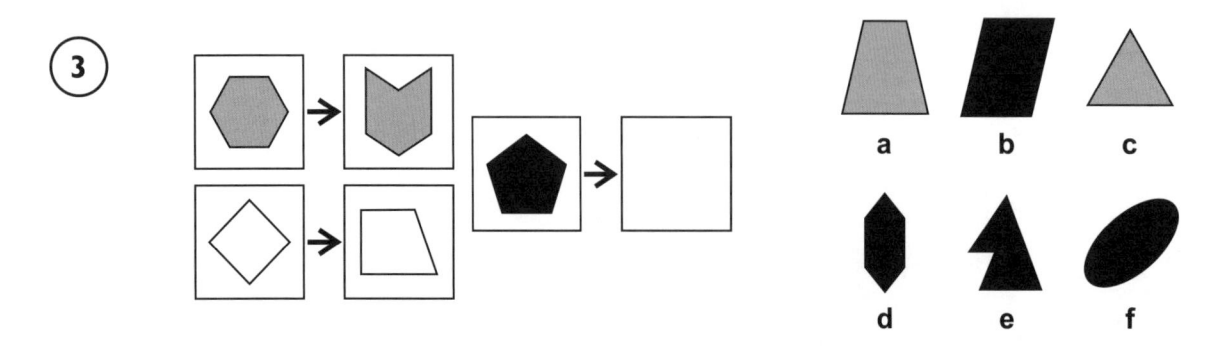

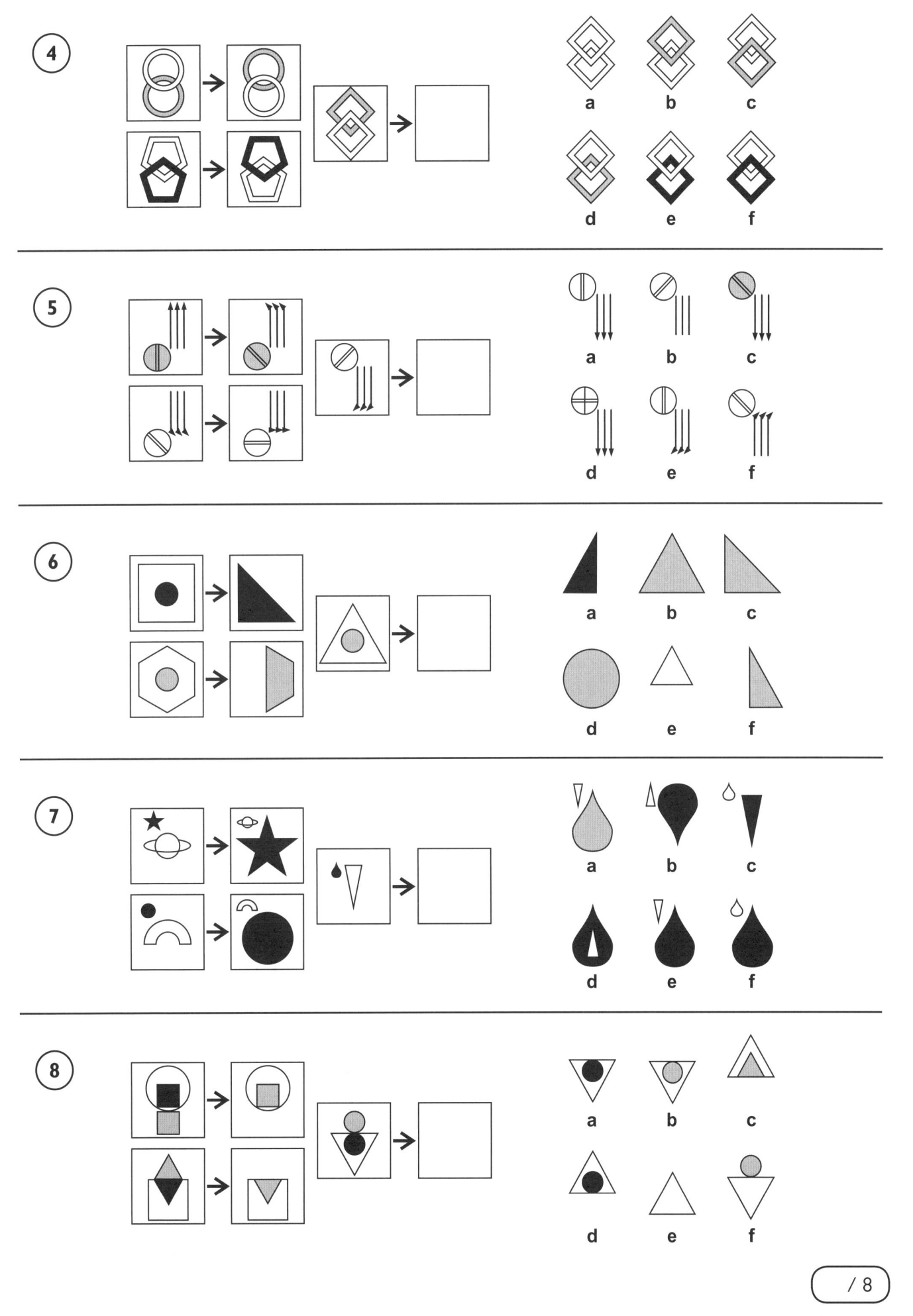

Carry on to the next question → →

Assessment Test 5

Section 4 — Rotate the Figure

Work out which option would look like the figure on the left if it was rotated.

Example:

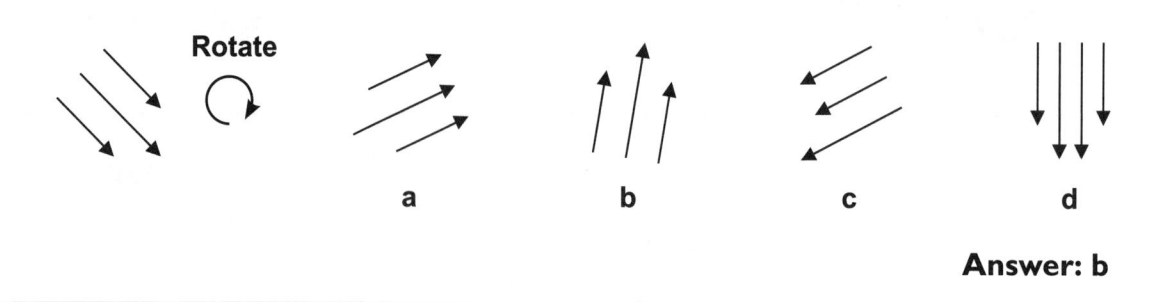

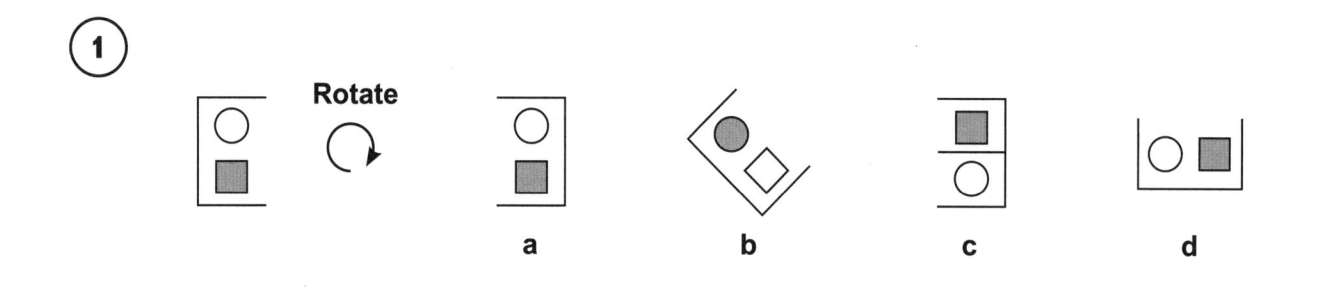

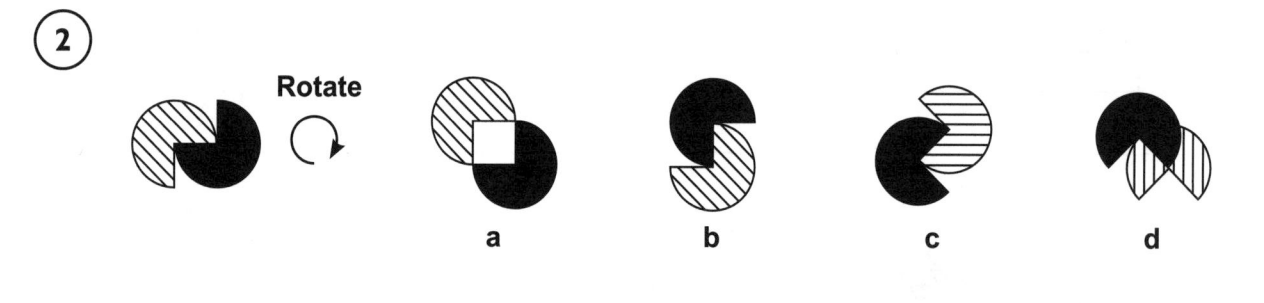

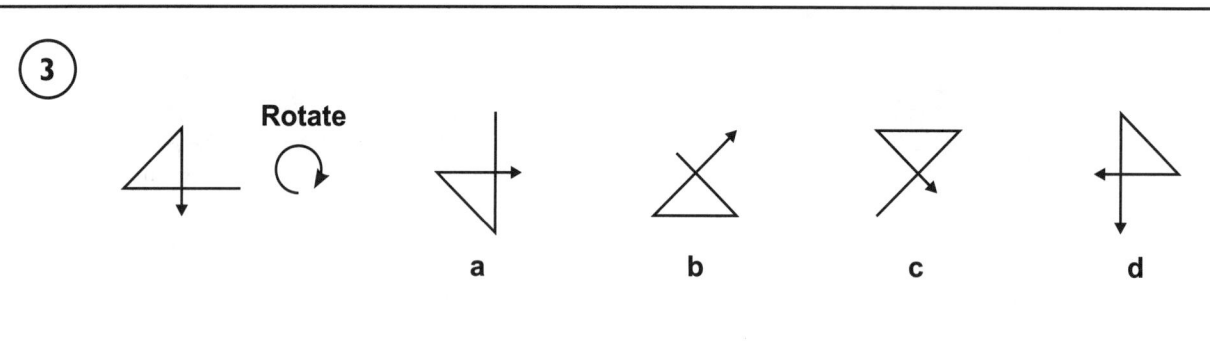

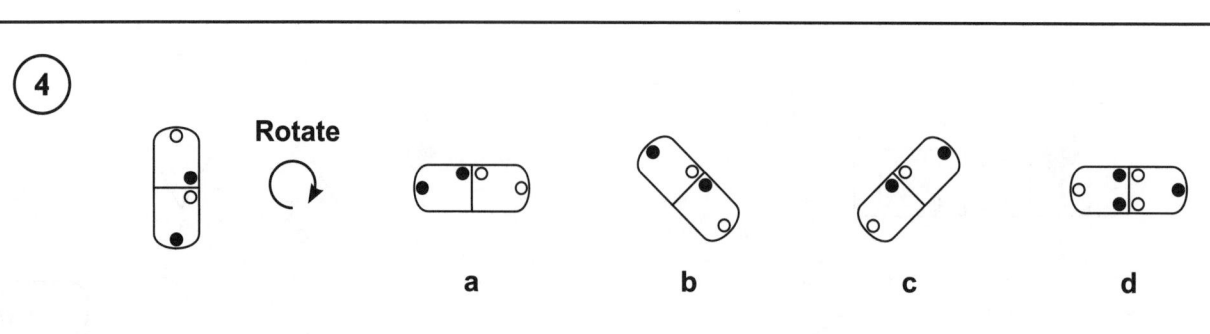

Rotate

a b c d

Answer: b

1

Rotate

a b c d

2

Rotate

a b c d

3

Rotate

a b c d

4

Rotate

a b c d

Assessment Test 5

5 Rotate

a b c d

6 Rotate

a b c d

7 Rotate

a b c d

8 Rotate

a b c d

9 Rotate

a b c d

10 Rotate

a b c d

/ 10

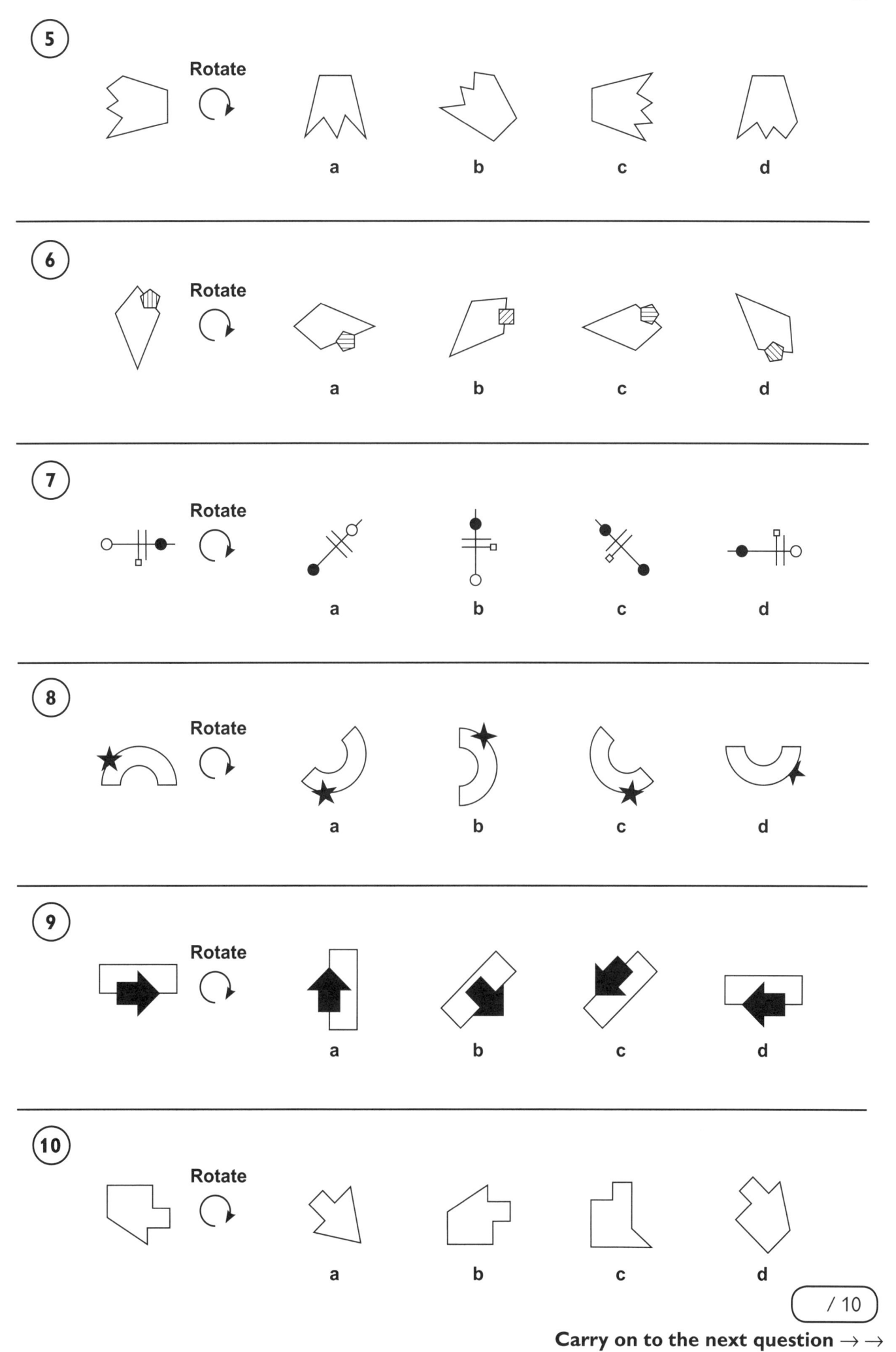

Carry on to the next question → →

Assessment Test 5

Section 5 — Complete the Series

Work out which of the options best fits in place of the missing square in the series.

Example:

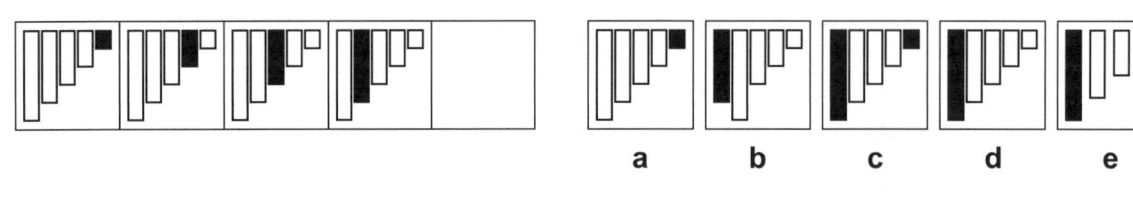

Answer: d

(1)

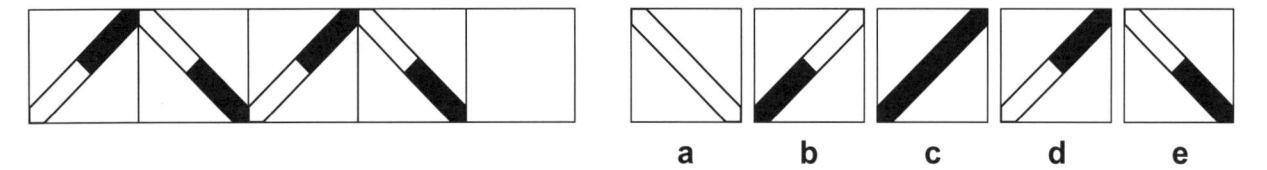

a b c d e

(2)

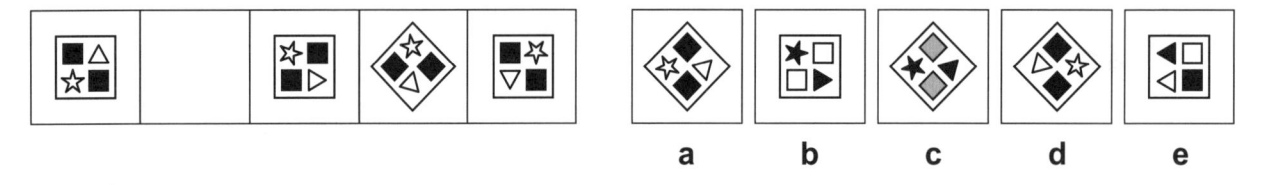

a b c d e

(3)

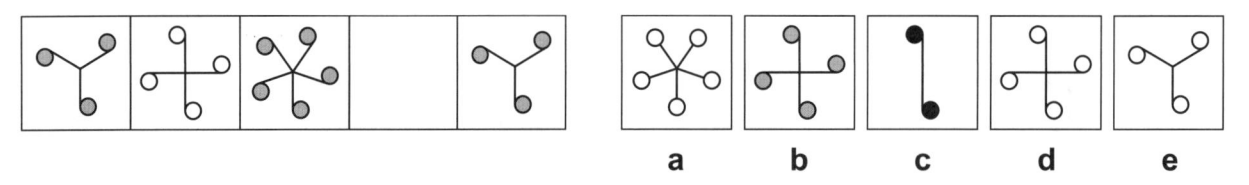

a b c d e

(4)

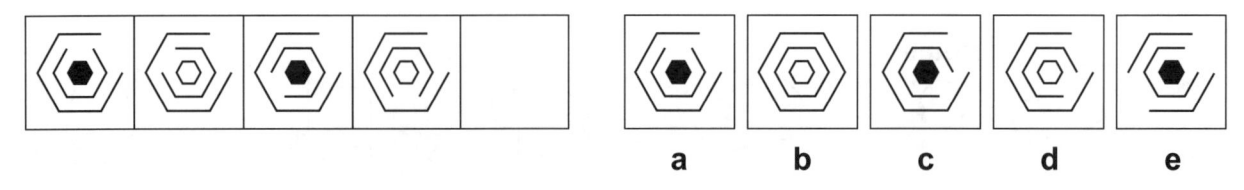

a b c d e

Assessment Test 5

5

6

7

8

9

10

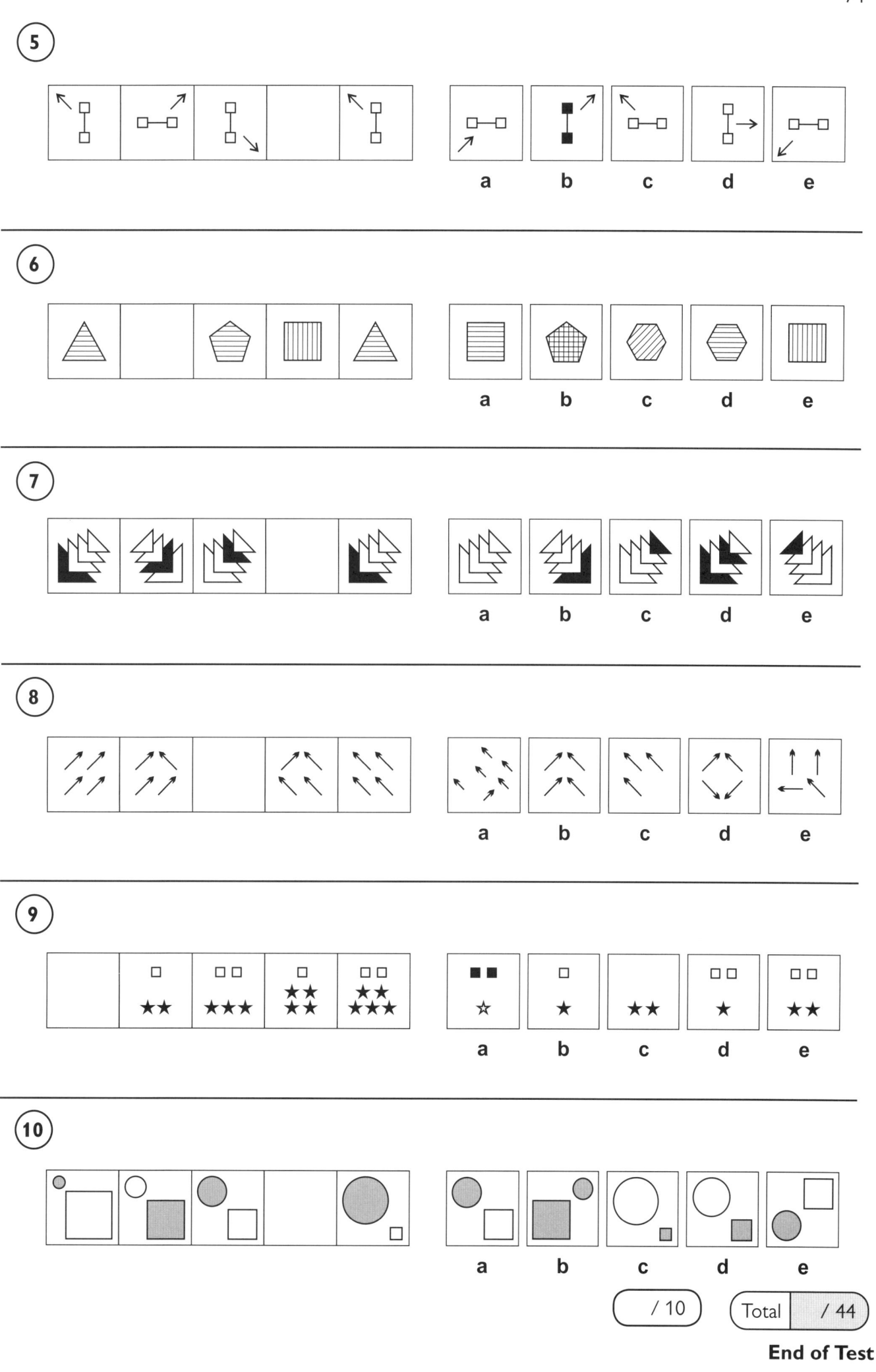

/ 10   Total / 44

End of Test

Assessment Test 5

Assessment Test 6

You can print **multiple-choice answer sheets** for these questions from our website — go to cgpbooks.co.uk/11plus/answer-sheets. If you'd prefer to answer them in standard write-in format, just circle the letter underneath your answer. The test should take around 20 minutes.

Section 1 — Changing Bugs

Look at how the first bug changes to become the second bug.
Then work out which option would look like the third bug if you changed it in the same way.

Example:

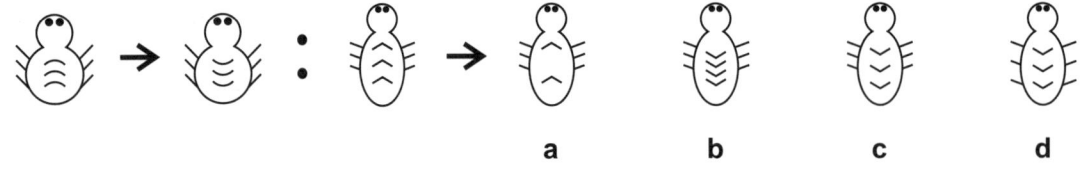

Answer: c

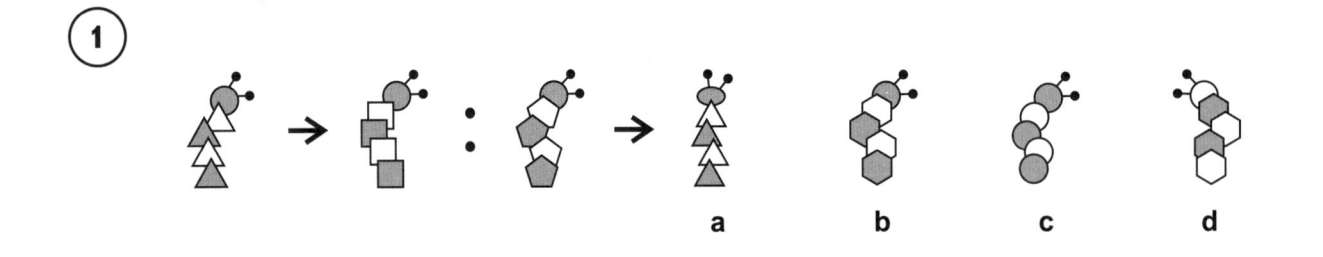

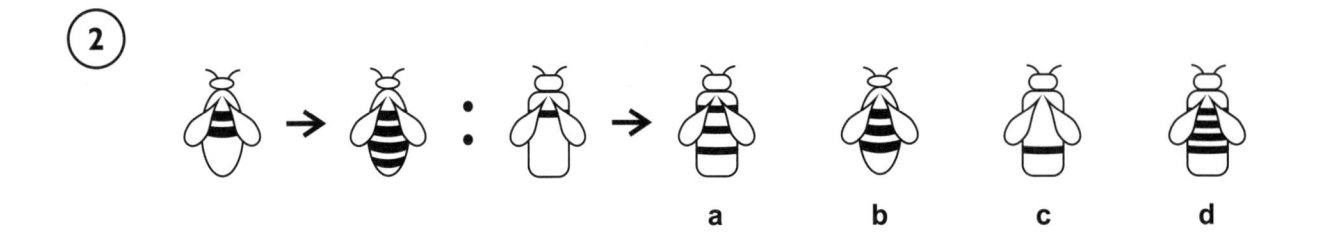

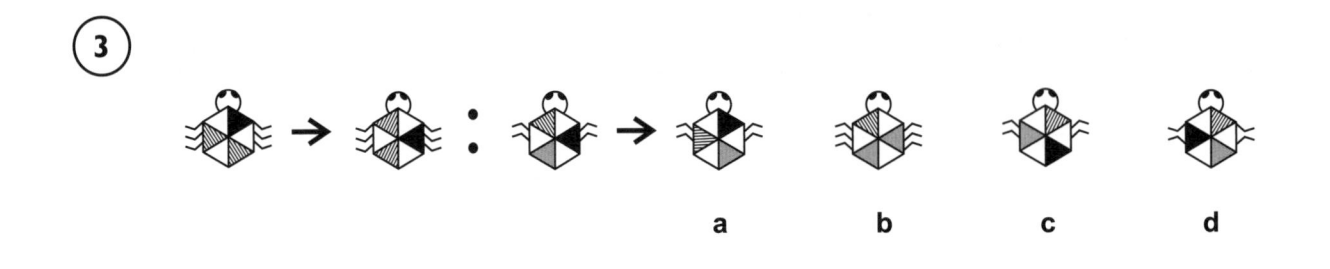

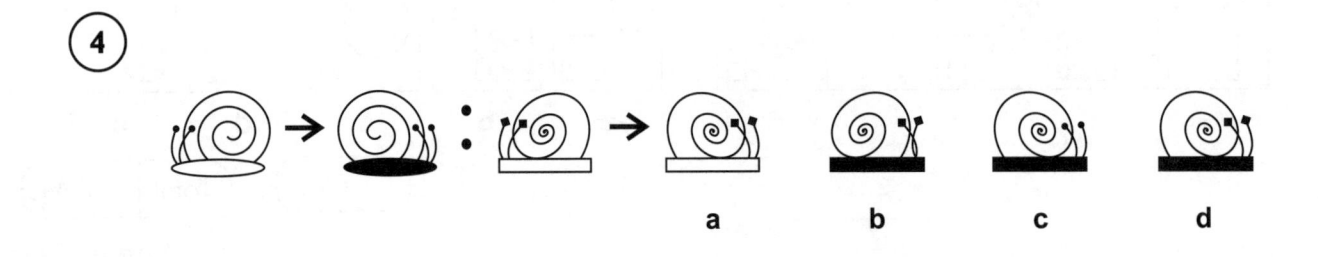

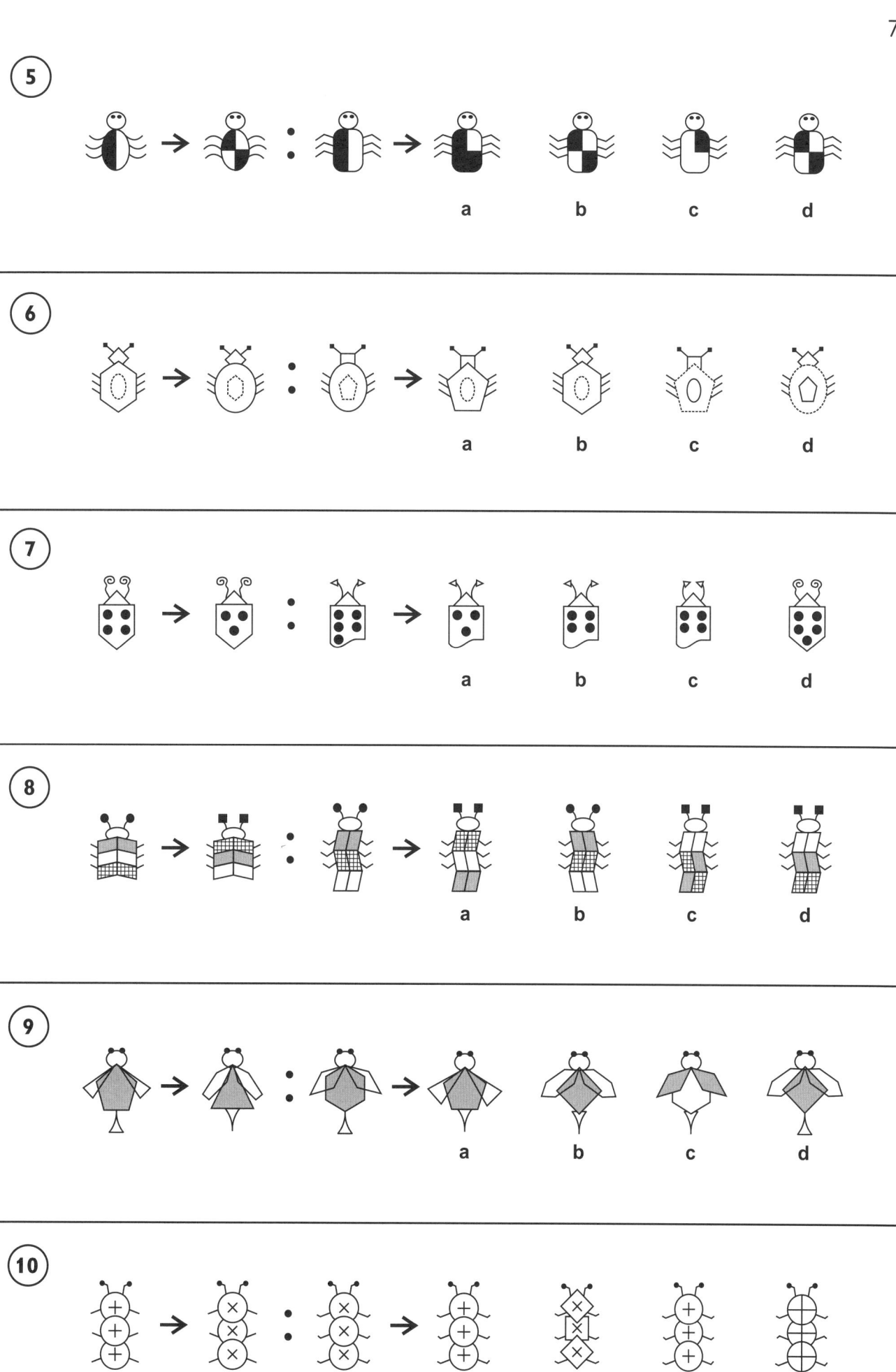

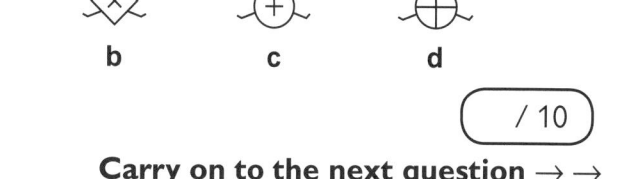

Assessment Test 6

Section 2 — Complete the Hexagonal Grid

Work out which of the options best fits in place of the missing hexagon in the grid.

Example:

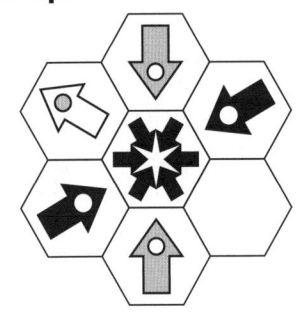

Answer: **b**

1

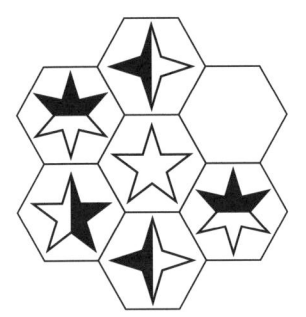

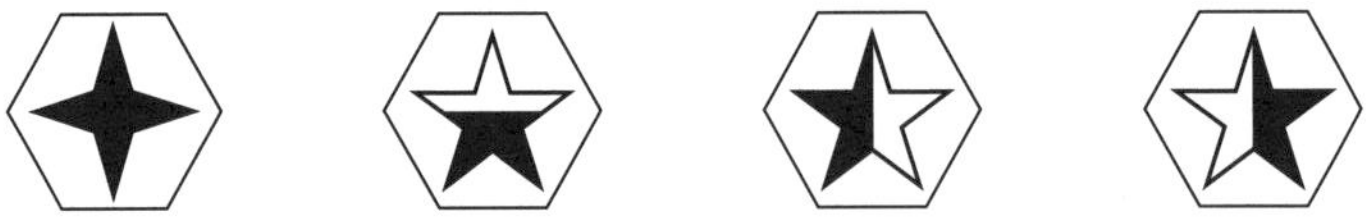

2

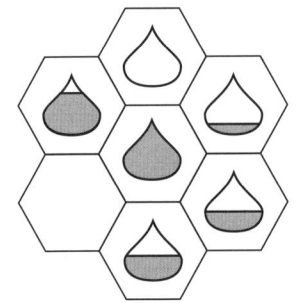

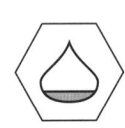

3

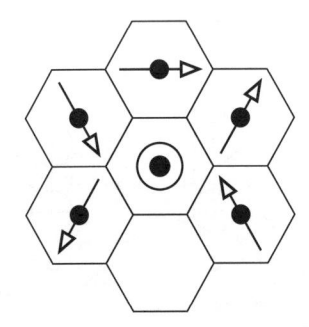

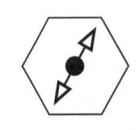

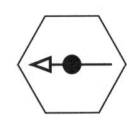

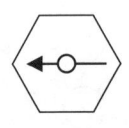

Assessment Test 6

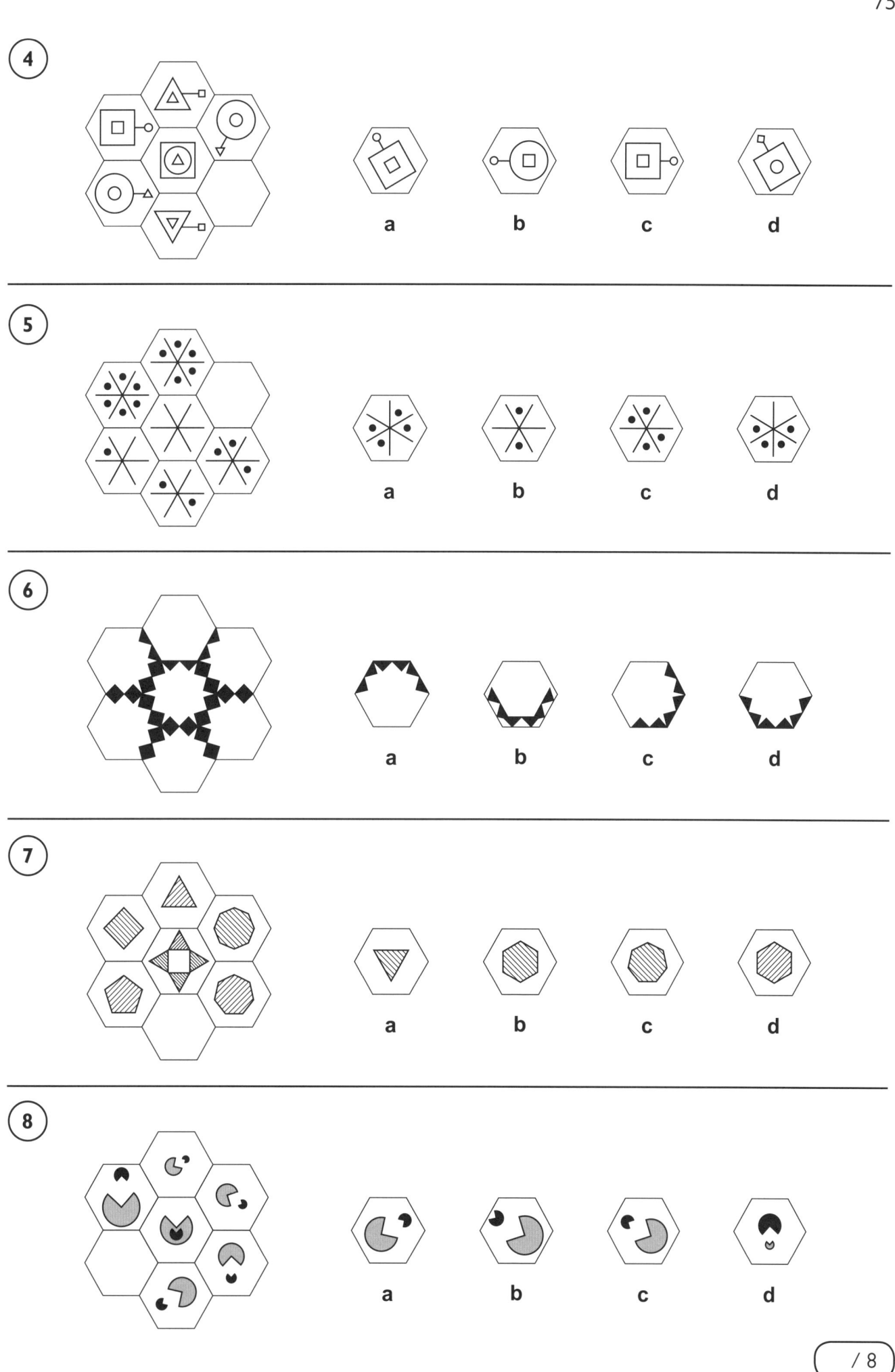

Assessment Test 6

/ 8

Carry on to the next question → →

Section 3 — Reflect the Figure

Work out which option would look like the figure on the left if it was reflected over the line.

Example:

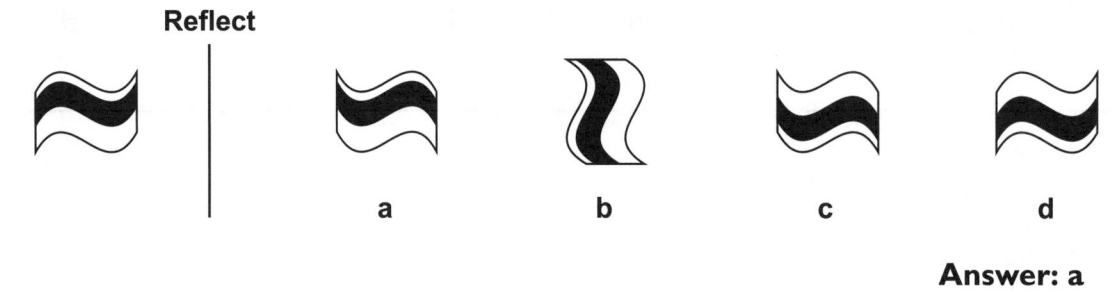

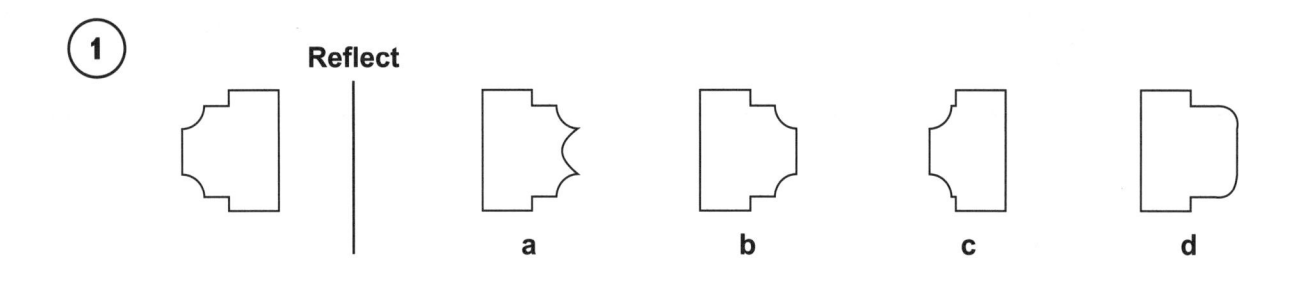

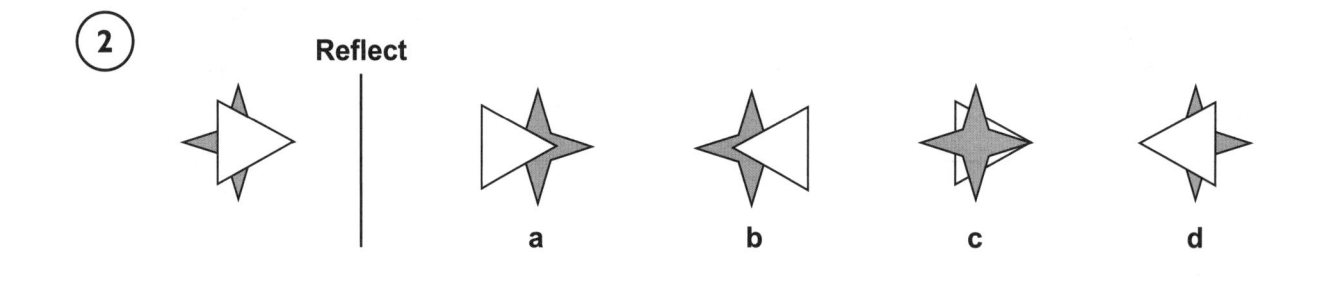

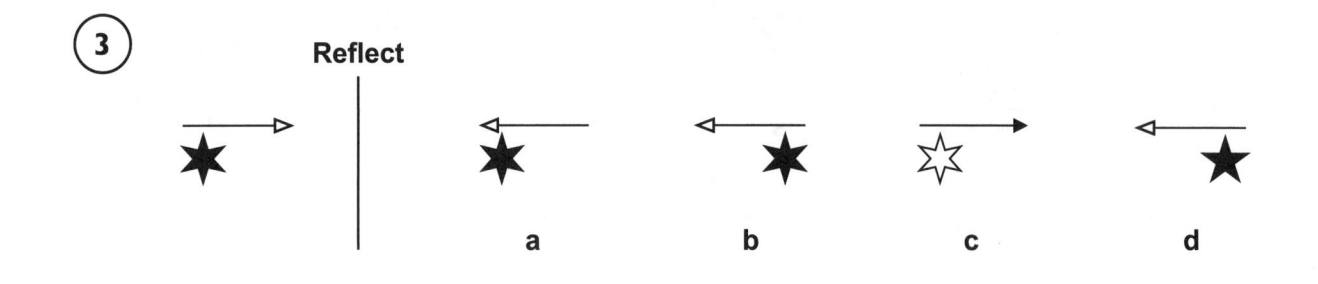

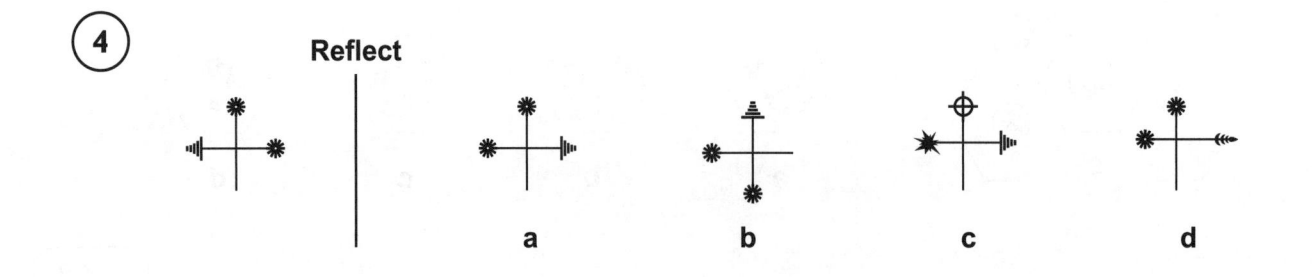

Reflect

a b c d

Answer: a

(1) Reflect

a b c d

(2) Reflect

a b c d

(3) Reflect

a b c d

(4) Reflect

a b c d

Assessment Test 6

5 Reflect

6 Reflect

7 Reflect

8 Reflect

9 Reflect

10 Reflect

/ 10

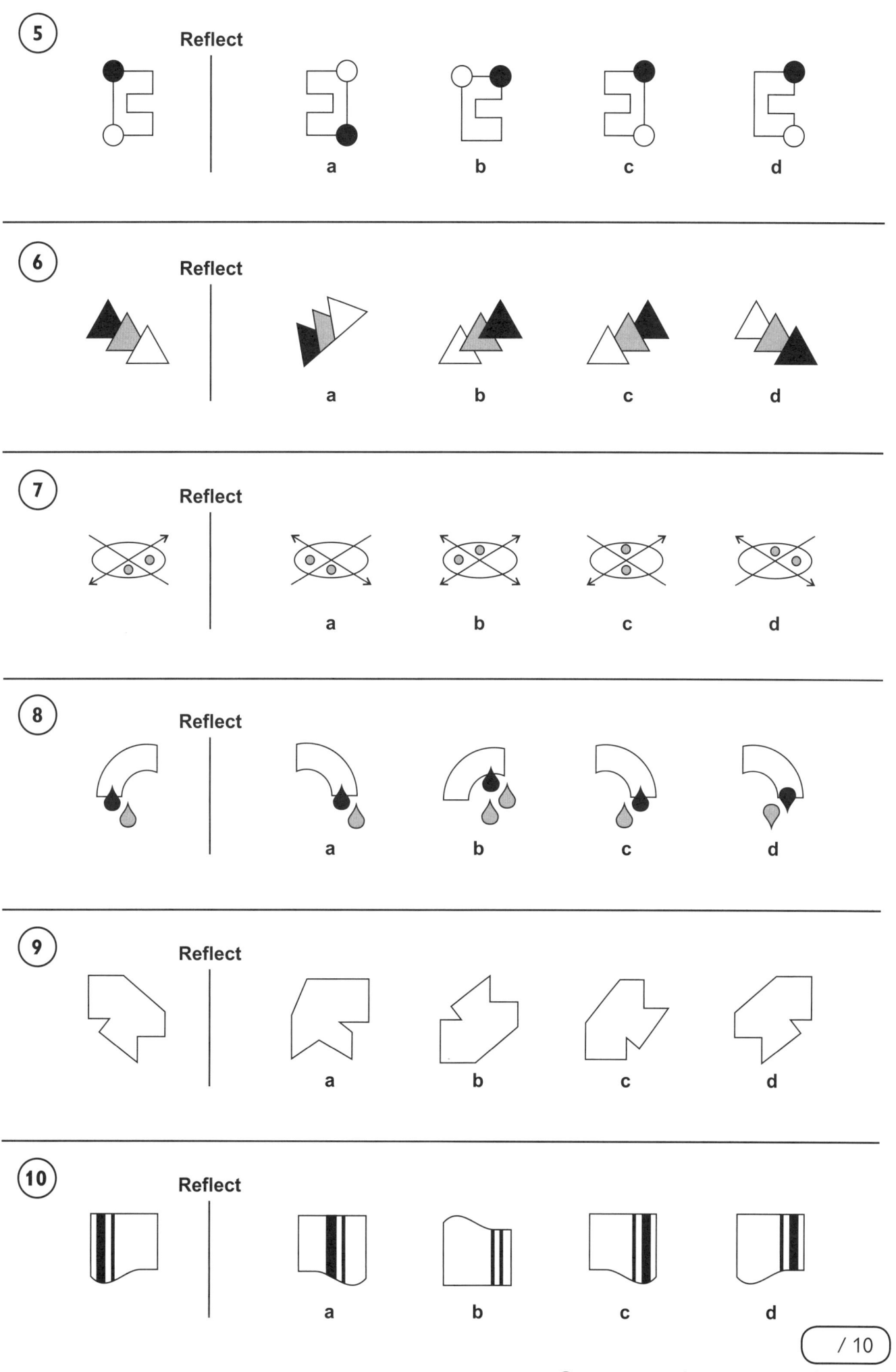

Carry on to the next question → →

Assessment Test 6

Section 4 — 3D Building Blocks

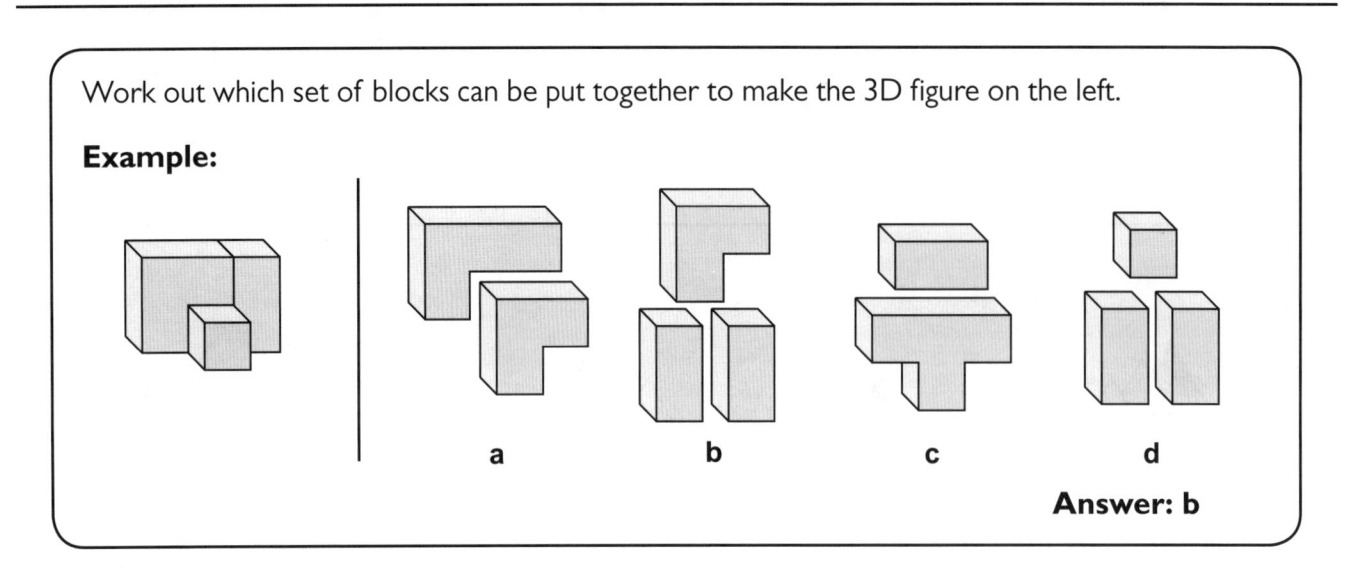

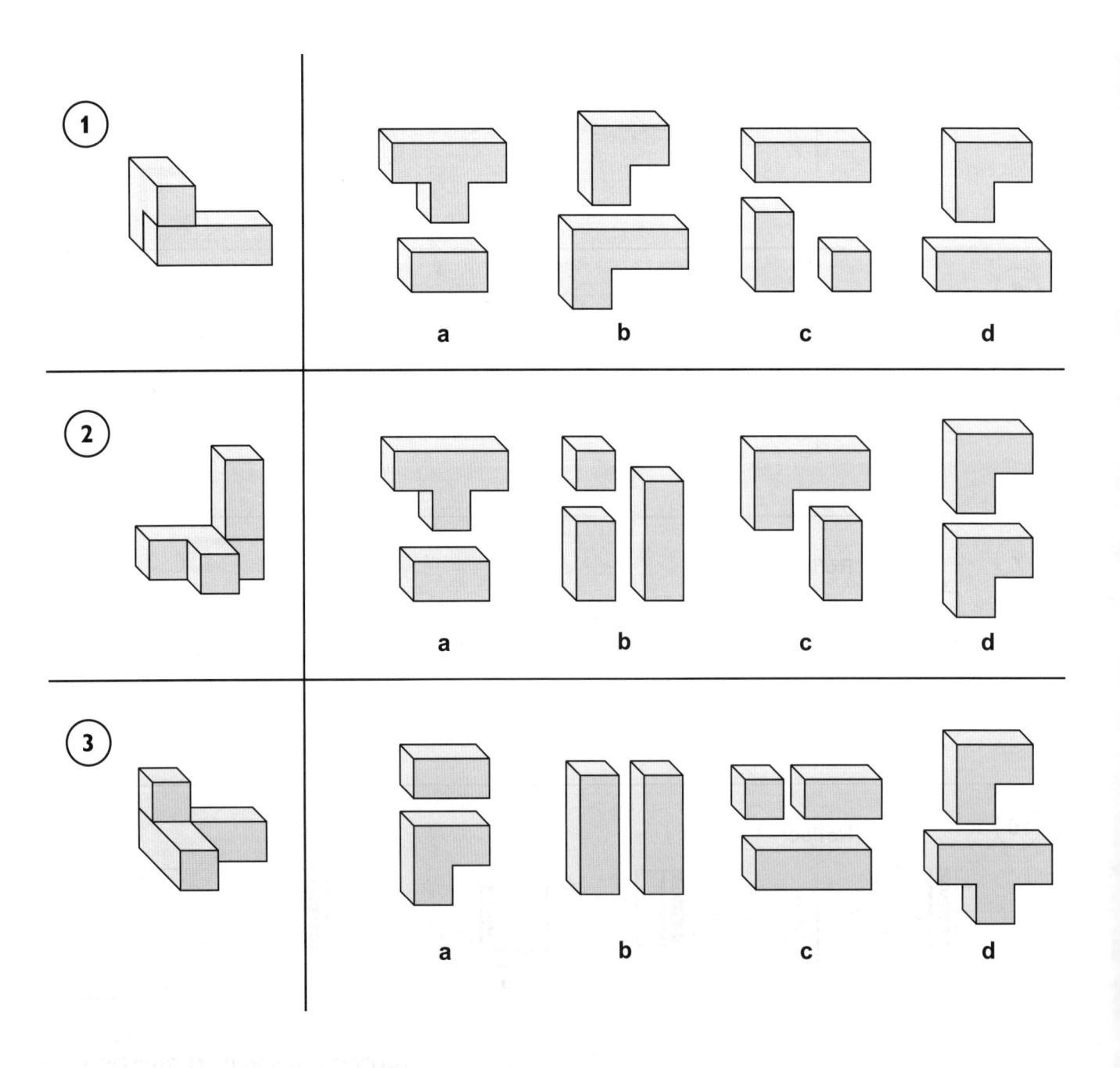

Work out which set of blocks can be put together to make the 3D figure on the left.

Example:

a   b   c   d

Answer: **b**

1.

a   b   c   d

2.

a   b   c   d

3.

a   b   c   d

Assessment Test 6

4

a b c d

5

a b c d

6

a b c d

7

a b c d

8

a b c d

/ 8

Carry on to the next question → →

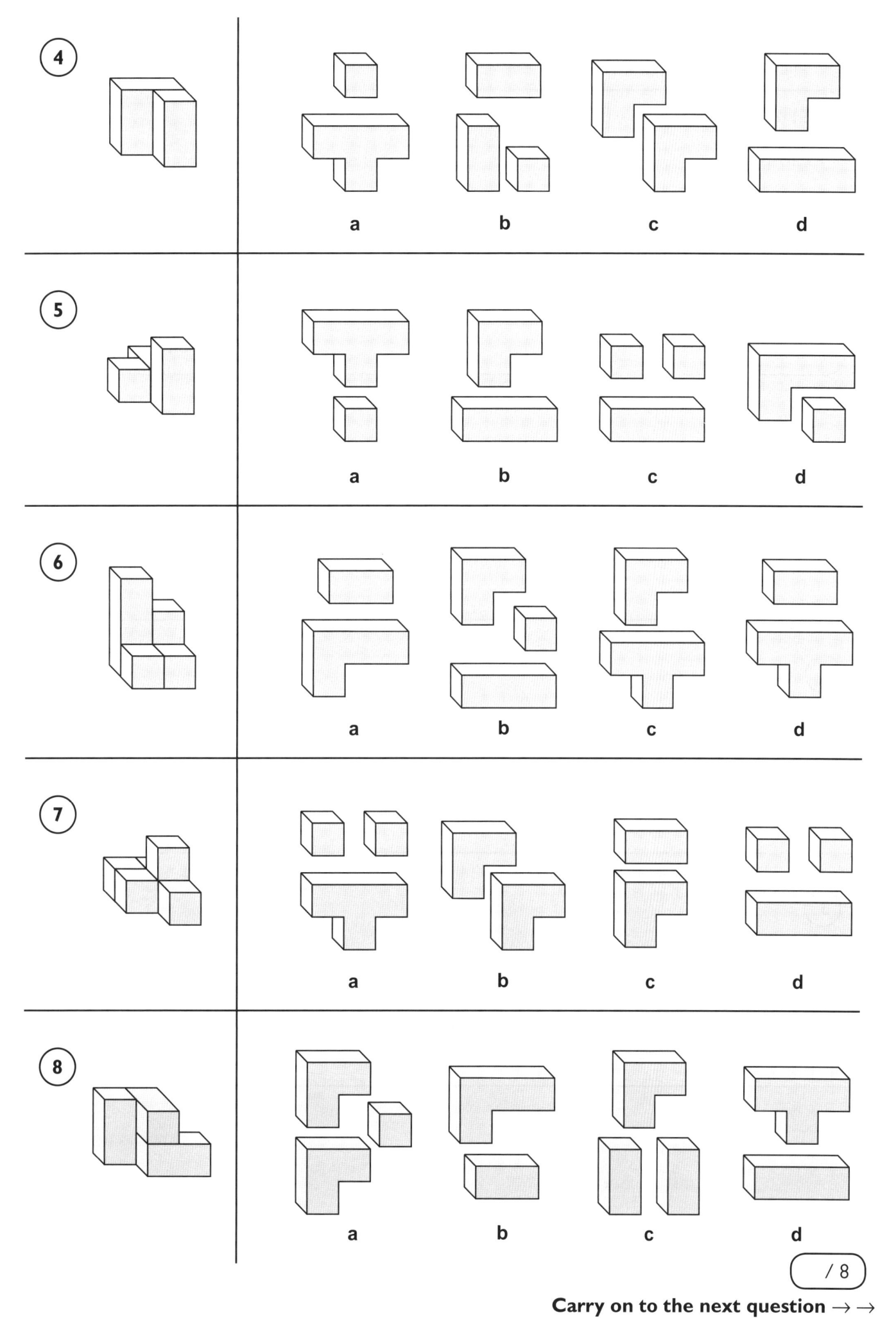

Assessment Test 6

Section 5 — Odd One Out

Find the figure in each row that is most unlike the other figures.

Example:

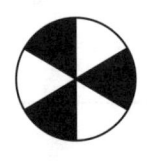

    a   b   c   d   e

Answer: a

(1) a b c d e

(2) a b c d e

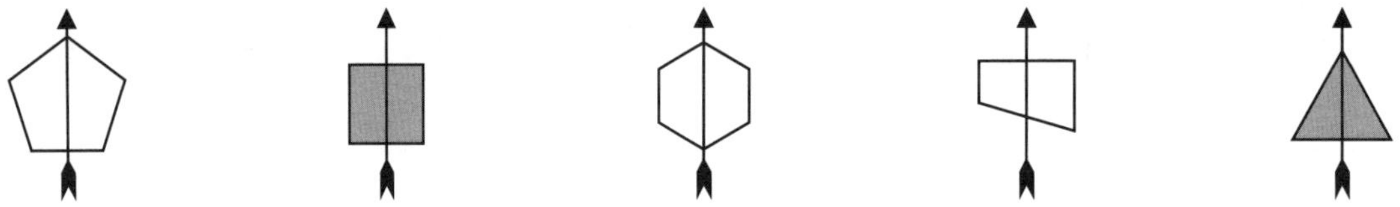

(3) a b c d e

(4) a b c d e

Assessment Test 6

5

a   b   c   d   e

6

a   b   c   d   e

7

a   b   c   d   e

8

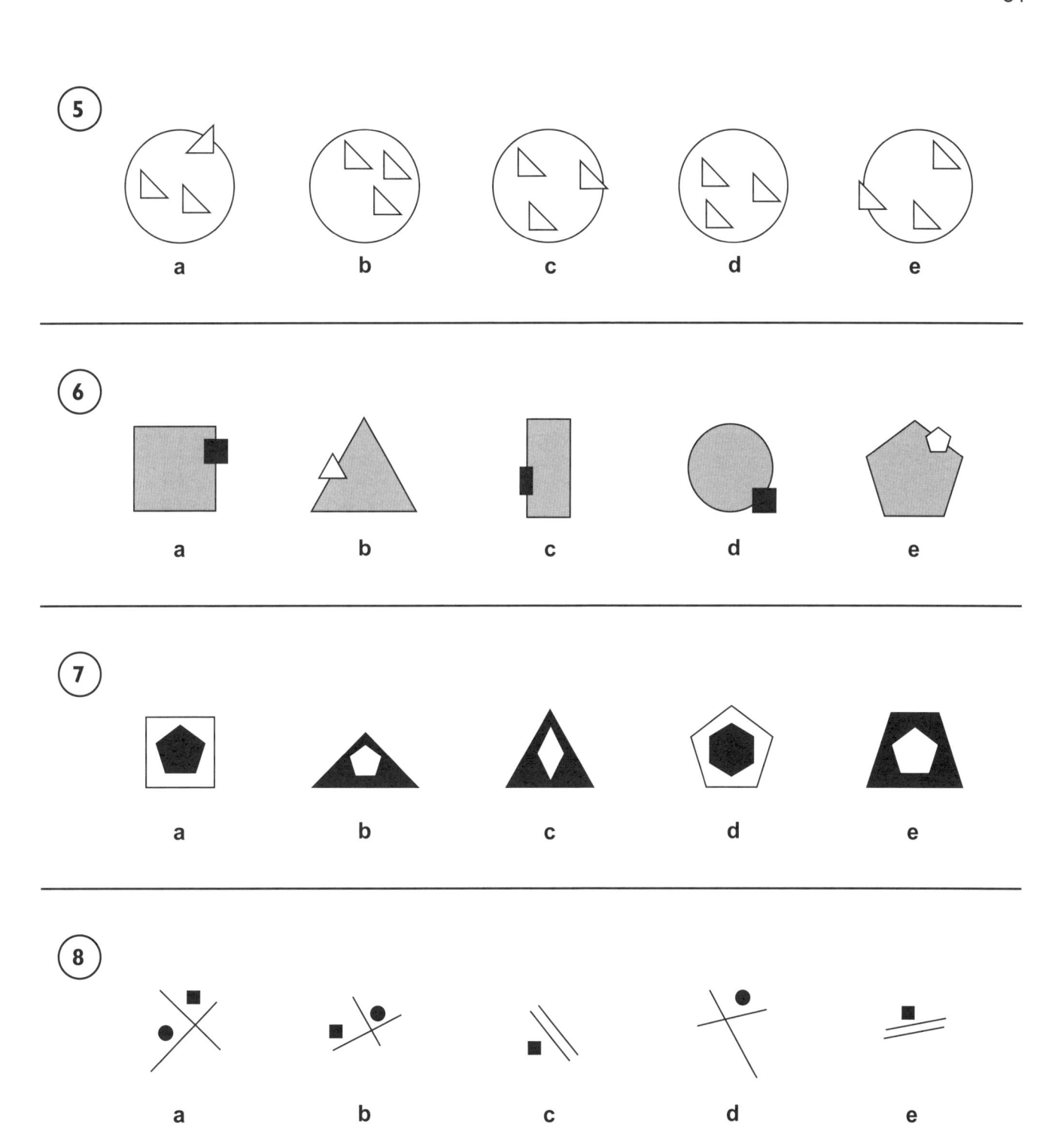

a   b   c   d   e

/ 8   Total / 44

End of Test

Assessment Test 6

Assessment Test 7

You can print **multiple-choice answer sheets** for these questions from our website — go to cgpbooks.co.uk/11plus/answer-sheets. If you'd prefer to answer them in standard write-in format, just circle the letter underneath your answer. The test should take around 20 minutes.

Section 1 — Rotate the Figure

Work out which option would look like the figure on the left if it was rotated.

Example:

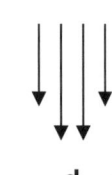

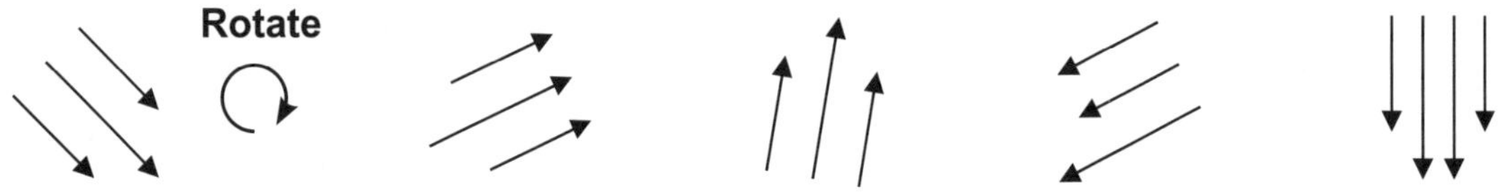

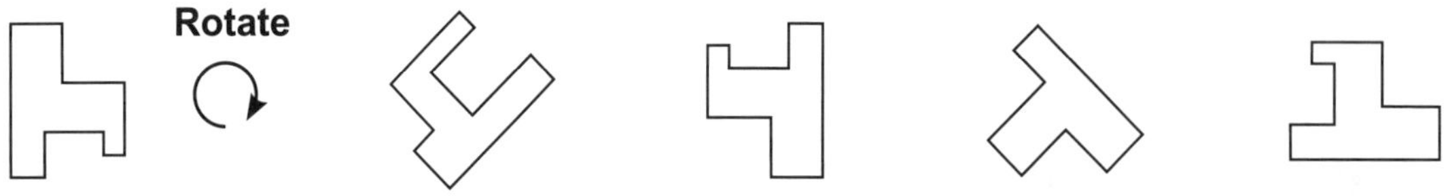

Answer: b

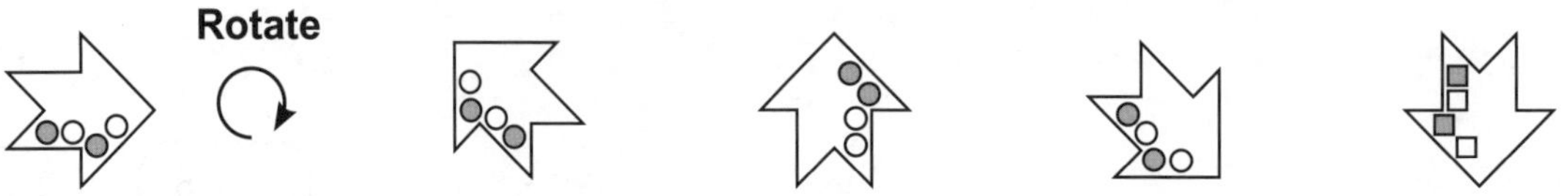

5
Rotate

a b c d

6
Rotate

a b c d

7
Rotate

a b c d

8
Rotate

a b c d

9
Rotate

a b c d

10
Rotate

a b c d

/ 10

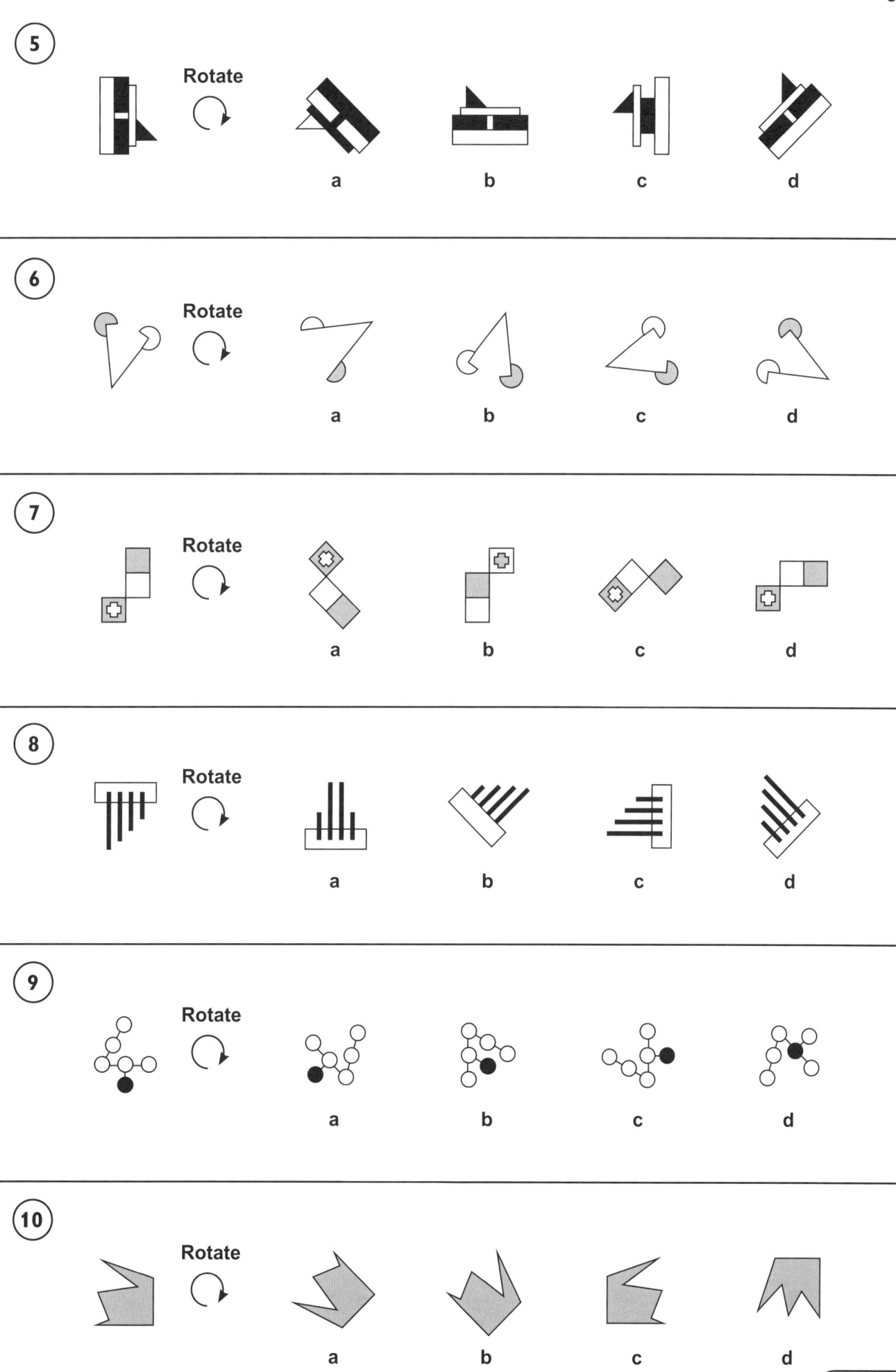

Carry on to the next question → →

Assessment Test 7

Section 2 — Find the Figure Like the First Three

Work out which option is most like the three figures on the left.

Example:

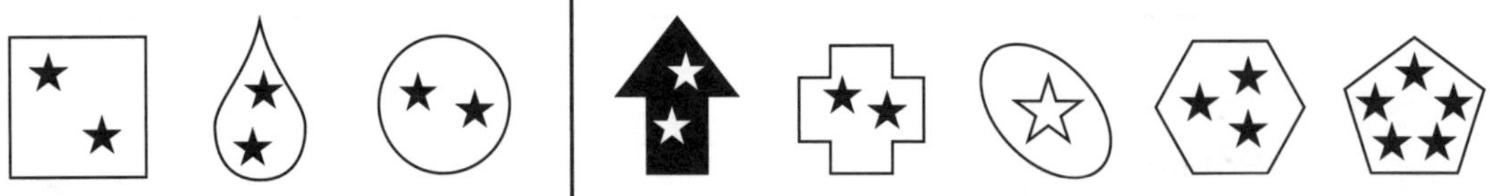

Answer: b

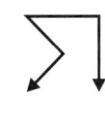

1.

2.

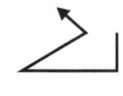

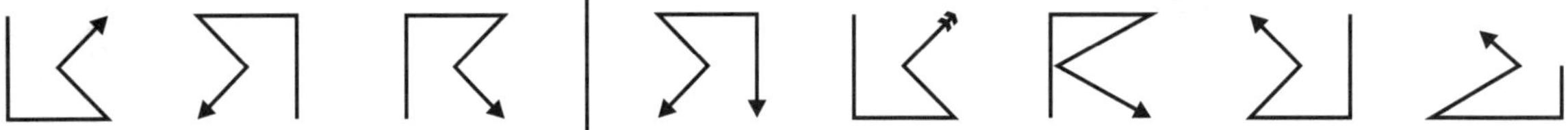

3.

4.

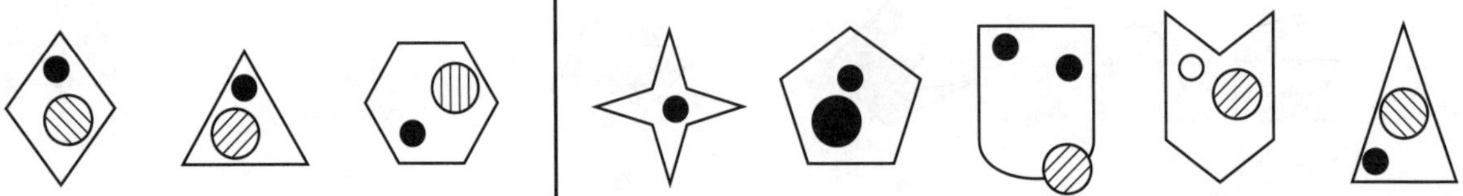

Assessment Test 7

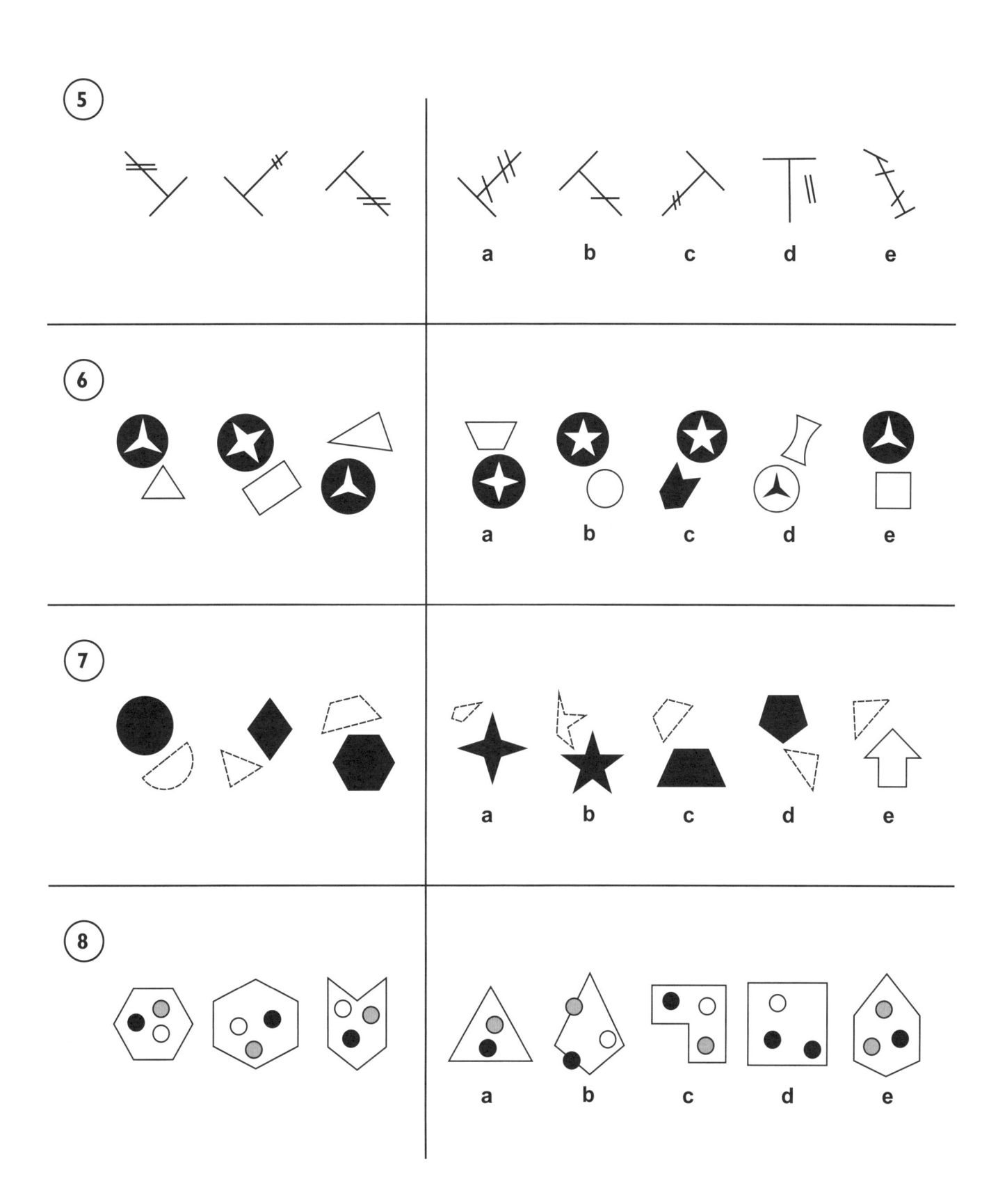

5

a b c d e

6

a b c d e

7

a b c d e

8

a b c d e

/ 8

Carry on to the next question → →

Assessment Test 7

Section 3 — 3D Rotation

Work out which 3D figure in the grey box has been rotated to make the new 3D figure.

Example:

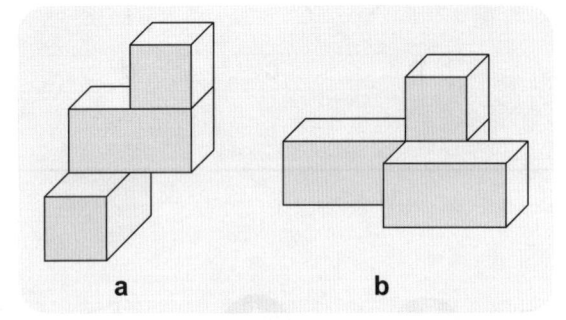

a   b

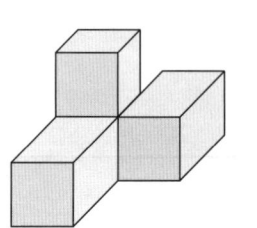

Answer: b

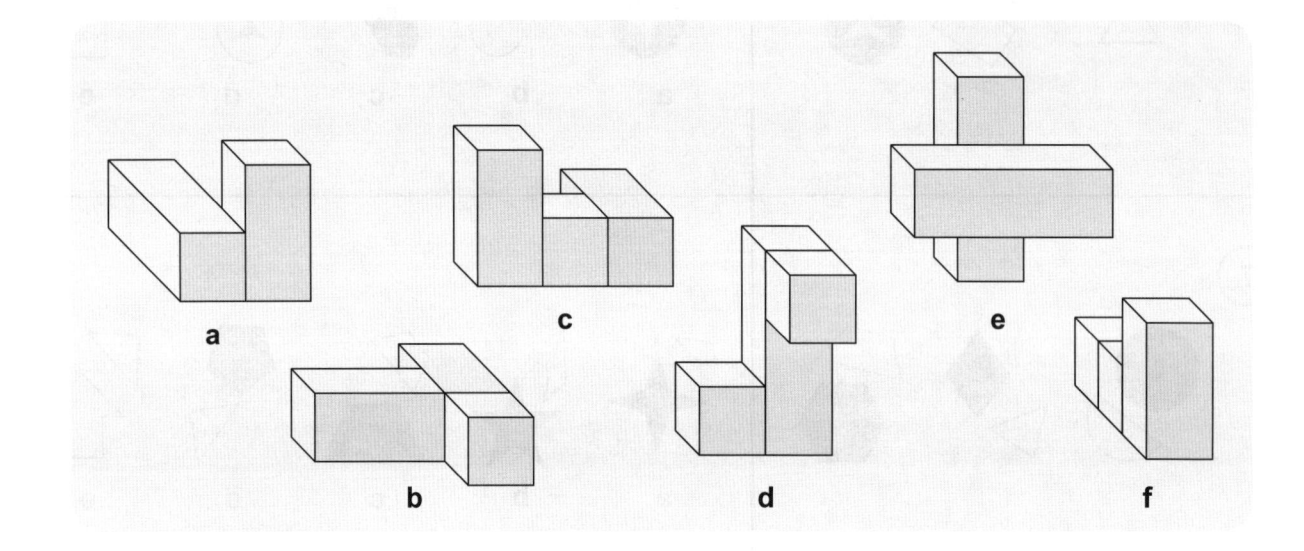

1

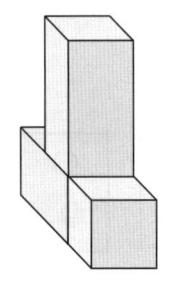

a   d
b   e
c   f

2

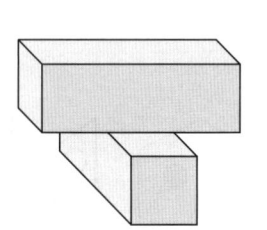

a   d
b   e
c   f

3

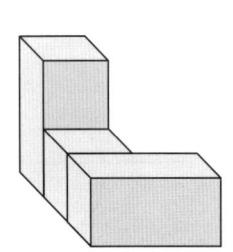

a   d
b   e
c   f

4

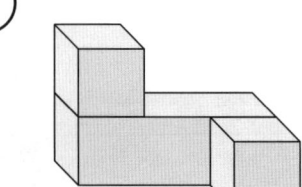

a   d
b   e
c   f

Assessment Test 7

87

a

b

c

d

e

f

(5)

a	d
b	e
c	f

(6)

a	d
b	e
c	f

(7)

a	d
b	e
c	f

(8)

a	d
b	e
c	f

(9)

a	d
b	e
c	f

(10)

a	d
b	e
c	f

/ 10

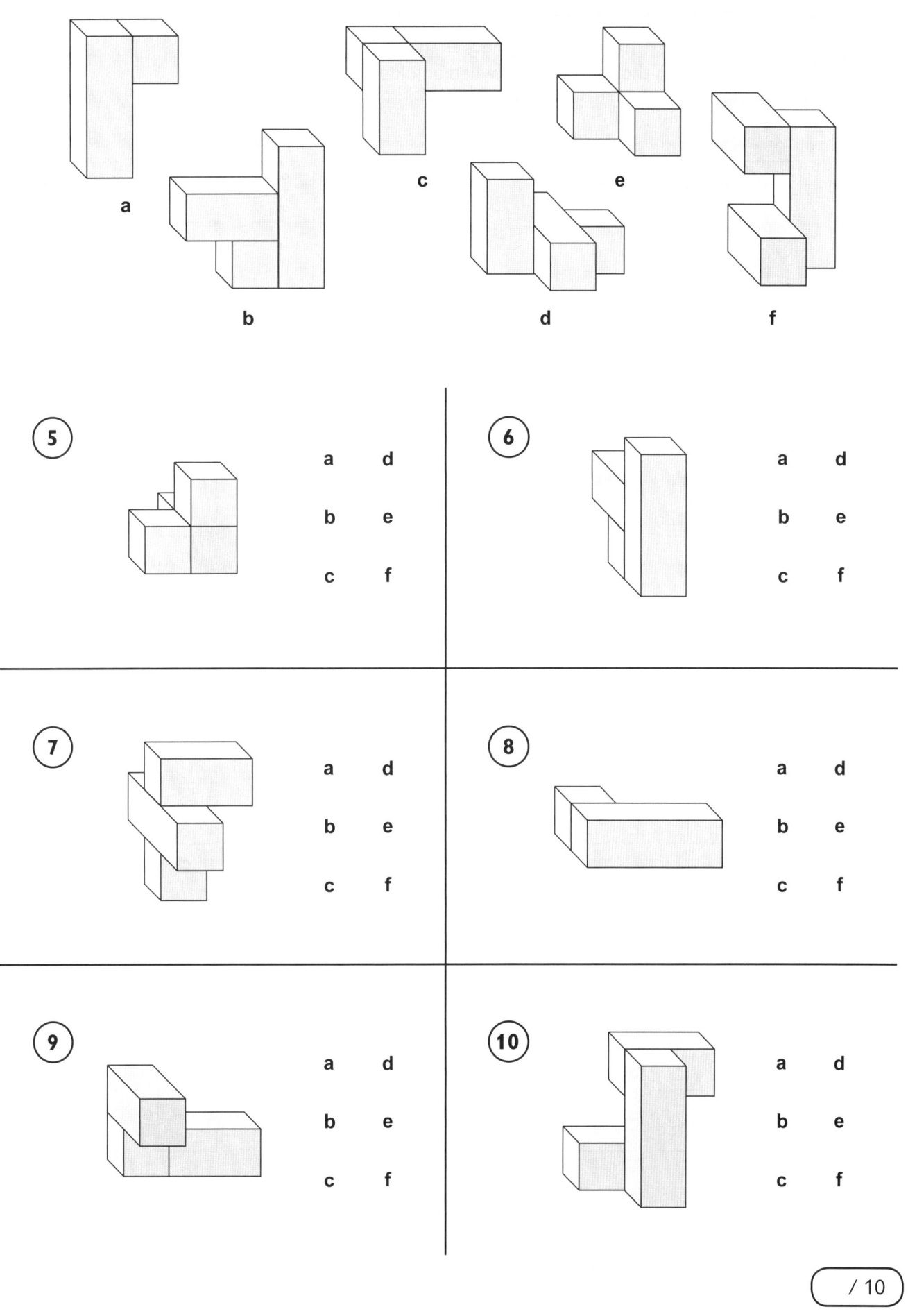

Carry on to the next question → →

Assessment Test 7

Section 4 — Fold and Punch

A square is folded and then a hole is punched, as shown on the left.
Work out which option shows the square when unfolded.

Example:

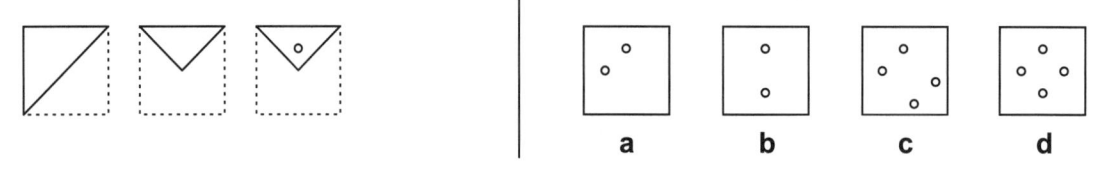

a   b   c   d

Answer: d

1.

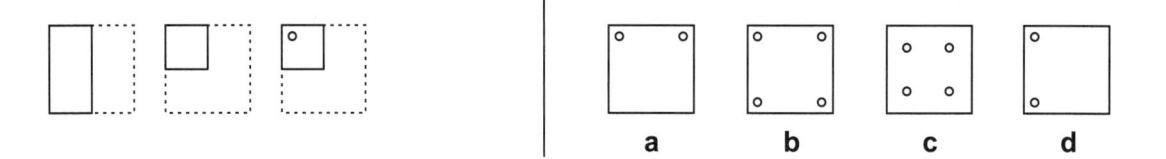

a   b   c   d

2.

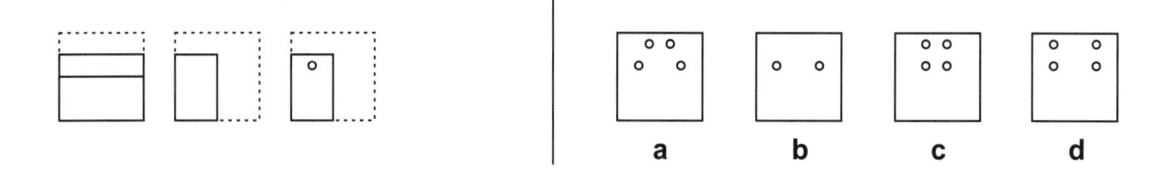

a   b   c   d

3.

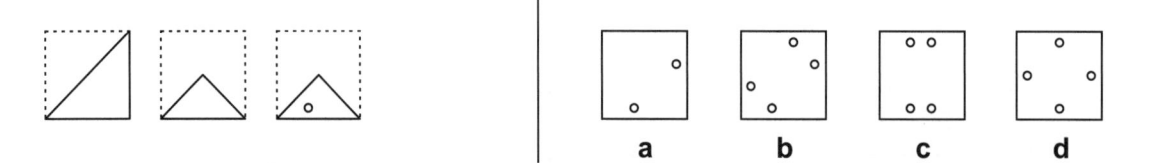

a   b   c   d

Assessment Test 7

89

4

5

6

7

8

/ 8

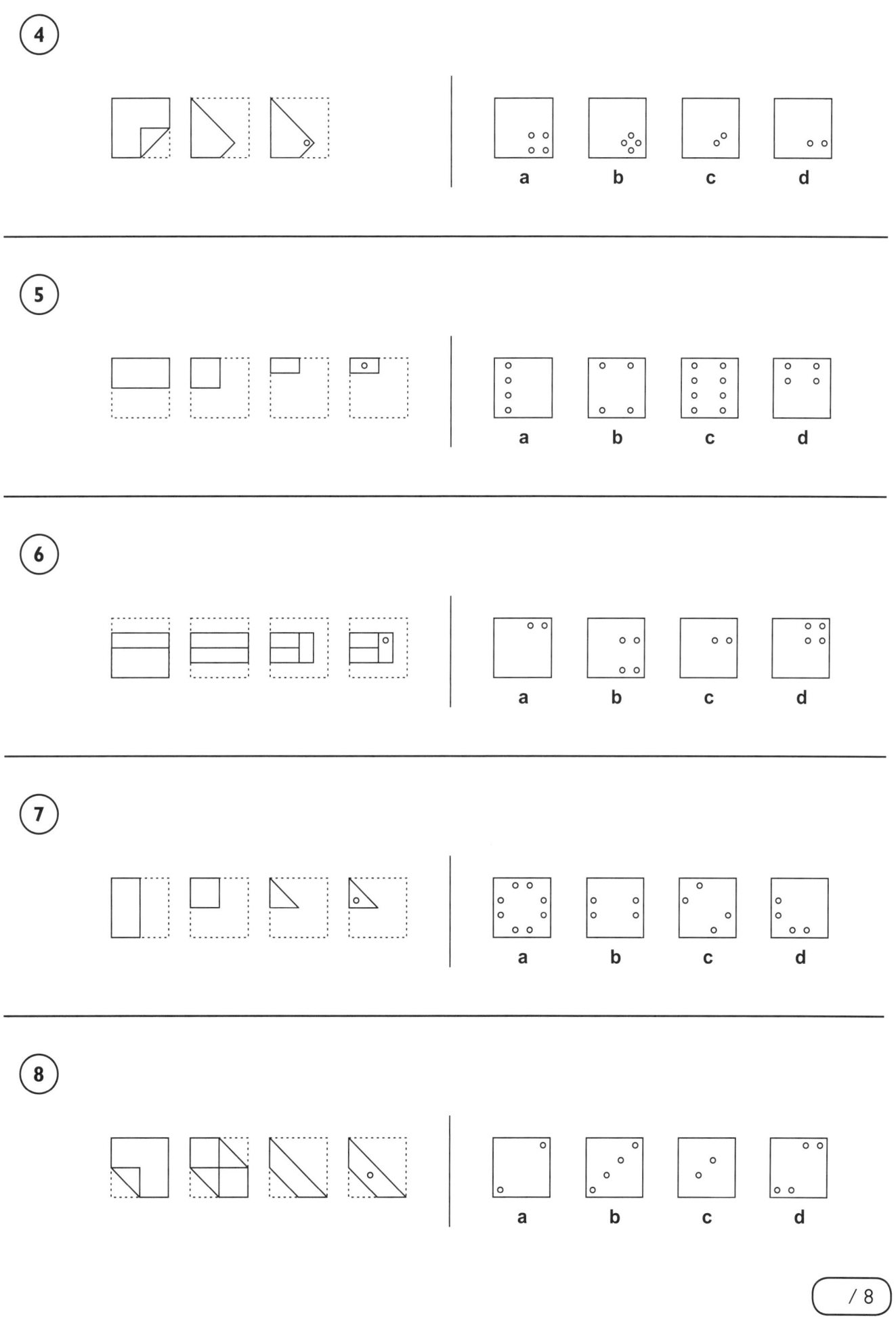

Carry on to the next question → →

Assessment Test 7

Section 5 — 2D Views of 3D Shapes

Work out which option is a top-down 2D view of the 3D figure on the left.

Example:

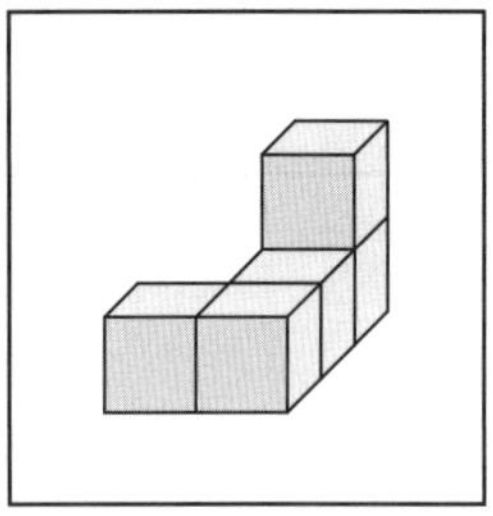

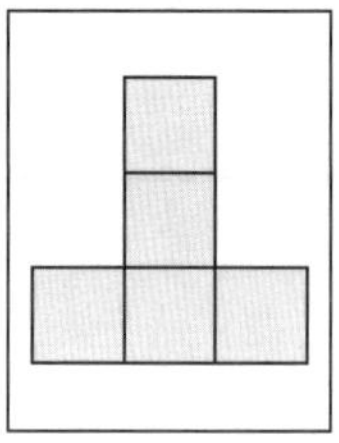

a 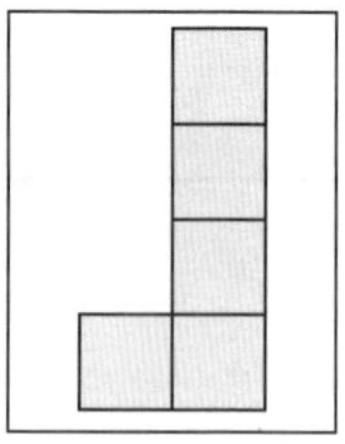 b 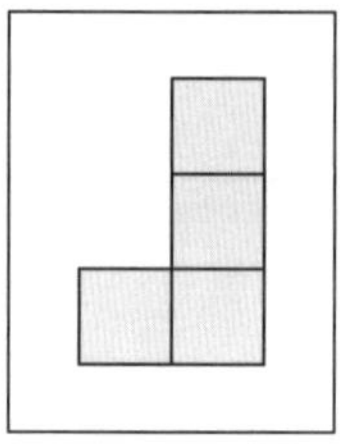 c 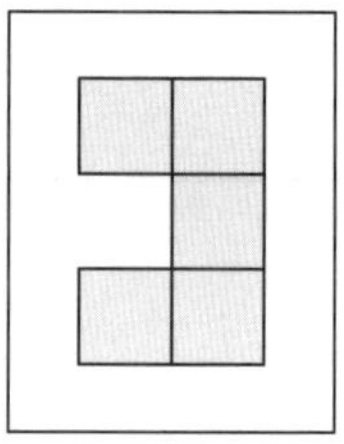 d

Answer: c

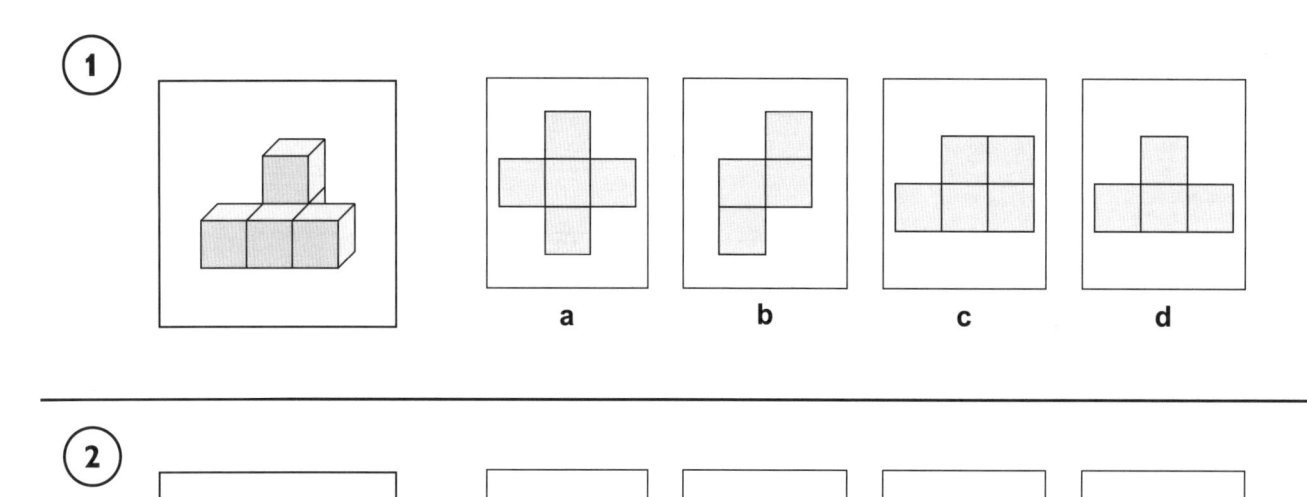

(1) a b c d

(2) a 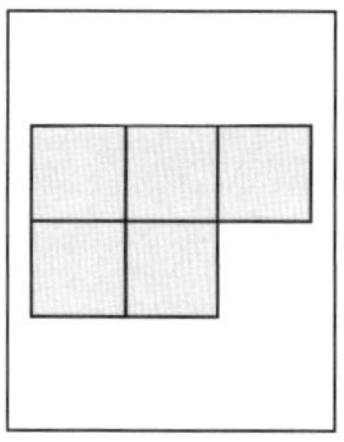 b 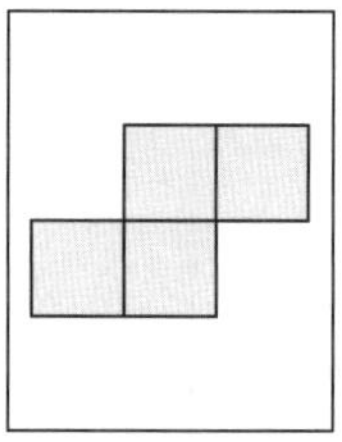 c 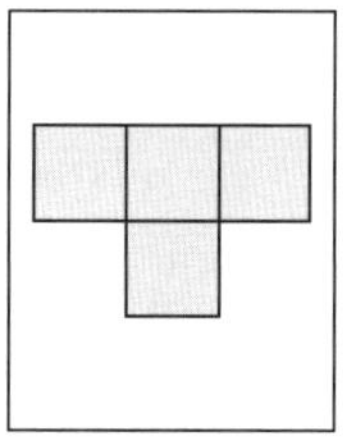 d

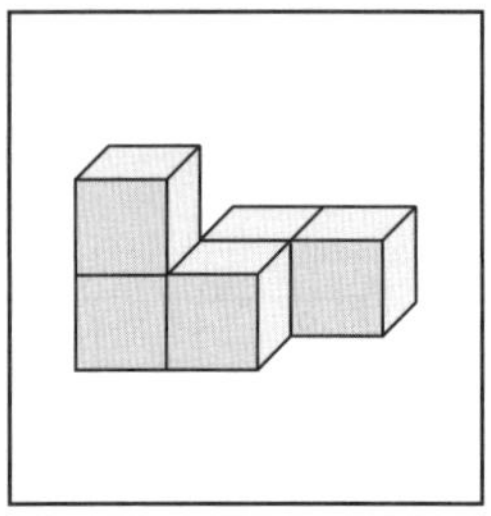

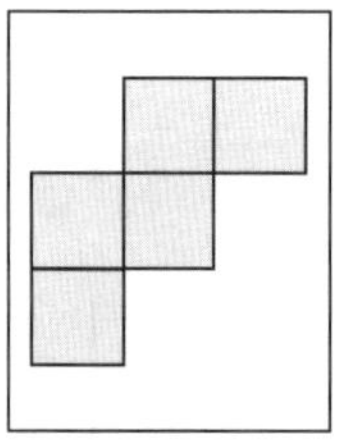

(3) a b c d

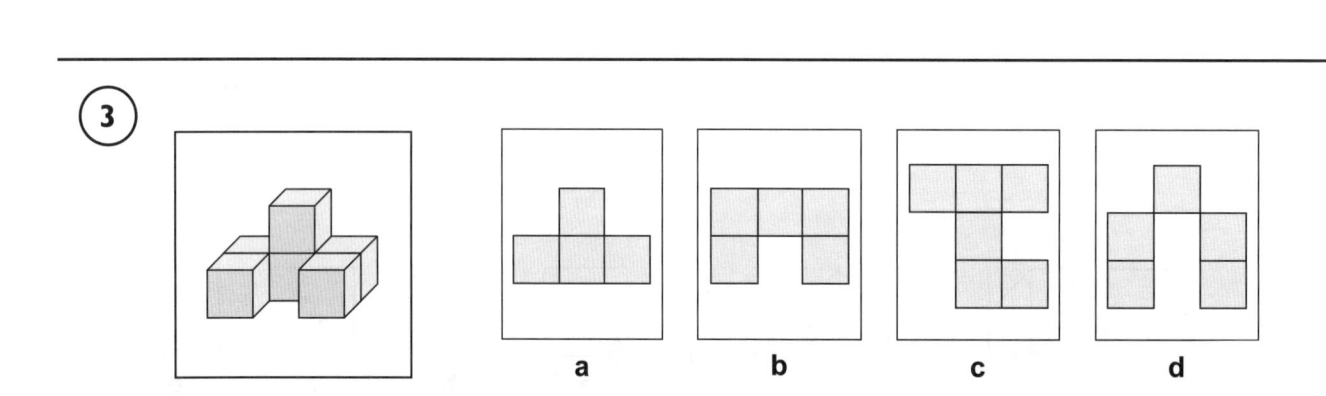

Assessment Test 7

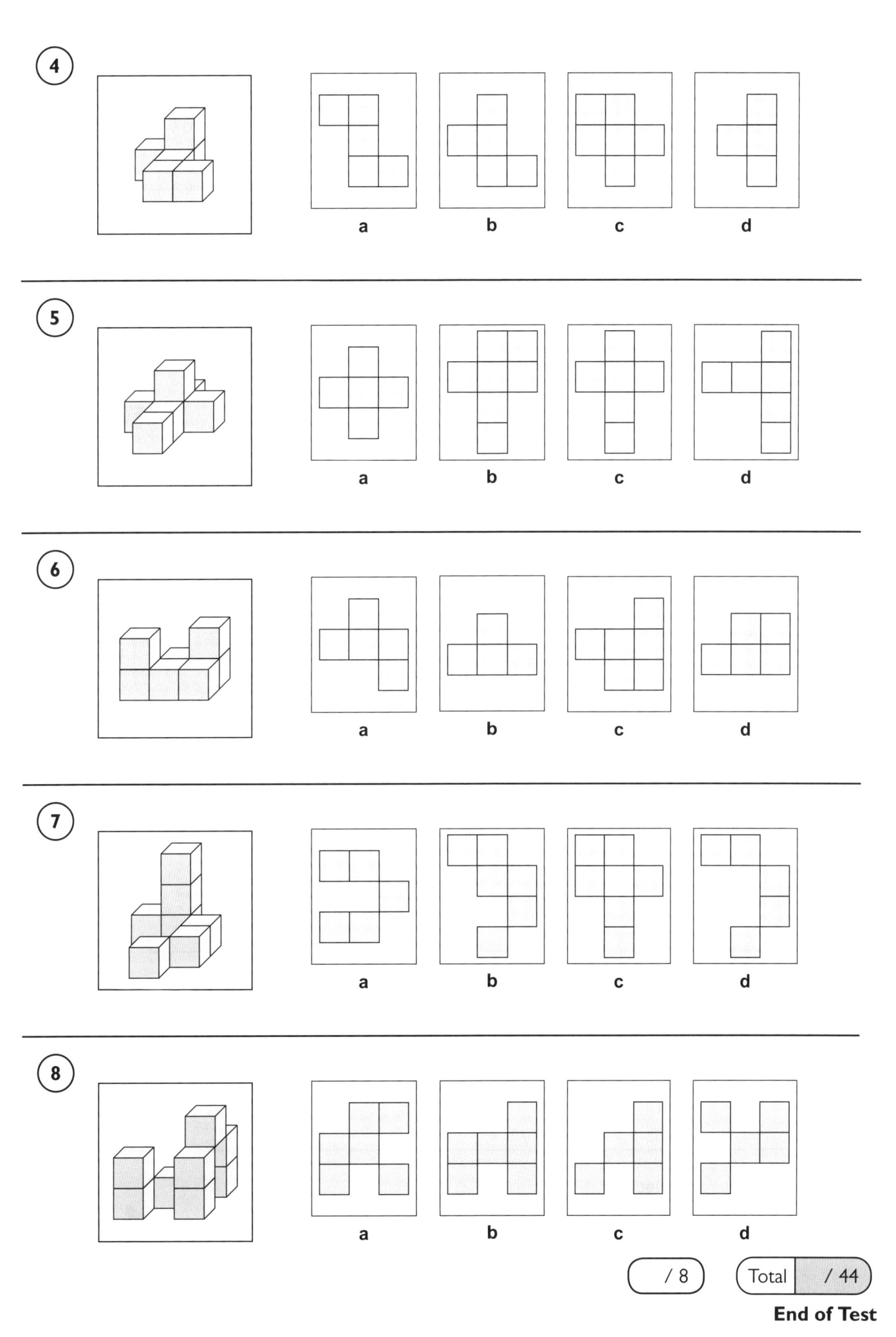

Assessment Test 7

/ 8   Total / 44

End of Test

Assessment Test 8

You can print **multiple-choice answer sheets** for these questions from our website — go to cgpbooks.co.uk/11plus/answer-sheets. If you'd prefer to answer them in standard write-in format, just circle the letter underneath your answer. The test should take around 20 minutes.

Section 1 — Reflect the Figure

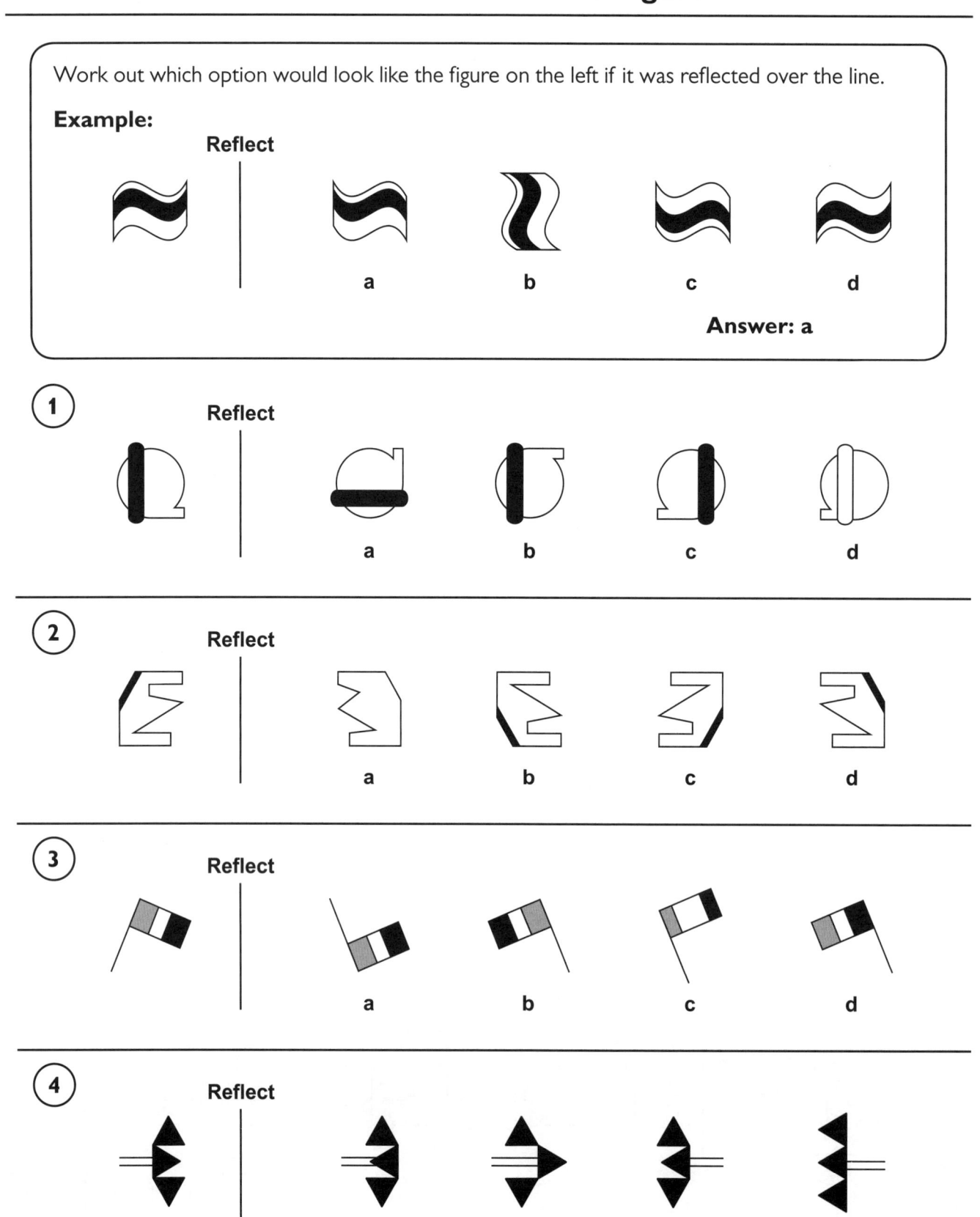

Work out which option would look like the figure on the left if it was reflected over the line.

Example:

Answer: a

5 Reflect

a b c d

6 Reflect

a b c d

7 Reflect

a b c d

8 Reflect

a b c d

9 Reflect

a b c d

10 Reflect

a b c d

/ 10

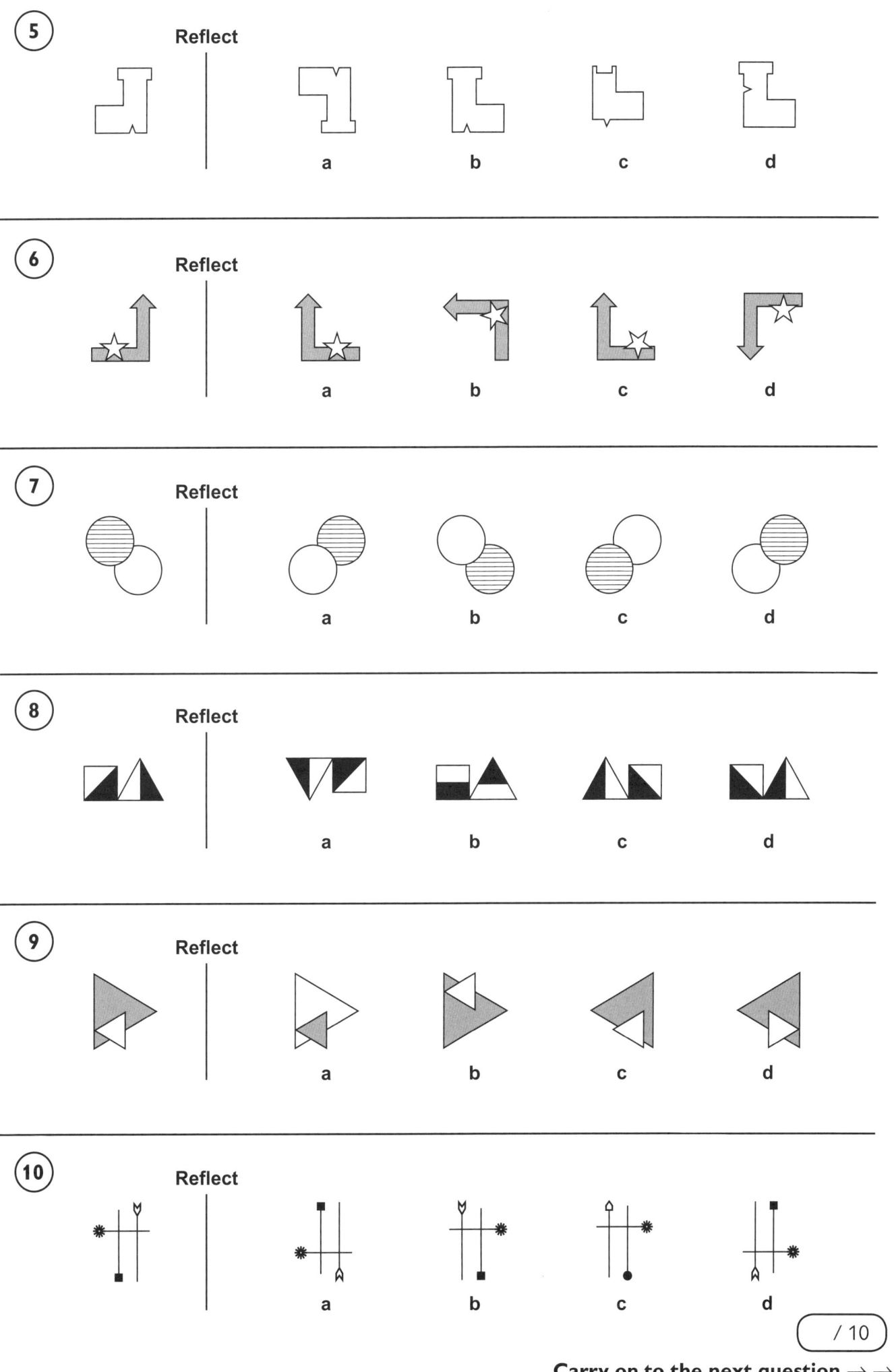

Carry on to the next question → →

Assessment Test 8

Section 2 — Complete the Square Grid

Work out which of the options best fits in place of the missing square in the grid.

Example:

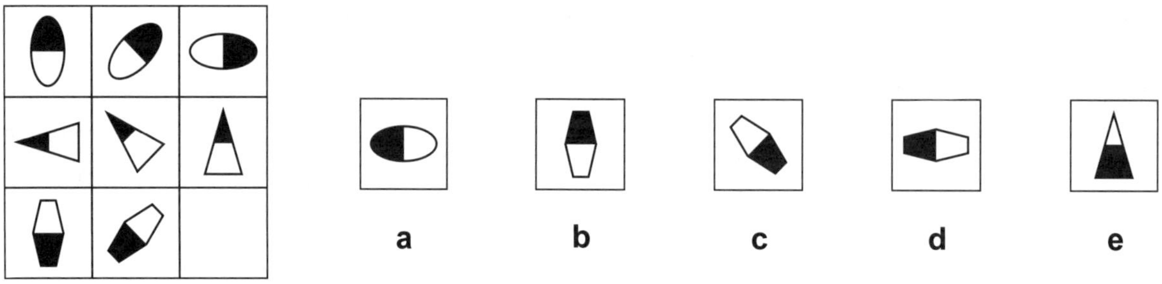

Answer: d

1

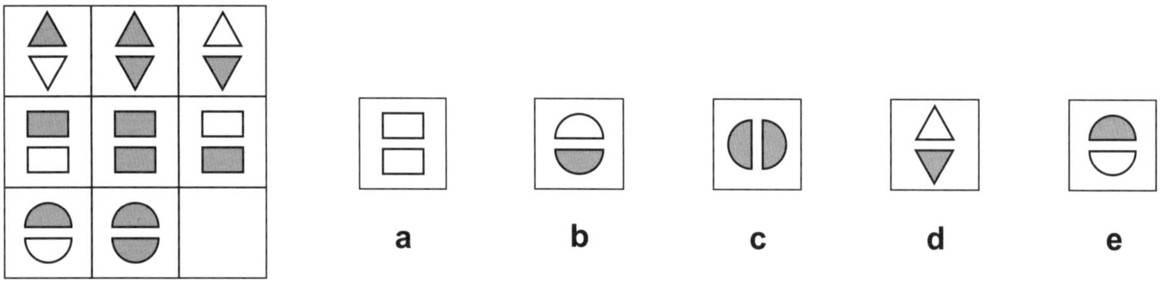

2

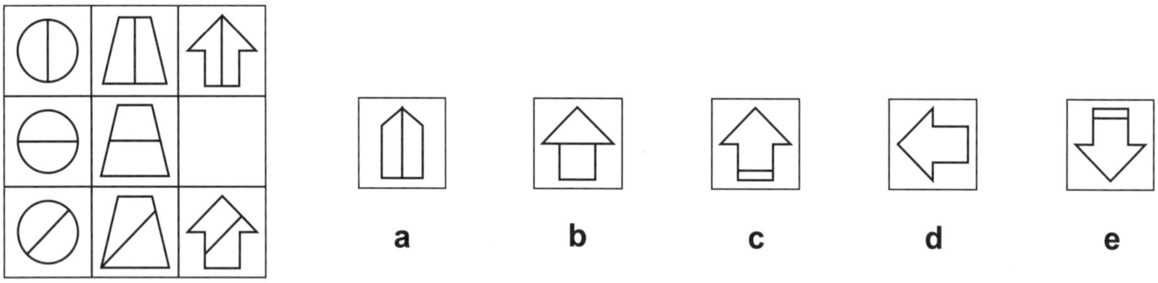

3

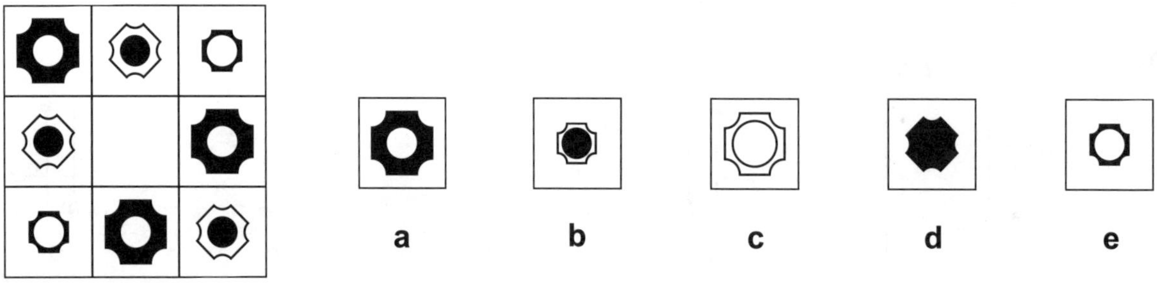

Assessment Test 8

95

(4) a b c d e

(5) a b c d e

(6) a b c d e

(7) a b c d e

(8) a b c d e

/ 8

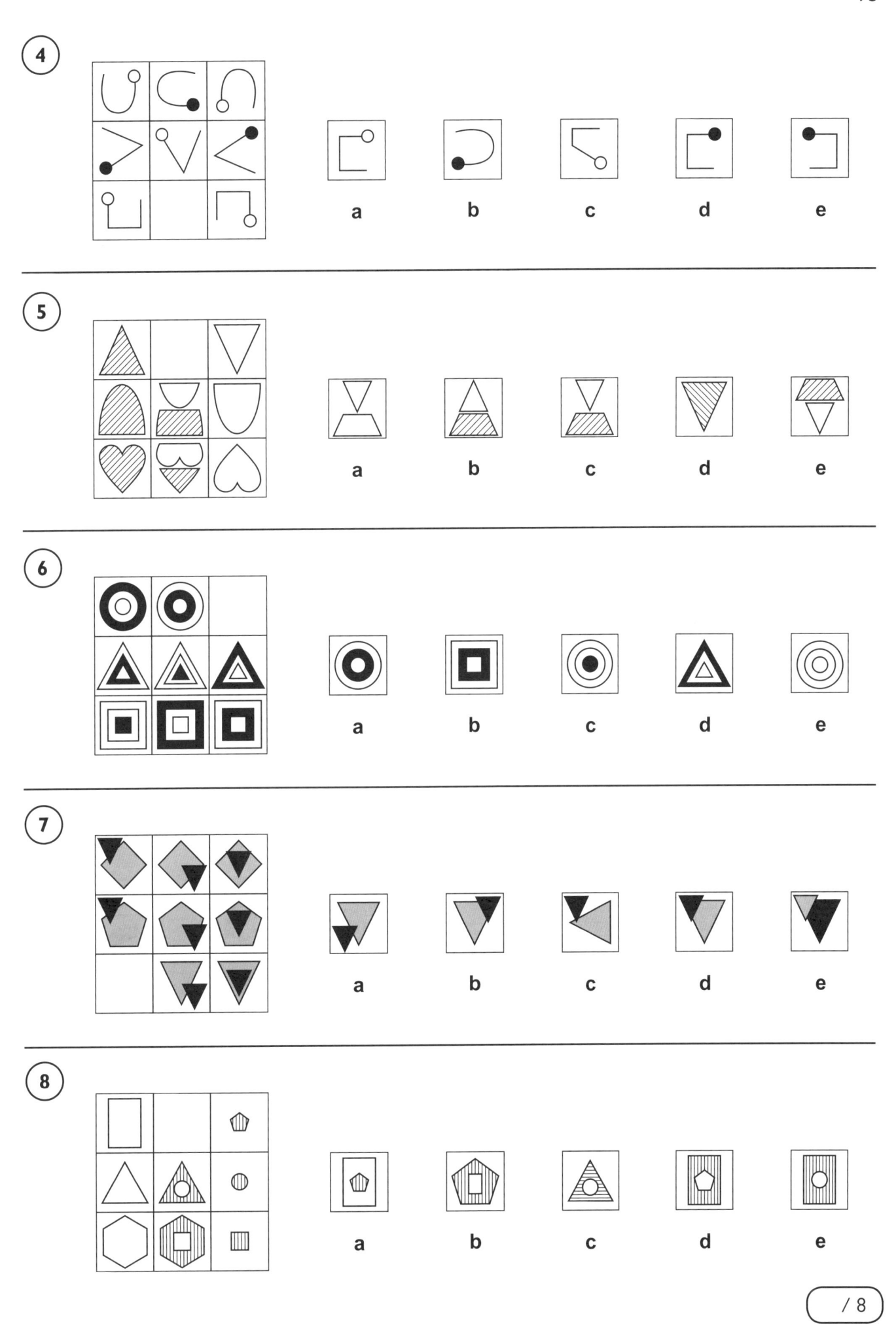

Carry on to the next question → →

Assessment Test 8

Section 3 — Cubes and Nets

Work out which of the four cubes can be made from the net.

Example:

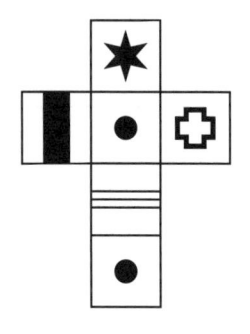

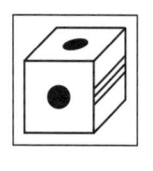

Answer: c

1

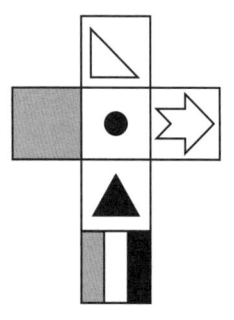

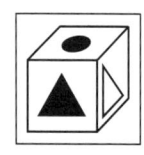

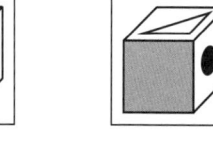

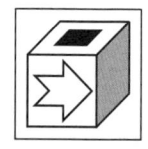

a   b   c   d

2

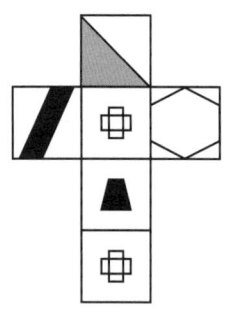

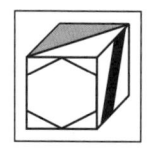

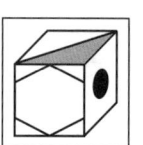

a   b   c   d

3

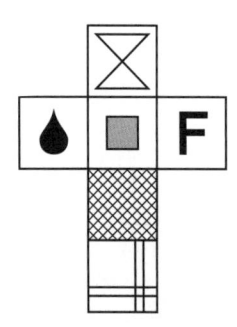

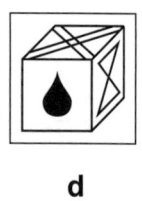

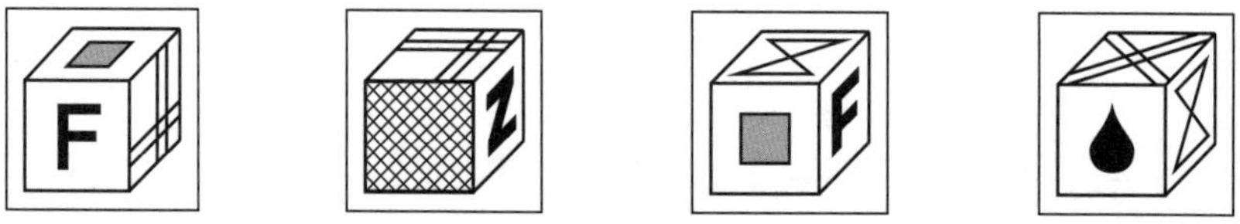

a   b   c   d

Assessment Test 8

Assessment Test 8

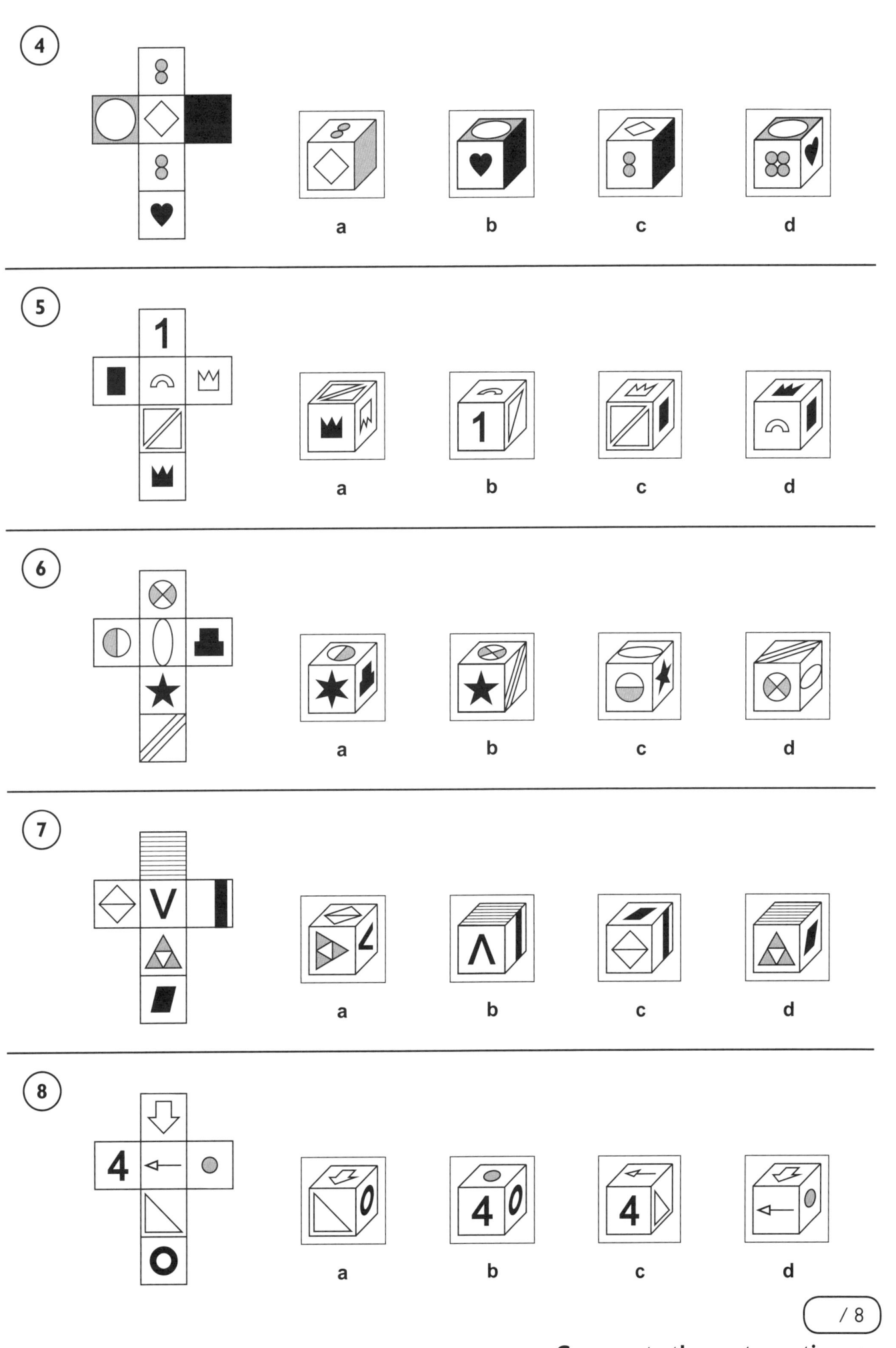

Section 4 — Complete the Pair

Look at how the first two figures are changed, and then work out which option would look like the third figure if you changed it in the same way.

Example:

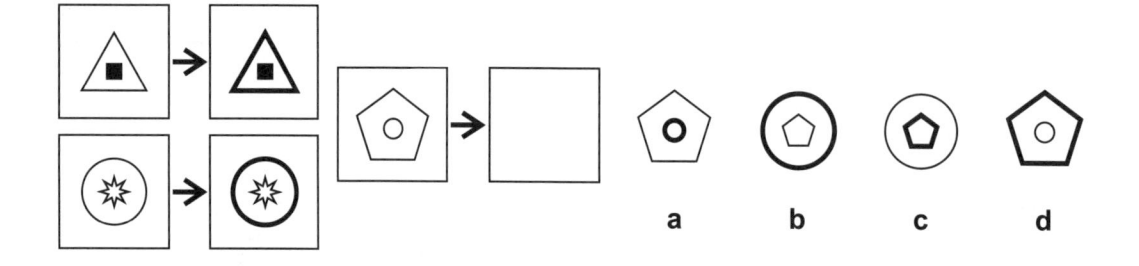

Answer: d

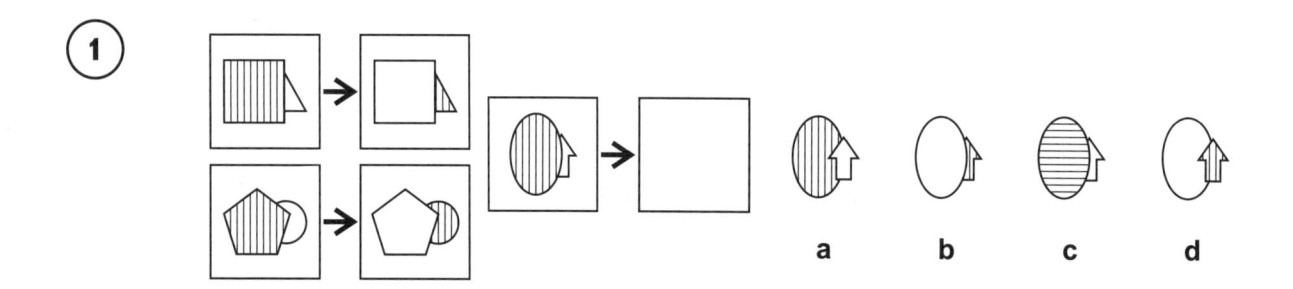

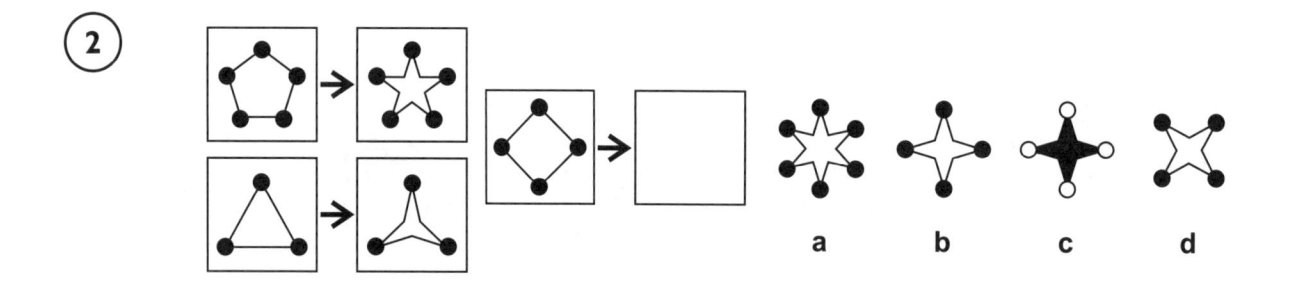

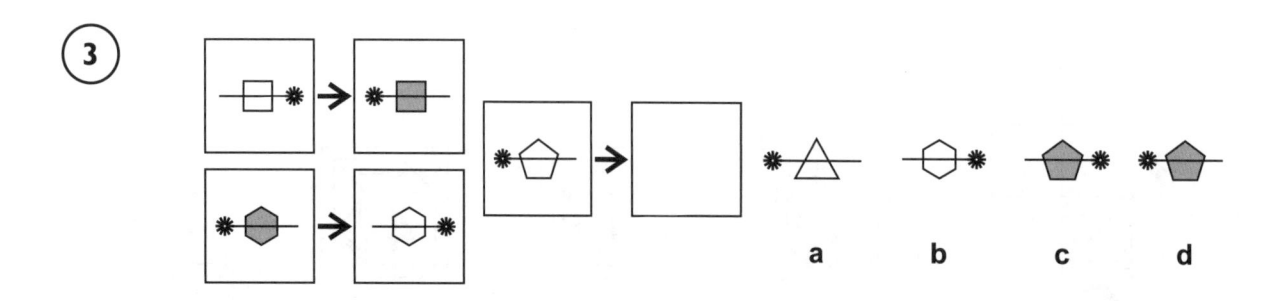

Assessment Test 8

4

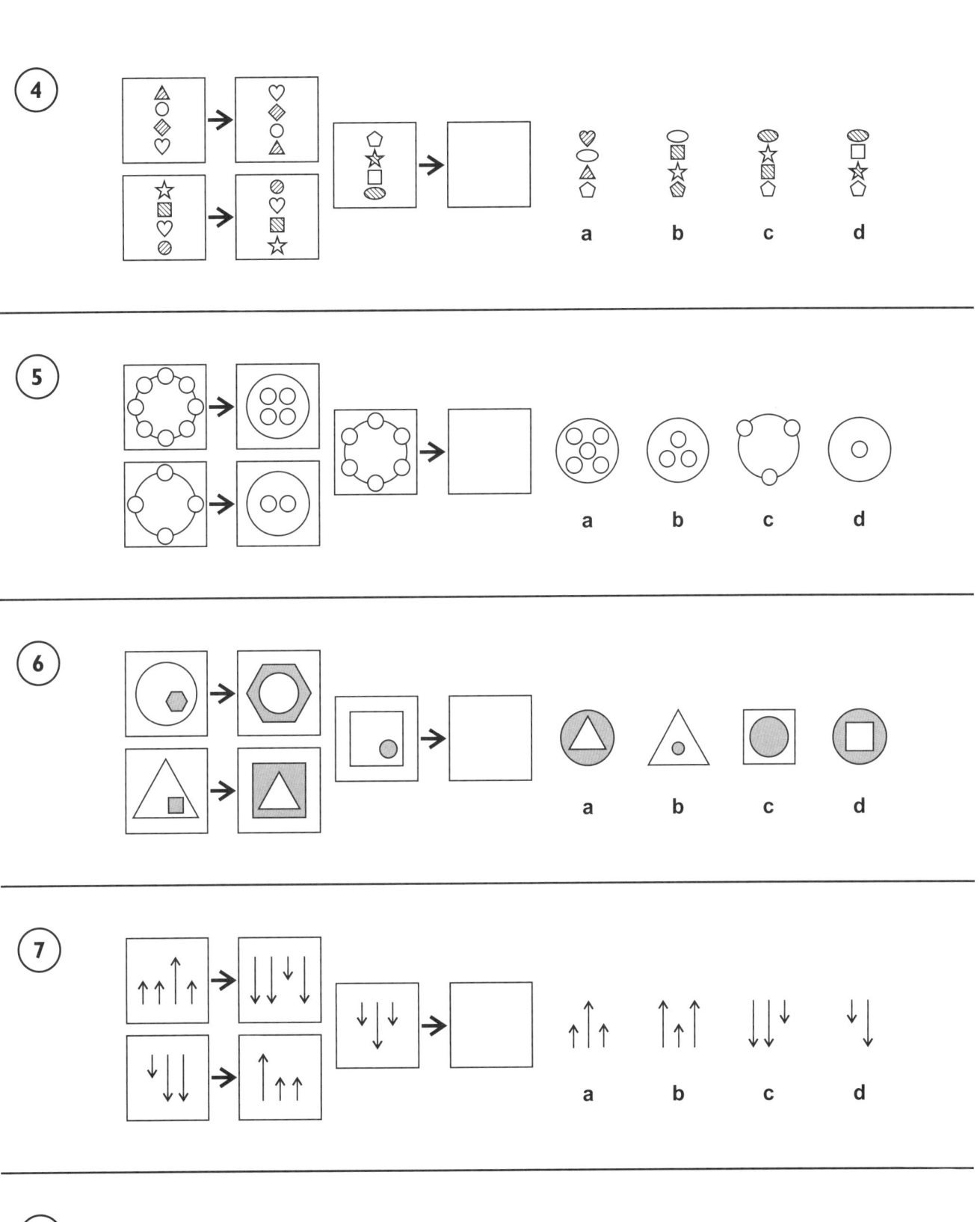

5

6

7

8

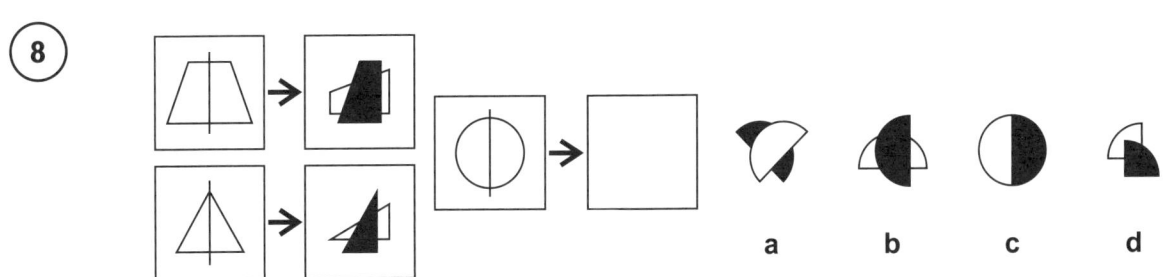

/ 8

Carry on to the next question → →

Assessment Test 8

Section 5 — Changing Bugs

Look at how the first bug changes to become the second bug.
Then work out which option would look like the third bug if you changed it in the same way.

Example:

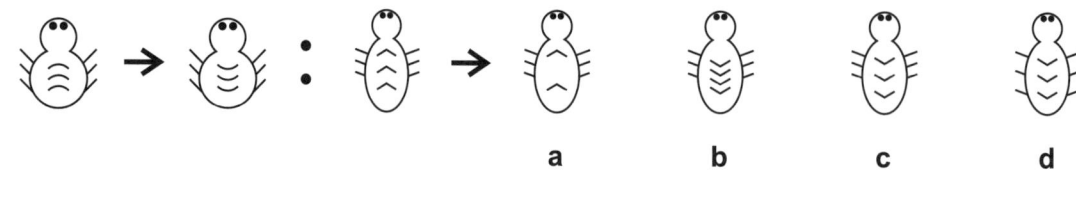

Answer: c

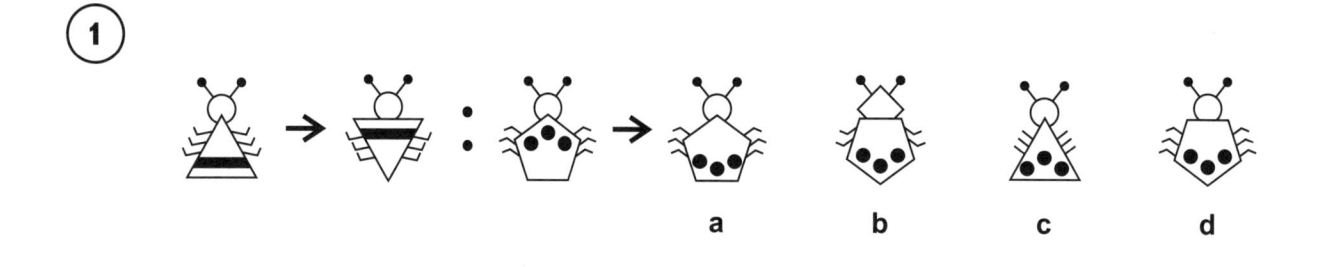

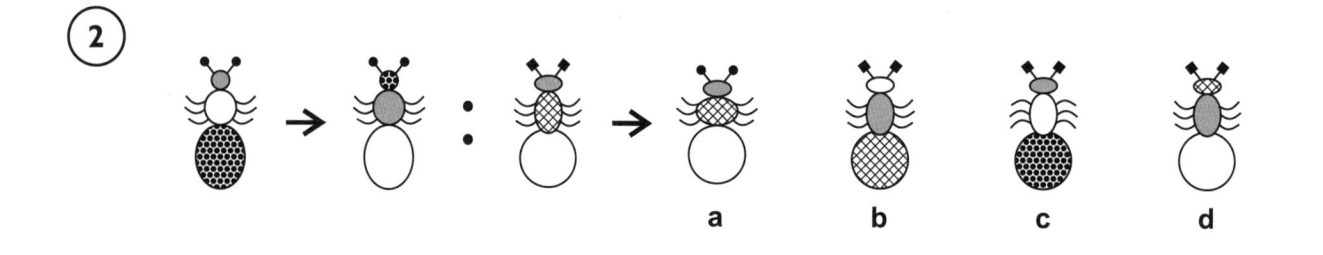

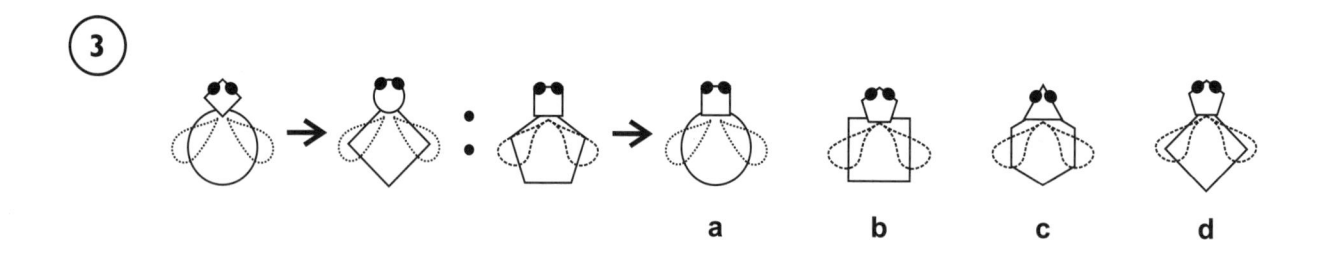

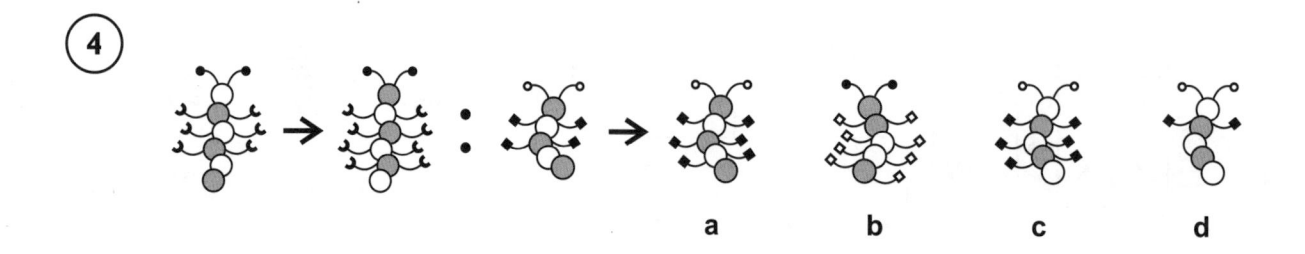

5

6

7

8

9

10

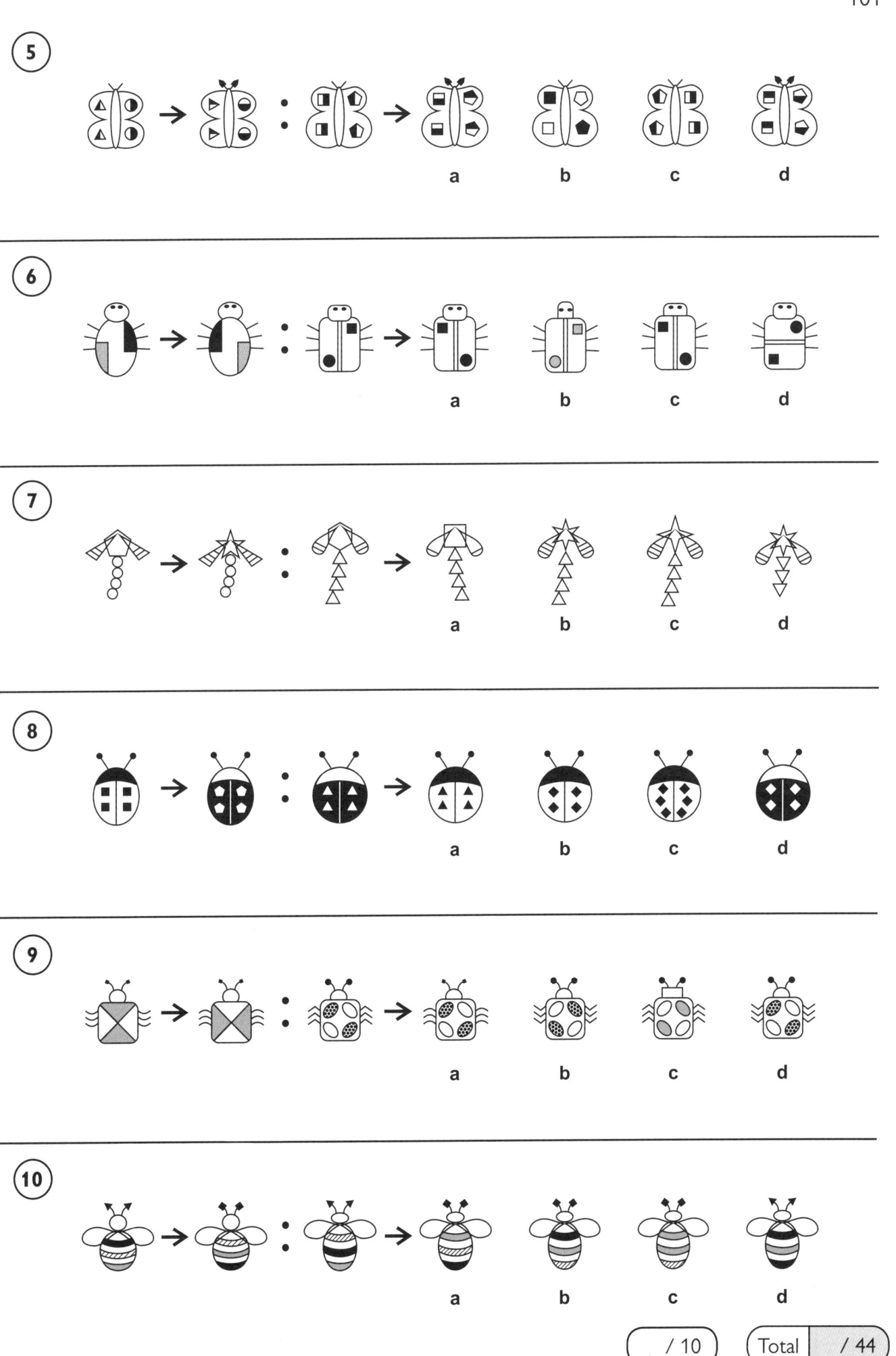

/ 10   Total / 44

End of Test

Assessment Test 8

Glossary

Rotation and Reflection

Rotation is when a shape is **turned** clockwise or anticlockwise.

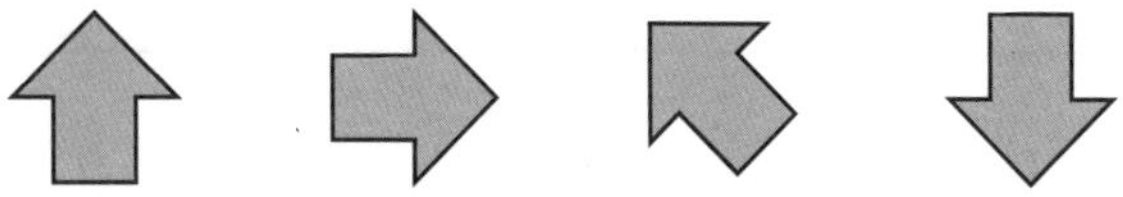

Example shape — 90 degrees clockwise rotation — 45 degrees anticlockwise rotation — 180 degrees rotation

The hands on a clock move **clockwise**: ↻
Anticlockwise is the **opposite** direction: ↺

Reflection is when something is **mirrored** over a visible or invisible line.

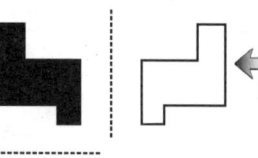

The black shape is reflected across to make the white shape.

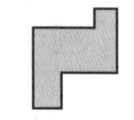

The black shape is reflected down to make the grey shape.

3D Rotation

There are **three planes** that a 3D shape can be rotated in.

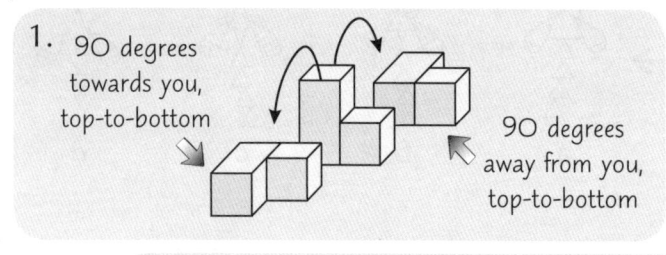

1. 90 degrees towards you, top-to-bottom / 90 degrees away from you, top-to-bottom

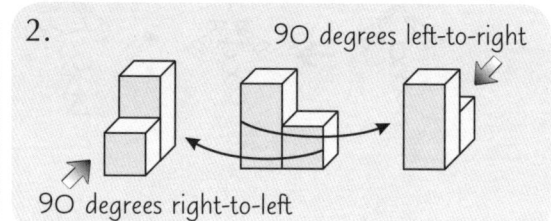

2. 90 degrees left-to-right / 90 degrees right-to-left

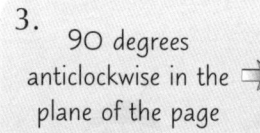

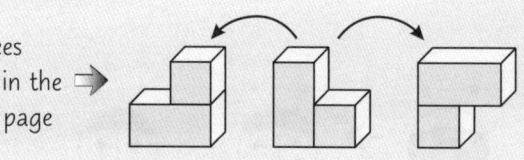

3. 90 degrees anticlockwise in the plane of the page / 90 degrees clockwise in the plane of the page

Other terms

Line Types: Thin, Thick, Dashed, Dotted, Curved

Shading Types: Black, Grey, White, Two types of hatching, Cross-hatched, Spotted

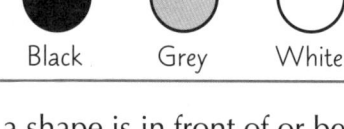

Layering — when a shape is in front of or behind another shape, or where two or more shapes overlap each other.

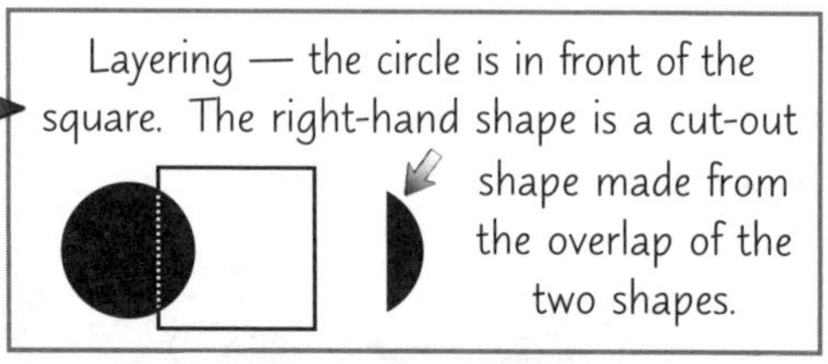

Layering — the circle is in front of the square. The right-hand shape is a cut-out shape made from the overlap of the two shapes.

Line of Symmetry — a line which splits a shape into halves that are reflections of each other.

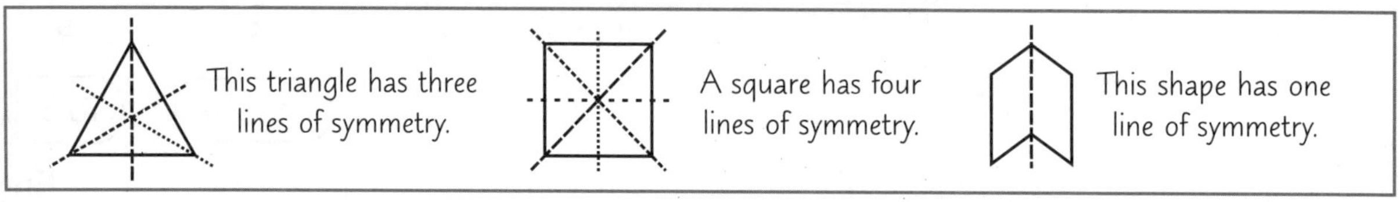

This triangle has three lines of symmetry.

A square has four lines of symmetry.

This shape has one line of symmetry.

Complete the Hexagonal Grid

4) A

Each hexagon has two rectangles and half an ellipse on its inner sides and a triangle on the side opposite the central hexagon.

5) B

Going in a clockwise direction around the hexagonal grid, each shape moves one side clockwise.

6) B

The figures reflect across the middle of the hexagonal grid.

7) A

Moving clockwise from the top hexagon, the position of the arrows changes from bottom, to middle, to top. Then it starts again from the bottom. The grey arrow is always on the left of the black arrow.

Find the Figure Like the First Three

8) E

In all figures, the large black shape must contain a small white square on the right and a small white circle on the left.

9) D

In all figures, the shape at the top must have fewer sides than the shape at the bottom.

10) A

If all figures are rotated so that the arrow points up, the grey circle must be in the bottom left-hand corner of the square.

Page 12 — Rotation

Warm Up

1) a) C   b) C   c) A   d) A   e) C   f) A   g) C
2) a) 45   b) 90   c) 45   d) 180 e) 90   f) 180 g) 45

Complete the Series

3) B

The figure rotates 45 degrees clockwise in each series square. The circle's shading alternates between black and white.

4) A

The entire series square rotates 90 degrees anticlockwise.

5) D

The entire series square rotates 90 degrees clockwise. The droplet's shading alternates between black and white.

Page 13 — Reflection

Warm Up

1) a) yes   b) yes   c) no   d) yes   e) no   f) no
2) a) reflected   b) rotated   c) reflected
   d) reflected   e) rotated

Reflect the Figure

3) B

In option A, the figure has not been reflected and the star has the wrong number of points. Option C is a 90 degree anticlockwise rotation. Option D is a downwards reflection.

4) C

Option A is a downwards reflection. Option B is a 90 degree anticlockwise rotation. In option D, the line is reflected but the ends of the line have been swapped over.

5) D

In option A, the shape has not been reflected. In option B, the hatching has not been reflected. Option C is a downwards reflection.

Pages 14-15 — Layering

Warm Up

1) a) rectangle   b) circle   c) hexagon
   d) cross   e) triangle f) star
2) a) white   b) black   c) white
   d) grey   e) white   f) grey
3) a) 3   b) 4   c) 5   d) 4   e) 6   f) 5   g) 3

Odd One Out

4) C

In all other figures, the white shape is at the front.

5) B

In all other figures, the white shape which is created by the overlap of the two grey shapes has four sides.

6) A

In all other figures, the circle is in front of the large shape.

7) D

In all other figures, the black-and-white shapes have their black half overlapping the big square.

Complete the Pair

8) D

The lines crossing the large shapes move to the back.

9) B

The grey shape moves to the front.

10) B

The small shape at the back moves to the front. The small shape at the front moves to the back.

3D Shapes and Folding

Pages 16-17 — Rotating 3D Shapes

Warm Up

1) Number of figures containing the block inside the square: 2
   (The second and fifth figures.)
2) a) Same.
      (The left-hand figure is rotated 90 degrees away from you, top-to-bottom to make the right-hand figure.)
   b) Different.
   c) Same.
      (The left-hand figure is rotated 90 degrees anti-clockwise in the plane of the page to make the right-hand figure.)

3D Building Blocks

3) B

One way is for the bottom two blocks of set B to each rotate 90 degrees left-to-right and become the blocks on the bottom of the figure on the left. The cube moves to become the top-left block of the figure.

4) B

One of the blocks at the bottom of set B rotates 90 degrees top-to-bottom and becomes the block at the bottom-left of the figure on the left. The other block from the bottom of set B moves to become the right-hand block. The top block from set B rotates 90 degrees in the plane of the page and becomes the top-left block of the figure.

5) A

The bottom block from set A rotates 180 degrees in the plane of the page and becomes the block at the back of the figure on the left. The other block from set A moves in front of the first block.

4

3D Rotation

6) A
Shape A rotates 90 degrees towards you, top-to-bottom.

7) C
Shape C rotates 90 degrees
clockwise in the plane of the page.

8) D
Shape D rotates 90 degrees left-to-right.

9) B
Shape B rotates 90 degrees away from you, top-to-bottom.

Pages 18-19 — 2D and 3D Shapes

Warm Up

1) a) 2   b) 3   c) 5   d) 3   e) 4   f) 5
2) a) C   b) E   c) F   d) D   e) B

2D Views of 3D Shapes

3) D
There are four blocks visible from above, which rules out options B and C. There is only one block visible on the right-hand side, which rules out option A.

4) A
There are five blocks visible from above, which rules out options B and D. There are three blocks visible on the right-hand side, which rules out option C.

5) D
There are five blocks visible from above, which rules out options A and C. There are three blocks visible on the left-hand side, which rules out option B.

Cubes and Nets

6) D
Option A is ruled out because there is no face with a black dot on the net. Option B is ruled out because the black face and the face with a heart should be on opposite sides. Option C is ruled out because the face with the grey hexagon and the face with the black arrow should be on opposite sides.

7) C
Option A is ruled out because there aren't two faces with crosses on the net. Option B is ruled out because the face with the grey rectangle and the face with the figure 8 should be on opposite sides. Option D is ruled out because there is no face with a grey star on the net.

8) A
Option B is ruled out because the face with the grey circle and the face with the black cross should be on opposite sides. Option C is ruled out because there aren't two faces with pentagons on the net. Option D is ruled out because the bottom of the letter F should be next to the face with the star on it.

Pages 20-21 — Folding

Warm Up

1) Figure D
2) a) 2   b) 3

Fold Along the Line

3) D
Options A and B are ruled out because the fold line has moved. Option C is ruled out because the part of the figure that has been folded is the wrong shape.

4) C
Option A is ruled out because the part of the figure originally to the right of the fold line is the wrong shape. Option B is ruled out because the part of the figure that has been folded is the wrong shape. Option D is ruled out because the part of the figure originally to the right of the fold line should still be visible.

5) C
Option A is ruled out because the part of the figure that has been folded is the wrong shape. Option B is ruled out because the part of the figure originally to the left of the fold line is the wrong shape. Option D is ruled out because the part of the figure originally to the right of the fold line is the wrong shape.

Fold and Punch

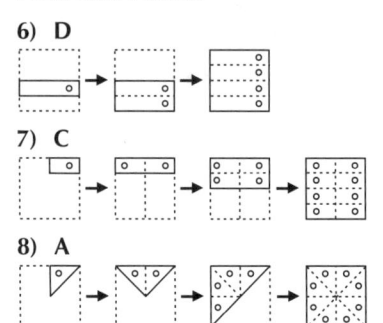

6) D

7) C

8) A

Pages 22-31 — Assessment Test 1

Section 1 — Complete the Pair

1) D
The circle alternates colour between black and white.

2) B
The small shape at the front moves behind the large shape.

3) D
The figure is rotated 90 degrees anticlockwise.

4) A
The two circles move to the right of the shapes and swap shadings.

5) B
The figure rotates 180 degrees and its outline changes.

6) B
The small shape at the front becomes the large shape at the back, and the large shape at the back becomes the small shape at the front.

7) C
Taken together, the bottom two shapes reflect downwards (or the shapes change places and the arrow points in the opposite direction).

8) C
The small white shape rotates 90 degrees clockwise. The large black shape becomes white and the small white shape becomes black.

Section 2 — Find the Figure Like the First Two

1) D
All figures must have a small white shape on a larger black shape on a large white shape.

2) C
All figures must have a black crescent on a white circle.

3) B
All figures must be made up of straight lines and right angles.

4) B
All figures must have a white four-pointed star inside a black shape.

5) A
All figures must have two shapes which overlap to make a smaller version of the two overlapping shapes.
6) D
All figures must have a large shape below a smaller version of the same shape which has been reflected upwards.
7) C
All figures must have a shape with a thick black outline containing two white triangles and one black triangle.
8) A
All figures must have three arrows, two pointing to the left and one pointing to the right.

Section 3 — Complete the Hexagonal Grid

1) A
The shapes are reflected across the middle of the hexagonal grid.
2) B
Going in a clockwise direction from the top-left hexagon, each outer hexagon gains one extra triangle. Each triangle added is smaller than the previous ones added.
3) C
Going in a clockwise direction from the top hexagon, each outer hexagon rotates 60 degrees clockwise.
4) B
Going in a clockwise direction from the bottom-left hexagon, each outer hexagon gains a vertical line to the left of the existing lines. The lines are then spaced equally inside the circle.
5) D
Going in an anticlockwise direction from the bottom-right hexagon, the square in each outer hexagon increases in size. The outline of the squares alternates between solid and dotted.
6) A
The shapes are reflected across the middle of the hexagonal grid.
7) D
Going in an anticlockwise direction from the bottom-left hexagon, the next circle down is shaded grey in each outer hexagon.
8) A
Each outer hexagon has a black semicircle on the innermost side and a black sector on each of the two middle corners.

Section 4 — Rotate the Figure

1) C
The figure is rotated 225 degrees clockwise (or 135 degrees anticlockwise). Option A is a reflected rotation. Options B and D are the wrong shape.
2) A
The figure is rotated 270 degrees clockwise (or 90 degrees anticlockwise). In options B, C and D, the black shading is the wrong shape.
3) A
The figure is rotated 135 degrees clockwise. In option B, the white triangle has been shaded grey. In option C, the triangles are positioned incorrectly. Option D is a reflected rotation.
4) D
The figure is rotated 90 degrees. Options A and C have the wrong number of grey circles. In option B, the circles line up with the sides of the hexagon instead of its corners.
5) B
The figure is rotated 45 degrees clockwise. In option A, the outline of the rectangle has become dotted and the outlines of the squares have become solid. In option C, the squares are positioned incorrectly. Option D is a reflected rotation.
6) C
The figure is rotated 180 degrees. Option A is a reflected rotation. Option B is the wrong shape. Option D has the wrong shading.
7) D
The figure is rotated 180 degrees. Option A doesn't have a line across the circle. Option B is a reflected rotation. Option C only has a semicircle.
8) C
The figure is rotated 135 degrees clockwise. Option A is a reflected rotation. In option B, the black diamond has become white. In option D, the white diamond has become black.
9) A
The figure is rotated 225 degrees clockwise (or 135 degrees anticlockwise). Option B is a reflected rotation. In options C and D, the arrowheads are positioned incorrectly.
10) B
The figure is rotated 270 degrees clockwise (or 90 degrees anticlockwise). Options A and D are the wrong shape. Option C is a downwards reflection.

Section 5 — Complete the Series

1) B
In this series, the pattern alternates between a small white circle on top of a large black circle, and a small black circle on top of a large white circle.
2) B
The arrow rotates 90 degrees anticlockwise in each series square.
3) C
In each series square, the shape gains an extra side.
4) B
The squares in this series are in two pairs. In each pair, the large star is removed so only the small star remains.
5) B
In each series square, the size of the pentagon increases. The pentagons rotate 180 degrees in each series square.
6) A
In each series square, the shape rotates 45 degrees anticlockwise. Its outline alternates between dashed and solid lines.
7) D
The different types of shading move clockwise to the next small triangle in each series square.
8) C
In each series square, the hexagon loses an arrow and gains a circle.
9) D
In each series square, a quarter of the grey circle is removed and is replaced by a quarter of the hatched circle. (In C, the hatching is going in the wrong direction.)
10) C
In each series square, the shape rotates 90 degrees anticlockwise and alternates between small and large.

Pages 32-41 — Assessment Test 2

Section 1 — Changing Bugs

1) C
The bug's body gains a shape which is the same shape as its body (but smaller) and the same colour as its head.
2) B
The bug loses one pair of lines from its wings.
3) D
The tail gains two segments and reflects across.
4) B
The inner shape on the bug's body rotates 180 degrees and its outline becomes dotted instead of dashed.

6

5) A

The four shapes on the wings split in half and the inner half of each shape is removed.

6) C

The small shape on the bug's body rotates 90 degrees. The bug's head moves under the bug's body.

7) A

The shadings of the small shapes on the bug's body move one place in a clockwise direction.

8) D

The bug's body gains two stripes. The legs each lose one line.

9) D

The shading on the bug's body segments moves up one segment. The shading on the top segment becomes the shading on the bottom segment.

10) C

The black shape on the bug's body changes to become a skewed star. The number of points on the star is the same as the number of sides on the shape. The bug's antennae change from curved to straight.

Section 2 — Complete the Square Grid

1) A

Working from left to right, each grid square rotates 90 degrees clockwise.

2) B

Working from left to right, the shape moves diagonally upwards from the bottom left-hand corner of the first grid square, to the top-right corner of the third grid square. The shading of the shape alternates between black and white.

3) D

The third grid square in each row contains the star from the first grid square in front of the shape from the second grid square.

4) B

Working from top to bottom, each grid square gains a raindrop.

5) A

Each shape (black star, grey heart and white circle) only appears once in each row and column.

6) B

In each row, the shape stays the same. Each colour (black, grey and white) only appears once in each row and column.

7) E

In each row, the figure in the left grid square is added to the figure in the right grid square to make the figure in the middle grid square.

8) B

Working from left to right, the figure in the grid square rotates 45 degrees clockwise. In the first grid square the small shapes are all grey. In the second grid square the middle shape is white and the outer shapes are grey. In the third grid square the middle shape is grey and the outer shapes are white.

Section 3 — Fold Along the Line

1) C

Options A and B are ruled out because the fold line has moved. Option D is ruled out because the part of the figure originally to the left of the fold line is the wrong shape.

2) B

Options A and D are ruled out because the fold line has moved. Option C is ruled out because the part of the figure originally above the fold line is the wrong shape.

3) B

Options A and D are ruled out because the fold line has moved. Option C is ruled out because the part of the figure originally to the right of the fold line is the wrong shape.

4) A

Option B is ruled out because the part of the figure that has been folded is the wrong shape. Options C and D are ruled out because the fold line has moved.

5) D

Option A is ruled out because the part of the figure originally to the left of the fold line should still be visible. Option B is ruled out because the part of the figure that has been folded is the wrong shape. Option C is ruled out because the fold line has moved.

6) A

Option B is ruled out because the part of the figure that has been folded is the wrong shape. Option C is ruled out because the fold line has been moved. Option D is ruled out because the part of the figure originally below the fold line should still be visible.

7) D

Option A is ruled out because the fold line has moved. Option B is ruled out because the part of the figure that has been folded is the wrong shape. Option C is ruled out because the part of the figure originally below the fold line is the wrong shape.

8) C

Options A and D are ruled out because the part of the figure that has been folded is the wrong shape. Option B is ruled out because the fold line has moved.

9) D

Option A is ruled out because the fold line has moved. Option B is ruled out because the part of the figure that has been folded is the wrong shape. Option C is ruled out because the part of the figure originally to the left of the fold line is the wrong shape.

10) C

Option A is ruled out because the fold line has moved. Option B is ruled out because the part of the shape originally to the right of the fold line is the wrong shape. Option D is ruled out because the part of the figure originally to the right of the fold line should still be visible.

Section 4 — 3D Building Blocks

1) C

The block on the left of set C moves to become the back right-hand part of the figure on the left. The block on the right of set C rotates 90 degrees anticlockwise in the plane of the page. It then rotates towards you 90 degrees, top-to-bottom, to become the front left-hand part of the figure.

2) D

The block on the right of set D rotates towards you 90 degrees top-to-bottom and moves to become the bottom left-hand part of the figure on the left. The block on the bottom-left of set D moves to become the right-hand part of the figure. The block on the top-left of set D moves to become the top left-hand part of the figure.

3) A

The block on the bottom-left of set A rotates 90 degrees in the plane of the page and moves to become the block at the back of the figure on the left. The block on the right of set A rotates 90 degrees right-to-left and moves to become the front left-hand part of the figure.

4) C

The block on the top of set C rotates 90 degrees in the plane of the page and moves to become the back left-hand part of the figure on the left. The block on the bottom of set C rotates towards you 90 degrees top-to-bottom and moves to become the front part of the figure.

5) A

The block on the bottom of set A rotates towards you 90 degrees top-to-bottom and moves to become the front part of the figure on the left. The block on the top of set A moves to become the back part of the figure.

6) B
The block on the bottom of set B rotates 90 degrees clockwise in the plane of the page. It then rotates 180 degrees left-to-right and moves to become the back part of the figure on the left. The block on the top of set B rotates 90 degrees in the plane of the page and moves to become the front part of the figure.
7) A
One of the bottom blocks of set A moves to become the back part of the figure on the left. The other bottom block of set A rotates 90 degrees in the plane of the page and moves to become the bottom-front part of the figure. The block at the top of set A moves to become the top-front part of the figure.
8) D
The block on the bottom of set D rotates 90 degrees clockwise in the plane of the page and moves to become the back part of the figure on the left. The block on the top of set D moves to become the front part of the figure.

Section 5 — Complete the Pair

1) C
The two shapes swap shadings.
2) A
The top-right shape is removed.
3) D
The shading of the top inner shape changes from white to black and the whole figure rotates 90 degrees clockwise.
4) C
The black and grey shading moves one shape towards the outside (when it reaches the outermost shape it goes back to the centre).
5) B
The inner shape becomes the outer shape and the outer shape becomes the inner shape. The inner shape is shaded with smaller versions of the shape.
6) C
The whole figure rotates 180 degrees. All black shapes turn white and all white shapes turn black.
7) A
The irregular shape becomes a regular shape with the same number of sides. The shading changes from grey to white or from white to grey.
8) D
The shape in front moves to the back. One of the lines disappears.

Pages 42-51 — Assessment Test 3

Section 1 — Complete the Series

1) A
In each series square, a quarter-circle is added. The first quarter is the bottom-left quarter and the others are added anticlockwise. The first quarter is white and the others are added in an alternating grey / white pattern.
2) C
In each series square, the black triangle rotates 90 degrees clockwise around the white square.
3) C
In each series square, the white circle gains an extra black dot. The arrow alternates between pointing right and pointing left.
4) B
The squares in this series are in two pairs. In each pair, the bottom shape rotates 90 degrees clockwise and changes shading from white to grey.
5) D
In each series square, an extra line crosses the triangle. The triangle alternates between pointing to the top-left and top-right corners.

6) B
In each series square, the figure rotates 45 degrees and gets bigger.
7) C
In each series square, an extra shape is added. The colours of the shapes alternate between black and white.
8) B
Each series square is reflected across and gains an extra black star.
9) A
Each series square rotates 90 degrees clockwise. The rectangles alternate between having a solid and dashed outline.
10) C
In each series square, the square rotates 90 degrees anticlockwise. The small black square alternates position between the bottom and top of the vertical line.

Section 2 — Find the Figure Like the First Three

1) C
All figures must have five sides.
2) C
All figures must have two triangles.
3) C
All figures must contain two crosses and one circle.
4) D
All figures must contain three versions of the same shape between two lines. One must be black and the other two must be white.
5) C
All figures must have two overlapping shapes with the same number of sides.
6) C
All figures must be identical apart from rotation. (D is a reflection.)
7) E
In each figure, the number of short lines equals the number of sides of the shape.
8) B
All figures must have two arrows going in a clockwise direction.

Section 3 — Rotate the Figure

1) C
The figure is rotated 180 degrees. Options A, B and D are the wrong shape.
2) B
The figure is rotated 90 degrees clockwise. In option A, the small triangle has become black and the thick black stripe has become white. In options C and D, the triangle is positioned incorrectly and in option C, the stripe is also positioned incorrectly.
3) D
The figure is rotated 135 degrees clockwise. Option A is a reflection. In option B, the triangle and arrow have swapped shadings. In option C, the arrow is positioned incorrectly.
4) A
The figure is rotated 225 degrees clockwise (or 135 degrees anticlockwise). Option B has the wrong arrowheads. In options C and D, the arrows are positioned incorrectly.
5) B
The figure is rotated 90 degrees clockwise. Options A and D are the wrong shape. Option C is a rotated reflection.
6) B
The figure is rotated 135 degrees clockwise. Options A and C have the wrong shading. Option D is a rotated reflection.
7) D
The figure is rotated 270 degrees clockwise (or 90 degrees anticlockwise). Option A has the wrong arrowhead. Option B is a rotated reflection. Option C is the wrong shape.

8

8) A

The figure is rotated 225 degrees clockwise (or 135 degrees anticlockwise). In option B, the parallelogram has the wrong shading. Option C is a rotated reflection. In option D, the parallelogram is positioned incorrectly.

9) C

The figure is rotated 90 degrees clockwise. Option A is a downwards reflection. In option B, there are too many lines inside the triangles. In option D, the lines in the triangles are positioned incorrectly.

10) C

The figure is rotated 135 degrees clockwise. In option A, the star only has four points. Option B is a reflected rotation. Option D has the wrong number of black lines.

Section 4 — 2D Views of 3D Shapes

1) B

There should be four blocks visible from above, which rules out options A and D. There are two blocks at the front of the shape, which rules out option C.

2) D

There should be four blocks visible from above, which rules out options A and B. There is only one block at the front of the shape, which rules out option C.

3) C

There should be four blocks visible from above, which rules out options A and D. There are three blocks at the front of the shape, which rules out option B.

4) A

There should be five blocks visible from above, which rules out options B and C. There are two blocks at the back of the shape, which rules out option D.

5) B

There should be five blocks visible from above, which rules out options A and C. There are two blocks on the right of the shape, which rules out option D.

6) B

There should be six blocks visible from above, which rules out options A and D. There are three blocks at the back of the shape, which rules out option C.

7) B

There should be six blocks visible from above, which rules out options C and D. There are two blocks on the right of the shape, which rules out option A.

8) C

There should be seven blocks visible from above, which rules out options A and B. There are three blocks at the front of the shape, which rules out option D.

Section 5 — Odd One Out

1) D

All other figures have a white shape on the end of the arrow-style line.

2) D

In all other figures, the line of symmetry is dashed.

3) E

In all other figures, the white shape has four sides.

4) E

In all other figures, there are three thick lines.

5) B

All other figures have two white shapes.

6) D

In all other figures, the shape at the end of the arrow-style line is the same as the large shape.

7) B

In all other figures, the two circles are on adjacent corners of the large shape.

8) C

In all other figures, the arrow is pointing at the small grey circle.

Pages 52-61 — Assessment Test 4

Section 1 — Complete the Hexagonal Grid

1) B

Going in a clockwise direction from the top hexagon, the heart shape increases in size.

2) B

The hexagons on opposite sides of the hexagonal grid are identical.

3) A

Going in an anticlockwise direction from the top hexagon, each circle gains an extra line. The lines are added end-to-end in an anticlockwise direction.

4) A

Each figure is reflected across the middle of the hexagonal grid.

5) D

Going in a clockwise direction, each outer hexagon rotates 60 degrees clockwise.

6) B

Each outer hexagon has a black triangle on its two innermost and two outermost corners.

7) C

Going in a clockwise direction from the top-right hexagon, each outer hexagon gains a grey triangle.

8) C

Going in a clockwise direction, each outer hexagon rotates 60 degrees anticlockwise.

Section 2 — Fold Along the Line

1) A

Option B is ruled out because the shape has been broken apart along the fold line. Options C and D are ruled out because the fold line has moved.

2) B

Options A and C are ruled out because the fold line has moved. Option D is ruled out because the part of the figure originally below the fold line should still be visible.

3) D

Options A and B are ruled out because the fold line has moved. Option C is ruled out because the part of the figure that has been folded is the wrong shape.

4) D

Options A and C are ruled out because the fold line has moved. Option B is ruled out because the shape has been broken apart along the fold line.

5) A

Option B is ruled out because the part of the figure originally to the right of the fold line should still be visible. Options C and D are ruled out because the part of the figure that has been folded is the wrong shape.

6) A

Option B is ruled out because the fold line has moved. Option C is ruled out because the part of the figure that has been folded is the wrong shape. Option D is ruled out because the part of the figure originally to the right of the fold line is the wrong shape.

7) **B**

Options A and C are ruled out because the part of the figure originally below the fold line is the wrong shape. Option D is ruled out because the fold line has moved.

8) **B**

Options A and C are ruled out because the part of the figure originally above the fold line is the wrong shape. Option D is ruled out because the fold line has moved.

Section 3 — Reflect the Figure

1) **B**

Option A is not reflected and there is only one line. Option C is a 90 degree anticlockwise rotation. Option D is a 180 degree rotation.

2) **C**

Options A and B are the wrong shape. Option D is a downwards reflection.

3) **B**

In option A, the stripe is positioned incorrectly and the shading is wrong. In option C, the stripe is positioned incorrectly. Option D is a 90 degree clockwise rotation.

4) **D**

In option A, the black quarter-circle's position has been reflected, but not the shape itself. In option B, the quarter-circle has been reflected, but its position has not been reflected. Option C is a 180 degree rotation.

5) **A**

Option B is the wrong shape. In option C, the shading of the circles is wrong. Option D is a downwards reflection.

6) **D**

Option A is not reflected but the shadings have swapped. In option B, the small grey rectangle has not been reflected. Option C is a downwards reflection.

7) **C**

Option A has an extra sun shape and the black line is in the wrong position. In option B, the sun shape is positioned incorrectly. Option D is a 180 degree rotation.

8) **C**

Options A, B and D are the wrong shape.

9) **D**

Option A is reflected but the triangle is behind the rectangle. Option B is reflected but the triangle is also reflected downwards. In option C, the triangle has rotated 90 degrees clockwise and there is only one line.

10) **D**

Option A is reflected but the hexagon is positioned incorrectly. Option B is a 180 degree rotation. Option C is not reflected and the hatching has been rotated 90 degrees.

Section 4 — Cubes and Nets

1) **B**

Option A is ruled out because the net doesn't have a face with a black triangle on it. Option C is ruled out because the net doesn't have a face with a 'W' on it. Option D is ruled out because the face with the grey ring and the face with the grey stripe must be on opposite sides.

2) **D**

Option A is ruled out because the face with the star and the grey face must be on opposite sides. Option B is ruled out because the net doesn't have a face with one grey circle on it. Option C is ruled out because the net doesn't have a face with a black square on it.

3) **A**

Option B is ruled out because the face with the three circles and the cross-hatched face must be on opposite sides. Option C is ruled out because the net doesn't have two identical faces. Option D is ruled out because the net doesn't have a face with a parallelogram on it.

4) **B**

Option A is ruled out because the face with the parallel lines and the face with the black circle must be on opposite sides. Option C is ruled out because the net doesn't have a face with four parallel lines on it. Option D is ruled out because the net doesn't have a face with an octagon on it.

5) **C**

Option A is ruled out because the face with the four squares and the face with the large white square must be on opposite sides. Option B is ruled out because the face with the white circle and the face with the black circle with the line through it must be on opposite sides. Option D is ruled out because the net doesn't have two identical faces.

6) **D**

Option A is ruled out because the face with the diamond shape and the face with the black and white circle must be on opposite sides. Option B is ruled out because the net doesn't have a grey face. Option C is ruled out because the face with the grey rectangle and the black face must be on opposite sides.

7) **A**

Option B is ruled out because the face with the white right-angled triangle and the face with the 'E' on it must be on opposite sides. Option C is ruled out because the face with the white isosceles triangle and the face with the five black circles must be on opposite sides. Option D is ruled out because the net doesn't have a face with a 'T' on it.

8) **C**

Option A is ruled out because the face with the white circle and the grey face with the white diamond must be on opposite sides. Option B is ruled out because the face with the arrow and the face with the 'T' on it must be on opposite sides. Option D is ruled out because the letter 'T' is rotated incorrectly.

Section 5 — 3D Rotation

1) **E**

Shape E has been rotated 90 degrees away from you, top-to-bottom.

2) **A**

Shape A has been rotated 90 degrees clockwise in the plane of the page.

3) **F**

Shape F has been rotated 90 degrees right-to-left.

4) **B**

Shape B has been rotated 90 degrees anticlockwise in the plane of the page.

5) **F**

Shape F has been rotated 90 degrees right-to-left.

6) **D**

Shape D has been rotated 90 degrees towards you, top-to-bottom.

7) **E**

Shape E has been rotated 90 degrees right-to-left.

8) **C**

Shape C has been rotated 90 degrees anticlockwise in the plane of the page.

9) **B**

Shape B has been rotated 90 degrees away from you, top-to-bottom.

10) **A**

Shape A has been rotated 90 degrees anticlockwise in the plane of the page.

Pages 62-71 — Assessment Test 5

Section 1 — Complete the Square Grid

1) B
Moving from left to right, the hatching of the shape rotates 45 degrees clockwise.

2) D
Moving from left to right, the shape rotates 90 degrees anticlockwise in each grid square.

3) C
The third grid square in each row is made up of the figure in the first grid square on top of the figure in the middle grid square.

4) B
Each shape only appears once in each row and column.

5) A
Working from top to bottom, the circles are in the same position in each grid square. Working from left to right, the arrows are in the same position and orientation in each grid square.

6) B
In each row, the right-hand grid square is formed by combining the shape from the left-hand grid square with the shading from the circle in the central grid square.

7) C
Working from top to bottom, the square in each grid square gains an extra line.

8) A
Working from right to left, one section of the shape is removed in each grid square, going in a clockwise direction. The shape changes colour from white to grey and then back to white.

Section 2 — Find the Figure Like the First Two

1) C
All figures must have a triangle overlapping a circle.

2) B
All figures must have six sides.

3) C
All figures must have a white rectangle in front of a black rectangle.

4) B
All figures must be identical apart from rotation.

5) D
In each figure, the larger shape must have one more side than the smaller shape.

6) D
All figures must have two parallel lines crossing a single longer line.

7) B
All figures must have a dashed line between two shapes of the same colour. (Or they must all have a dashed line and a triangle.)

8) B
All figures must have a grey shape in front of a white shape.

Section 3 — Complete the Pair

1) E
The circles change position, but keep the same shading.

2) B
The figure rotates 90 degrees anticlockwise.

3) E
The shape changes into another shape with the same number of sides.

4) D
The figure rotates 180 degrees.

5) A
The circle and the arrowheads rotate 45 degrees anticlockwise.

6) F
The large shape splits in half and becomes the same colour as the circle.

7) E
The black shape becomes larger and moves to the centre. The white shape gets smaller and moves to the top-left of the black shape.

8) B
The grey shape reflects onto the black shape.

Section 4 — Rotate the Figure

1) D
The figure is rotated 270 degrees clockwise (or 90 degrees anticlockwise). Option A is a reflection. In option B, the shadings of the circle and the square have swapped. Option C has an extra line across the middle.

2) C
The figure is rotated 225 degrees clockwise (or 135 degrees anticlockwise). Options A and D are the wrong shape. Option B is a reflected rotation.

3) A
The figure is rotated 270 degrees clockwise (or 90 degrees anticlockwise). Options B and D are the wrong shape. Option C is a reflected rotation.

4) C
The figure is rotated 225 degrees clockwise (or 135 degrees anticlockwise). In option A, the shading of the circles is wrong. Option B is a reflected rotation. Option D has too many circles.

5) B
The figure is rotated 45 degrees clockwise. Options A and C are the wrong shape. Option D is a reflected rotation.

6) D
The figure is rotated 135 degrees clockwise. In option A, the pentagon is positioned incorrectly. Option B has a small square instead of a pentagon. Option C is a reflected rotation.

7) B
The figure is rotated 270 degrees clockwise (or 90 degrees anticlockwise). In option A, the shadings of the circles have swapped and there is no small square. Option C is a reflected rotation and both circles are shaded black. In option D, the parallel lines are positioned incorrectly.

8) C
The figure is rotated 225 degrees clockwise (or 135 degrees anticlockwise). Option A is a reflected rotation. Option B has the wrong number of points on the star. In option D, the star is behind the arch instead of in front of it.

9) C
The figure is rotated 135 degrees clockwise. Option A is a reflected rotation. In option B, the arrow is positioned incorrectly. Option D is a reflection.

10) D
The figure is rotated 225 degrees clockwise (or 135 degrees anticlockwise). Options A and C are the wrong shape. Option B is a reflected rotation.

Section 5 — Complete the Series

1) D
The series alternates between the first two figures.

2) A
The entire contents of the series square rotates 45 degrees clockwise.

3) D
The number of 'arms' changes in the sequence: three, four, five, four, three. The shading of the circles alternates between grey and white.

4) C
In each series square, the missing side of the inner hexagon moves anticlockwise. The shading of the smallest hexagon alternates between black and white.
5) E
The entire contents of the series square rotates 90 degrees clockwise.
6) E
The sequence of the number of sides of each shape goes: three, four, five, four, three. The hatching alternates between horizontal and vertical.
7) E
Each series square is reflected across and the black shading moves up into the next triangle.
8) B
In each series square, one more arrow rotates so it is pointing diagonally up to the left.
9) D
In each series square, there is one more star. The number of squares alternates between two and one.
10) D
In each series square, the circle gets bigger and the square gets smaller. Each shape alternates between grey and white.

Pages 72-81 — Assessment Test 6
Section 1 — Changing Bugs
1) B
The shapes of the bug's body segments each gain an extra side.
2) A
Two stripes are added to the bug's body.
3) C
The bug's body rotates 60 degrees clockwise.
4) D
The whole bug reflects across and the shading of its base changes from white to black.
5) B
The bug's body becomes shaded as quarters and the legs reflect downwards.
6) A
The inner dotted shape on the bug's body becomes the solid outer shape and the solid outer shape becomes the inner dotted shape.
7) C
The bug's body loses a black circle and the antennae each reflect across.
8) D
All the shading on the bug's body moves down one segment. The shading at the bottom starts again from the top. The shapes at the ends of the bug's antennae change from circles to squares.
9) B
The shape of the bug's body becomes the shape of each of the bug's wings and the shape of the bug's wings becomes the shape of the bug's body. The tail reflects downwards.
10) C
The bug's body segments rotate 45 degrees and the middle segment moves below the top and bottom segments.

Section 2 — Complete the Hexagonal Grid
1) D
The hexagons on opposite sides of the hexagonal grid are identical.

2) B
Going in a clockwise direction from the top hexagon, the level of grey shading in the raindrop increases in each outer hexagon.
3) B
Going in a clockwise direction from the top hexagon, the arrow rotates 60 degrees anticlockwise in each outer hexagon.
4) A
Each figure is reflected across the middle of the hexagonal grid.
5) C
Going in an anticlockwise direction from the bottom-left hexagon, each outer hexagon gains an extra black circle. (In options A and D, the lines have been rotated.)
6) D
Each outer hexagon has two black triangles along each of its three inner sides. The triangles point towards the centre of the hexagon.
7) B
Going in an anticlockwise direction from the top hexagon, the shape in each outer hexagon gains an extra side. The hatching alternates between going diagonally down to the left and diagonally down to the right.
8) C
Going in a clockwise direction from the top hexagon, the figure rotates 60 degrees clockwise in each outer hexagon. The figure also increases in size.

Section 3 — Reflect the Figure
1) B
Options A, C and D are the wrong shape.
2) D
In options A and B, the triangle is positioned incorrectly in relation to the star. In option C, the shape has not been reflected, and the star has moved to the front.
3) B
In option A, the arrow has been reflected but the star is positioned incorrectly. In option C, the figure is not reflected and the star and arrowhead have swapped shading. In option D, the star has the wrong number of points.
4) A
Option B is a rotated reflection. Options C and D have the wrong shapes at the ends of their lines.
5) C
Option A is a reflection, but the circles have swapped shading. In options B and D, the large white shape is not reflected.
6) C
In option A, the triangles are positioned incorrectly in relation to each other. In option B, the triangles are reflected but the layering is incorrect. Option D is not reflected (the black and white triangles have just swapped shading).
7) A
In option B, both of the lines have arrowheads. In option C, the grey circles are positioned incorrectly. Option D is reflected downwards.
8) C
In option A, the arch is reflected but the raindrops have not reflected. In option B, the arch is not reflected and there is an extra raindrop. In option D, the arch is reflected across but the raindrops are also reflected downwards.
9) D
Option A is the wrong shape. Option B is a downwards reflection. Option C is a 90 degree anticlockwise rotation.

10) C

In option A, the black lines are positioned incorrectly. In option B, the white shape is reflected downwards and the lines are the wrong thickness. In option D, the white shape has not been reflected.

Section 4 — 3D Building Blocks

1) D
The block on the bottom of set D moves to become the bottom-front part of the figure on the left. The block on the top of set D rotates 90 degrees right-to-left and moves to become the left-hand part of the figure.

2) A
The block on the top of set A rotates away from you 90 degrees top-to-bottom and moves to become the bottom part of the figure on the left. The block on the bottom of set A rotates 90 degrees in the plane of the page and moves to become the top right-hand part of the figure.

3) C
The block on the bottom of set C rotates 90 degrees left-to-right to become left-hand part of the figure on the left. The top right-hand block of set C moves to become the right-hand part of the figure. The top-left block of set C moves to become the top block in the figure.

4) C
One of the blocks from set C rotates 90 degrees anticlockwise in the plane of the page. It then rotates 90 degrees left-to-right and moves to become the right-hand part of the figure on the left. The other block from set C moves to become the left-hand part of the figure.

5) D
The block on the top of set D rotates 180 degrees towards you top-to-bottom. It then rotates 90 degrees left-to-right and moves to become the right-hand part of the figure on the left. The block on the bottom of set D moves to become the left-hand part of the figure.

6) B
The block on the bottom of set B rotates 90 degrees in the plane of the page and moves to become the back left-hand part of the figure on the left. The block on the top of set B rotates 90 degrees anticlockwise in the plane of the page. It then rotates 90 degrees right-to-left and moves to become the right-hand part of the figure. The small cube in set B moves to become the front left-hand part of the figure.

7) A
One way is for the block on the bottom of set A to rotate 90 degrees away from you top-to-bottom. It then rotates 90 degrees right-to-left and moves to become the bottom part of the figure on the left. One cube from the top of set A moves to become the block at the back left-hand part of the figure. The other cube from set A moves to become the block at the top right-hand part of the figure.

8) C
One way is for one of the blocks from the bottom of set C to rotate 90 degrees in the plane of the page and move to become the bottom-front block in the figure on the left. The block on the top of set C rotates 90 degrees right-to-left and moves to become the middle block in the figure. The other block on the bottom of set C moves to become the left-hand part of the figure.

Section 5 — Odd One Out

1) D
All other figures have a circle inside the large shape.

2) D
In all other figures, the arrow marks a line of symmetry.

3) E
In all other figures, the hatching is horizontal.

4) C
In all other figures, the corner with the smallest angle is shaded.

5) A
In all other figures, the three triangles are facing the same way.

6) D
In all other figures, the small shape is the same shape as the large grey shape.

7) B
In all other figures, the inner shape has one more side than the outer shape. (B is also the only figure where the total number of sides is an even number.)

8) D
All other figures have one square.

Pages 82-91 — Assessment Test 7

Section 1 — Rotate the Figure

1) D
The figure is rotated 90 degrees clockwise. Option A has a black rectangle instead of a black triangle. Option B is a reflected rotation. In option C, the trapezium is rotated differently from the rest of the figure.

2) B
The figure is rotated 180 degrees. Options A and C are the wrong shape. Option D is a reflected rotation.

3) A
The figure is rotated 135 degrees clockwise. Option B has two black triangles. Option C is a reflected rotation. In option D, the triangles are positioned incorrectly.

4) C
The figure is rotated 45 degrees clockwise. Option A is a reflected rotation. In option B, the circles are shaded incorrectly. In option D, there are squares instead of circles.

5) D
The figure is rotated 225 degrees clockwise (or 135 degrees anticlockwise). In option A, the black shapes and white shapes have swapped shadings. Option B is a reflected rotation. Option C is the wrong shape.

6) B
The figure is rotated 180 degrees. Options A and D are the wrong shape. Option C is a reflected rotation.

7) A
The figure is rotated 135 degrees clockwise. In option B, the grey and white shapes have swapped shadings. In option C, the white cross is positioned incorrectly. Option D is a reflected rotation.

8) D
The figure is rotated 135 degrees clockwise. Option A is the wrong shape. In option B, the white rectangle is in front of the black lines. Option C is a reflected rotation.

9) C
The figure is rotated 270 degrees clockwise (or 90 degrees anticlockwise). Option A is a reflected rotation. Option B is the wrong shape. Option D is a reflected rotation and the black circle is in the wrong position.

10) B
The figure is rotated 45 degrees clockwise. Option A is a reflected rotation. Option C is a reflection. Option D is the wrong shape.

Section 2 — Find the Figure Like the First Three

1) B
All figures must have four sides.

2) D
All figures must be reflections or rotations of the same arrow.

3) E
All figures must have four versions of the same shape. Two of the shapes must be black and two of the shapes must be white.
4) E
All figures must contain a large hatched circle and a small black circle.
5) C
In all figures, a T-shape must be crossed by two parallel lines.
6) A
In all figures, the number of points on the star must equal the number of sides of the white shape.
7) B
In all figures, the shape with the dotted outline must be half of the black shape.
8) C
All figures must have one white circle, one grey circle and one black circle. In all figures, the large shape must have six sides.

Section 3 — 3D Rotation
1) B
Shape B has been rotated 90 degrees clockwise in the plane of the page.
2) E
Shape E has been rotated 90 degrees away from you top-to-bottom.
3) C
Shape C has been rotated 90 degrees right-to-left.
4) D
Shape D has been rotated 90 degrees clockwise in the plane of the page.
5) E
Shape E has been rotated 90 degrees right-to-left.
6) B
Shape B has been rotated 90 degrees right-to-left.
7) D
Shape D has been rotated 90 degrees clockwise in the plane of the page.
8) A
Shape A has been rotated 90 degrees anticlockwise in the plane of the page. It has then been rotated 90 degrees away from you top-to-bottom.
9) C
Shape C has been rotated 90 degrees away from you top-to-bottom.
10) F
Shape F has been rotated 90 degrees right-to-left.

Section 4 — Fold and Punch
1) B
2) D
3) B
4) B
5) C
6) D
7) A
8) B

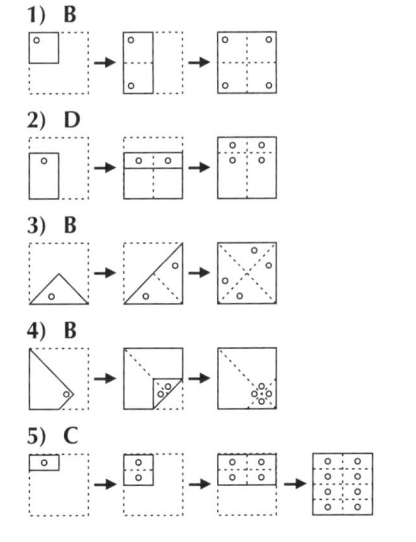

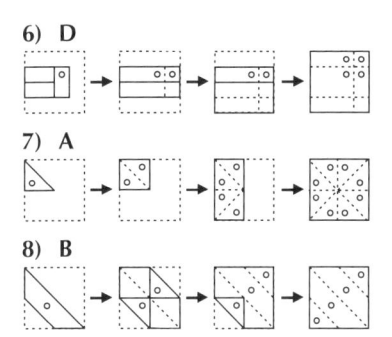

Section 5 — 2D Views of 3D Shapes
1) D
There are four blocks visible from above, which rules out options A and C. There are three blocks at the front of the shape, which rules out option B.
2) C
There are four blocks visible from above, which rules out options A and B. There are two blocks at the front of the shape, which rules out option D.
3) B
There are five blocks visible from above, which rules out options A and C. There are three blocks in a row at the back of the shape, which rules out option D.
4) A
There are five blocks visible from above, which rules out options C and D. There are two blocks at the back of the shape, which rules out option B.
5) C
There are six blocks visible from above, which rules out options A and B. There is only one block on the right-hand side of the shape, which rules out option D.
6) D
There are five blocks visible from above, which rules out options B and C. There are three blocks at the front of the shape, which rules out option A.
7) D
There are five blocks visible from above, which rules out options B and C. There is one block at the front of the shape, which rules out option A.
8) C
There are five blocks visible from above, which rules out options A and B. There are two blocks at the front of the shape (with a gap between them), which rules out option D.

Pages 92-101 — Assessment Test 8
Section 1 — Reflect the Figure
1) C
Option A is a 90 degree anticlockwise rotation. Option B is a downwards reflection. In option D, the black shape has become white.
2) D
Option A is the wrong shape. Option B is a downwards reflection. Option C is a 180 degree rotation.
3) B
Option A is a downwards reflection. Option C is a rotation (and the stripes have changed). Option D is a reflection but the black and grey shading has swapped.
4) C
In option A, the triangles are reflected but the parallel lines are positioned incorrectly. Options B and D are the wrong shape.
5) B
Option A is a downwards reflection. Options C and D are the wrong shape.

6) **A**

In option B, the arrow has been rotated 90 degrees anticlockwise and the star has moved. Option C is a reflection across but the star has also been reflected downwards. In option D, the arrow has been rotated 180 degrees and the star has then rotated 180 degrees.

7) **D**

Option A is a reflection but the white circle is in front of the hatched circle. Option B is not a reflection and the white and hatched circles have swapped positions. Option C is a downwards reflection.

8) **C**

Option A is a 180 degree rotation. Option B has the wrong shading and is not a reflection. In option D, the individual shapes have been reflected, but not the figure as a whole.

9) **D**

Option A has not been reflected and the shading has swapped. Option B is a downwards reflection. In option C the grey triangle has been reflected but not the white triangle.

10) **B**

Option A is a downwards reflection. In option C the arrowheads are incorrect. Option D is a 180 degree rotation.

Section 2 — Complete the Square Grid

1) **B**

Working from left to right, just the top shape is shaded grey, then both shapes are shaded grey, and then just the bottom shape is shaded grey.

2) **B**

The shapes in each column are the same and the positions of the lines through the shapes stay the same in each row.

3) **E**

Each figure only appears once in each row and column.

4) **D**

Working from left to right, the figure rotates 90 degrees clockwise. The circle alternates between black and white.

5) **C**

In each row, the middle grid square is made up of the bottom half of the first grid square placed under the bottom half of the third grid square.

6) **C**

In each row, all three shapes are the same. In each grid square one of the layers is shaded black. Each layer of the shape is only shaded black once in each row and column.

7) **D**

The large grey shape stays the same across each row. The black triangle stays in the same position in each column.

8) **D**

Working from left to right, the middle grid square in each row is made up of the shape from the third grid square on top of the shape from the first grid square. The two shapes swap shadings.

Section 3 — Cubes and Nets

1) **B**

Option A is ruled out because the face with the black triangle and the face with the white triangle must be on opposite sides. Option C is ruled out because the net doesn't have a face with a five-sided shape on it. Option D is ruled out because the net doesn't have a face with a black square on it.

2) **D**

Option A is ruled out because the net doesn't have a face with a black triangle on it. Option B is ruled out because the face with the hexagon and the face with the black stripe must be on opposite sides. Option C is ruled out because the net doesn't have a face with a black circle on it.

3) **C**

Option A is ruled out because the face with the grey square and the face with the parallel lines must be on opposite sides. Option B is ruled out because the net doesn't have a face with a 'Z' on it. Option D is ruled out because the net doesn't have a face with double parallel lines crossing in the centre on it.

4) **C**

Option A is ruled out because the net doesn't have a grey face. Option B is ruled out because the grey face with the white circle and the black face must be on opposite sides. Option D is ruled out because the net doesn't have a face with four grey circles on it.

5) **A**

Option B is ruled out because the net doesn't have a face with one triangle on it. Option C is ruled out because the face with the black rectangle and the face with the white crown must be on opposite sides. Option D is ruled out because the face with the black crown and the face with the white arch must be on opposite sides.

6) **C**

Option A is ruled out because the net doesn't have a face with a six pointed star on it. Option B is ruled out because the face with the black star and the face with the circle shaded in quarters must be on opposite sides. Option D is ruled out because the face with the three lines and the face with the white ellipse must be on opposite sides.

7) **A**

Option B is ruled out because the top of the 'V' must be next to the face with the stripes. Option C is ruled out because the face with the two joined white triangles and the face with the black stripe must be on opposite sides. Option D is ruled out because the striped face and the face with the white triangle inside the grey triangle must be on opposite sides.

8) **D**

Option A is ruled out because the face with the large white arrow and the face with the white triangle must be on opposite sides. Option B is ruled out because the face with the '4' and the face with the grey circle must be on opposite sides. Option C is ruled out because the line arrow should point towards the '4'.

Section 4 — Complete the Pair

1) **B**

The small shape becomes hatched, while the large shape becomes white.

2) **B**

The shape becomes a star with the same number of points as the shape had corners. The corners are marked with black circles which stay in the same position.

3) **C**

The figure is reflected and the shading of the shape changes from white to grey or grey to white.

4) **D**

The order of the shapes is reversed.

5) **B**

Half of the small circles move inside of the large circle. The other half disappear.

6) **D**

The grey shape gets bigger and goes to the back. The white shape gets smaller and goes in front of the centre of the grey shape.

7) **B**

The short arrows become long and the long arrows become short. The whole figure is reflected downwards.

8) **B**

The figure divides in half along the line (which disappears) and the left-hand half turns black. The white half rotates 90 degrees anticlockwise and moves behind the black half.